VOM Books
The publishing division of

Serving persecuted Christians since 1967
vom.org

Hearts of Fire 2

Twelve inspiring stories
of costly faith from today's
persecuted Christians

VOMBOOKS
The Voice of the Martyrs

Hearts of Fire 2

Published by VOM Books
A division of The Voice of the Martyrs
1815 SE Bison Road
Bartlesville, OK 74006

The Voice of the Martyrs

is a registered trademark of The Voice of the Martyrs, Inc. and
may not be reproduced in whole or in part in any form without
written consent of The Voice of the Martyrs, Inc.

Unless otherwise noted, Scripture quotations are from the ESV® Bible (The Holy
Bible, English Standard Version®), Copyright © 2001 by Crossway, a publishing
ministry of Good News Publishers. Used by permission. All rights reserved.

Scripture quotations marked "NIV" taken from The Holy Bible, New
International Version® NIV® Copyright © 1973, 1978, 1984, 2011 by Biblica,
Inc. Used with permission. All rights reserved worldwide.

Scripture quotations marked "NKJV" taken from the New King James Version®.
Copyright © 1982 by Thomas Nelson. Used by permission. All rights reserved.

ISBN 978-0-88264-234-5
eBook 978-0-88264-235-2
Audiobook - 978-0-88264-245-1
Library of Congress Control Number: 2022951021

Lead Writer and Researcher: Rebecca George
Edited by Sheryl Martin Hash
Interior Layout by Vicki Frye

Printed in the United States of America

202205p002a1

Therefore let us be grateful for receiving

a kingdom that cannot be shaken,

and thus let us offer to God acceptable worship,

with reverence and awe, for our God is a consuming fire.

Hebrews 12:28–29

Contents

Introduction

The dynamic witness of the twelve women whose true stories you will read in this book bring to life the words penned by the writer of Hebrews: "Therefore let us be grateful for receiving a kingdom that cannot be shaken, and thus let us offer to God acceptable worship, with reverence and awe, for our God is a consuming fire" (12:28–29).

As these women counted the cost of obeying and serving Christ, their own lives were turned upside down by those who opposed the activity of their faith. As written in Hebrews, their earthly kingdoms were shaken . . .

Sara has been on the run from guerrilla fighters in Colombia.
Semse's husband was brutally murdered by Islamists in Turkey.
Susanna's husband was kidnapped in Malaysia, and his whereabouts are still unknown.
Bianca risked bodily harm to reach Russian soldiers — the enemy occupying her country of Romania.
Gracia was kidnapped and held captive by Abu Sayyaf terrorists in the Philippines.

Tamara's husband was shot and killed in their home in Tajikistan.
Boupha was apprehended and questioned by police in Laos.
Huldah's husband was killed by Hindu extremists in India.
Marziyeh and Maryam were imprisoned in Iran.
Anita's husband was gunned down by Islamists in Libya.
Hannelie's family was slain by the Taliban in Afghanistan.
Helen was incarcerated in a shipping container in Eritrea.

Each woman clung to the hope found only in the unshakeable eternal kingdom of Jesus Christ our Lord. Though not always expressed immediately, their hope-filled response to suffering and loss allowed them to forgive their loved ones' killers, to sing worship songs in prison, to continue advancing the gospel, to experience intimacy with Christ amid tragedy, and to know that following Jesus is worth it — even if it means death.

In this follow-up to the first volume published in 2003, we have added eleven testimonies from women who, much like those in the feature stories, share how God sustained and strengthened them when they faced life-altering trials while doing God's work in some of the world's most difficult and dangerous places to follow Christ. These first-person accounts, called "In Her Words," represent women from a variety of nationalities — American, Australian, Chinese, Cuban, Czech, Iranian, Laotian, Nepalese, Nigerian, Romanian, Russian. Yet their message is united in gratitude for God's power and goodness as they entrusted their pain and suffering to Him.

You are not exempt from trials and difficulties shaking your earthly kingdom; no follower of Christ is. Therefore, we pray these stories inspire you to pursue God's unshakeable kingdom, pouring yourself out as an offering of worship to the Lord while placing your hope in the truth that God is an all-consuming fire who, one day, will make all things right. As you enter into fellowship with these women and the Holy Spirit speaks to you through their stories, may your heart be set ablaze to pursue and advance God's kingdom wherever you live—no matter the cost.

—The Voice of the Martyrs

Sara

The Guerrilla Evangelist

COLOMBIA

2001

Eighteen-year-old Sara Gómez sat anxiously on the long bench in the truck bed as the vehicle raced along the mountainous roads on Colombia's eastern border. A large tarp shaded her and other passengers from the scorching sun.

As weary travelers pressed against her on both sides, Sara tucked her arms in close, making herself as small as possible. She tensed as the truck slowed to stop at the checkpoint. A trickle of sweat dripped down her brow, but she didn't wipe it away. Her attention was focused on the man who had just hopped onto the back of the jungle taxi to hitch a ride.

The tarp shielding the passengers stretched just below the man's chin, concealing his face from Sara's sight, but she could see the dirty boots of a guerrilla fighter. She felt a heavy *thud* as the man dropped a sack of ammunition with bullets poking out of the burlap bag.

Sara lowered her head and held her breath. This was her only hope of escape. If the man ducked his head even inches, he would have a clear view of the passengers sitting beneath the tarp. If he saw her, she knew what would happen next.

He would kill her.

༄

Sara's life growing up was marked with suffering. Her mother had married at age fourteen; by age eighteen, she was a widow with two small children to raise. Willing to do anything to keep food on the table, Sara's mother linked her young family with a man who had thirteen children of his own. Sara was the oldest child of this union.

The family lived in a small village in an area of fertile farmland two hours from the city of Cúcuta. Her stepfather was a farmhand, and they grew their own food. They lived in a rustic house made of wooden planks on a dirt floor. When it rained, the cheap tin roof thundered as if under heavy artillery fire. The children slept on mattresses fashioned from sacks stuffed with straw and reeds. For pillows, they rolled worn clothes into soft bundles, which they tucked under their heads each night.

One of her new brothers had nicknamed Sara "Big Cheeks," a fitting moniker for the round-faced, brown-eyed, friendly little girl. As a child, Sara dreamed of becoming a doctor, but she knew the dream was impossible. How could her family afford the schooling? And even if they could, Sara lived on a rural farm, miles away from the educational opportunities of the city. Plus, her friendliness with boys had become a distraction and a bit of a problem for her.

For Sara, home never felt like a safe haven. While he was married to her mother, her father had two children with two other women, including one with the woman hired to care for Sara's mom after the birth of her last child. Her parents' relationship was volatile—a marriage wrought with violence—and Sara was also abused. Two of her much-older stepbrothers sexually assaulted her for more than five years. It would take years for Sara to break free.

Her country was also in turmoil. Since 1964, Marxist rebel groups had sought revolution in Colombia. Borrowing the strategies of Che Guevara, the Marxist revolutionary who had joined Fidel Castro in overthrowing Cuba's dictatorship, the militant groups fought the government for control over the country. Fueled by their Communist hybrid of Marxism and social programs, these fierce guerrillas recruited young boys and girls to join their cause in liberating Colombia's impoverished population. The guerrillas used whatever violent, rogue tactics were necessary to expand their influence, including kidnapping.

By the late '90s and early 2000s, the guerrilla groups discovered that drug trafficking could fund their movements, and the violence increased. Various paramilitary groups also sprang up in defense against the guerrillas, and those groups also entered the drug trade. Battles were waged on three fronts among guerrillas, paramilitary groups, and government soldiers. And when guerrilla fighters moved into Sara's village, her stepfather relocated the large family to Cúcuta. There, he thought, they'd be safe—away from the threat of Sara and her siblings getting recruited into the guerrillas' violent movement.

But life in the city was far from easy. The children in Cúcuta called Sara and her siblings "dirty farmers." When the same children invited Sara and her siblings to play, she quickly realized their ulterior motives: the children just wanted an opportunity to make fun of their accents.

Sara soon developed a feisty protectiveness over her younger brothers, with a readiness to fight anyone who made fun of them or tried to hurt them. When she saw an older boy trying to drown her brother, she jumped on the assailant and bit a chunk of tissue from his back. When the boy showed up later with a machete to fight Sara and her brother, the family was forced to move once again. Sara was heartbroken. Though the transition to living in the city was hard, Sara had grown accustomed to it and didn't want to start over again. Her family was the happiest they'd ever been while living in that neighborhood, and now they had to leave.

When Sara was twelve, her mother and stepfather separated. Sara and her two younger siblings drifted with their mother from city to city, from home to home, crossing large swaths of the country as their mother searched for work and love.

Sara's mother unleashed her frustrations on her children, kicking Sara viciously and hitting her with a wooden broomstick so hard that it cracked in half. One time, her mother lunged at her with a scalding-hot iron. The only thing that stopped her from blistering her daughter's flesh was the short cord tethering the appliance to the wall.

While Sara's stepfather had been a terrible husband, he'd always been loving toward Sara. He'd looked out for her needs and kept her on the right path; and she missed him desperately.

In December 1997, hope finally burst through the darkness. Her stepfather was coming for a visit. He promised to take her to the safety of his new home. And even more exciting was his second promise, one that was sure to change her entire life: in just a few short years, he would pay for her medical school.

The night before he arrived, however, Sara's mother woke her with devastating news. Her stepfather had died unexpectedly from an undiagnosed heart condition. His death crushed Sara. She fell back onto her pillow and stared up at the ceiling as her last bit of hope for her future slipped away.

Three weeks later, on a holiday visit to the countryside, Sara encountered a group of National Liberation Army or ELN guerrilla fighters, armed and dressed in green camouflage with red and black masks covering their faces. Sara knew to avoid them and crossed to the other side of the street.

"We're going to change Colombia," they called out to her. "You can change Colombia, too."

Sara stopped walking and slowly turned to face the men.

"What's your dream?" one of the fighters asked. "What do you want for your life?"

"I want to be a doctor," Sara said.

"You can be a doctor with us. Come with us, and you'll be able to do so much good."

For seven years, Sara's stepfather had kept her on the right path. But now, with him gone forever, her life felt pointless. That day, fourteen-year-old Sara returned home, packed her one special dress, told her mother she was joining a convent, and left to become a guerrilla fighter.

ele

As a new member of the ELN, Sara first learned how to fight, how to kill, and how to shoot someone with an AK-47 semi-automatic rifle. "Scar Face," the man responsible for her military training, was a fighter nicknamed for the machete slice that spanned the length of his cheek.

"Once you learn the weapons and complete your training," Scar Face explained to her, "you can begin your medical training."

While Sara was scared of the weapons, her fear of being called a coward was even greater, so she familiarized herself with them as quickly as possible.

When Sara graduated from combat school, she knew her role with ELN was permanent. From that point on, anyone who abandoned the cause would be punished by death. "*Not one step backward,*" she chanted along with the other fledgling militants. "*Liberation or death!*"

At age fifteen, Sara had become a trained killer.

With her military training completed, Sara began training to become a medic. The ELN recruited Cuban doctors to teach the nursing classes. This impressed Sara because in Colombia, Cuban doctors were known to be the best. They taught her how to remove bullets from a body, bind wounds, and perform other medical tasks common to jungle combat.

Sara finished her medical training in a few months. And her guerrilla colleagues now gave her the title of "healer."

⟋⟍

Hiding from the Colombian military, the guerrilla fighters of the ELN cloistered themselves within the lush vegetation of the Amazon rainforest, Sara's home as a teenager. Her new family—a military company of about a hundred armed rebels—could walk for eight days straight without leaving the jungle. The vast jungles of Colombia were the perfect breeding ground for guerrilla "red zones"—areas controlled by rebel fighters—where the Colombian military had been driven out. In these red zones, crime ran rampant.

Engineers, architects, students, and peasants were among those in Sara's squad, a smaller group of ten composed of three triads and a commander. Nearly half the fighters of the ELN—from the lowest to the highest ranks—were women. Many of these women joined because, like Sara, life in Colombia didn't offer any better opportunities. Others joined to escape home situations riddled with sexual assault. Some joined to flee poverty, while others wanted to lend their services in the political fight to secure representation for the poor. Still others were tricked, their naiveté making them easy targets for the persuasive ELN recruiters.

Sara learned to survive in the wild rainforest and how to navigate the rivers that snaked through the tropical terrain. She became skilled with the machete, a tool that proved useful for blazing a trail when her troop was on the move.

But life in the jungle was difficult. The ground, a mixture of clay and mud, became intolerable in the wet season. Moisture seeped into Sara's boots, creating painful blisters, and caused the dreaded trench foot that plagued the guerrillas. She knew that trench foot, which resulted from continual exposure to damp conditions, could lead to infection or even amputation if left untreated.

Sara's thighs chafed from all the walking, and thick calluses formed on her back where her gun and ammunition bag rubbed her skin. The troop would march for eight or twelve hours a day, changing locations to avoid being found by the Colombian military and also to fight their many enemies—military brigades, paramilitary groups, or other rebel combatants. Most weeks, they would march to a new campsite and set up camp all over again. Deep in the rainforest, when the troop felt hidden from their enemies, they might set up camp for two months or more. But when they were near small towns, they stayed only a few days.

Sara kept a tight routine in camp. Each day at 4:45 a.m., the guard on watch walked tent to tent to sound the alarm and wake the troops. Sara washed herself as best she could and dressed in her green camouflage shirt and black pants. Within fifteen minutes, she stood in formation, ready to sing the unifying anthem of the ELN hymn and salute the group's red and black flag.

An hour of physical training followed before the company broke ranks in search of breakfast, which usually consisted of rice and potatoes. If they had recently slaughtered a cow, the soldiers also feasted on beef. Sara noticed that the ELN always paid for their food, in contrast to other guerrilla and paramilitary groups roaming the jungle. Mostly, they secured it from local villagers and peasant farmers, but other times they received shipments from ELN leaders, which they then transported on their backs.

Following breakfast was weapons training, then lunchtime and a quick break before honing their battle skills late into the afternoon. After an early communal dinner, Sara and the others would wash their uniforms in the river and engage in ideological discussions about the philosophical writings of their leaders, along with those of Lenin, Marx, and even Castro. By 6:00 p.m. the jungle was dark, and by 8:00 p.m. she was asleep. An early bedtime allowed Sara to rest before her two-hour nightly shift on guard duty.

When they were near towns, the ELN spread out to meet the physical needs of the inhabitants. Some built houses; others helped with agricultural work. As the medic, Sara spent her time tending to the needs of the community. For the first time, she began to feel her life had value. Townspeople flocked to greet her, and she relished her newfound purpose.

Combat, however, proved a much different experience. Sometimes, she was allowed to stay at the camp to treat injured soldiers, but more often than not, she worked on the frontlines, surrounded by exploding grenades and incoming gunfire.

On one occasion, as they cut their way through the thick jungle, ELN guerrillas came across a young fighter who had been wounded a week earlier. His body, riddled with bullets, had been shot either by the Colombian military or a paramilitary group.

By the time the group brought him to Sara, the holes had become putrid with infection. She examined the wounds in his chest and stomach. Maggots oozed from the tunnels carved into his body.

Without any sort of anesthesia, Sara stuffed a rag into his mouth. "Hold him down," she instructed another fighter. She plucked the maggots from the boy's body, along with the sticks, leaves, and fragments of uniform that had entered the wounds. His hellish screams sent sharp chills down Sara's spine. When she had finished and removed the soaked rag from the boy's lips, he unleashed a raging torrent of curses in her direction.

Six times a day, for three days, Sara cleaned the boy's wounds and packed them with fresh gauze to prevent infection. By the seventh day, she knew he would survive.

But not all fighters could be saved. Whenever an ELN guerrilla was killed, it was Sara's job to perform an autopsy on the body. She carefully removed the organs and determined whether or not it would be possible to return the body to the family. For the fighters who accidentally stepped on landmines placed by the Colombian military, Sara left the bodies for the jungle to consume.

One night, as one of Sara's medical partners held a flashlight between her shoulder and her cheek in order to free her hands, a Colombian military operative saw the light and fired his machine gun through the jungle brush. The shots struck their target and obliterated the lower half of the young woman's face. Sara's comrades packed the gaping wound left where the woman's jaw had been and sent her off for treatment. When Sara saw her colleague again a year later, the poor woman was unrecognizable.

⁓ele⁓

Sara had witnessed so much suffering, bloodshed, and death that it was taking a toll on her. When another rebel group killed a family of farmers in retaliation for helping Sara and her fellow rebels, she felt like she had caused their deaths. She was sickened by the kidnapping of young men and women by a cause that preached justice.

Sara also sensed something missing from her heart, absent from her soul. Additionally, she was losing her closest friends. One friend was wounded in combat and left to die in the jungle. Another spoke out against a commander and was taken up a mountain to be shot. One by one, they were being erased.

In the four years since she'd joined the guerrillas, Sara saw her mother only once. One day, Sara's mother heard a rumor that Sara's squad would temporarily be in a town many miles away from the rebel warfare. Her mother desperately missed her daughter and headed to the town to find Sara.

As the ELN squad passed through the town, Sara's mother scoured the band of rebel fighters, finally spotted her daughter, and begged her to return home. At the time, Sara had been too brainwashed to leave her duties and abandon her responsibilities. But now, the desire to see her mother again was strong. The idea of going home consumed her thoughts.

Finally, Sara had seen enough death and violence, and she decided to leave the ELN. She'd seen how little they cared for her friends and how they killed anyone who dared to disagree. Sara wanted out.

"I want to stop," she told her friend, a young woman tasked with monitoring the group's radio communications. The two women concocted a story—they would claim Sara was pregnant and needed to be transported to town to be cared for in the home of a trusted confidant. Somehow, their plan worked.

But Sara's friend was not so lucky. Days after helping Sara escape, her friend served on watch duty when she, too, decided to flee the ELN. When the girl ran, the guards chased her, caught her, and shot her dead.

Sara was bored in town, and with nothing to do, she passed the time out on her balcony. One day, she met her neighbors: a kind, older Christian couple. The husband worked in a bakery, and to him, Sara looked depressed. Every day, he checked in on his new neighbor.

"My patient is showing some sadness," he'd say.

"No, no, no," she protested. "I'm fine."

Finally, all of Sara's burdens came spilling out to her kind neighbor. She wanted to escape the ELN, but she was afraid to leave since she knew she would encounter both friends and enemies on her journey home.

"My son can help you," the man said. Both he and his son were Christians who opposed the ELN's methods, and they were eager to help Sara escape.

Though Sara was far away in the mountains, a ten-day drive from Cúcuta, the man's son drove a small transportation truck and volunteered to transport her.

Sara knew it would be a dangerous mission. In addition to armed groups who might stop the vehicle at any time, the police often halted vehicles at checkpoints to verify travelers' papers. Without the right document in hand, the national ID card known as a *cedula*, the police would naturally assume Sara was a rebel. Without her *cedula*, she would need a copy of her birth certificate. Her neighbor contacted Sara's brother to secure hers.

Like the Colombian military, the ELN set up their own checkpoints, scrutinizing passing vehicles and searching for escaping fighters they recognized. Many guerrilla fighters like Sara were leaving the ELN, and the rebel group was on high alert for deserters. Sara had heard the rumors from her friends in the ELN and had good reason to be afraid. If they found a deserter, they killed him or her in the most brutal ways imaginable.

On the morning of Sara's escape, her neighbor's wife styled her hair and applied her makeup. They exchanged her uniform for civilian clothes. The more Sara looked like a city girl, the more convincing she would be that she was not a guerrilla.

The driver helped Sara into the back of his truck. The U-shaped bench was already full of passengers, and Sara ducked under the large tarp and squeezed between two of them. Sara was terrified of being discovered, but she knew she needed to escape. This was the only way.

⁓

Sara held her breath, staring at the guerrilla fighter's boots as he stood at the foot of the truck. The vehicle accelerated through the checkpoint with the guerrilla fighter still onboard. For thirty horrifying minutes, Sara kept her eyes locked on the man as he held onto the frame of the tarp covering the truck bed. With every second that passed, she feared he would recognize her.

As the truck approached the next checkpoint, Sara craned her neck to look around. Immediately, she recognized the green camouflage of the ELN rebels. The men approached the truck just as Sara lowered her chin to her chest, trembling. The guerrillas were just feet away.

Without warning, one of them started shouting. Sara braced herself, but instead of coming toward her, the men ran to the car behind her.

"Go, go, go!" one of the soldiers said to the truck driver, waving him forward. Amazingly, Sara had escaped detection.

The truck wove through the jungle roads until it slowed once more at the next checkpoint. Sara felt her pulse quicken again, and beads of cold sweat formed on her upper lip. She lowered her head and cut her eyes toward the back of the truck. As the truck came to a stop, she watched the guerrilla loosen his grip on the tarp frame and shift his feet.

Why is he moving? Has he seen me?

All of a sudden, the man reached down, grabbed his sack of ammunition, and jumped from the truck. For several excruciating seconds Sara held her breath, but the man never looked back. As he walked farther away from the truck, Sara finally allowed herself to exhale. It seemed as though she had become invisible, somehow protected from being discovered by the man who could have thwarted her escape.

Days later, the truck finally reached a city. Sara looked around as the truck pulled up to a bus station. The driver brought his vehicle to a stop, stepped out onto the dusty ground, and motioned for Sara to stay seated. "Don't get out," he said. "I'll let you know when." Sara's eyes followed him as he walked into the bus station.

When he returned, he waved to Sara and she stood, her back aching from the jarring trip. Climbing past the other passengers and sliding out the back of the truck, she took the bus ticket in the driver's outstretched hand.

"You'll be okay," he said. "Go get on the bus." He bid her farewell, and she watched him climb back into his truck and drive away.

Stepping up into the waiting bus, she handed the driver her ticket. She found an empty seat next to another woman and settled in for the next leg of her long journey home.

For hours, the bus rumbled along the dusty roads until finally, it began to slow. Sara groaned. *Not another checkpoint.* She dreaded these distressing interruptions, each one an opportunity for her to be discovered and taken back to the ELN.

More than a dozen Colombian military boarded the bus and made their way down the aisle, checking passengers' identification cards. Sara gripped her birth certificate and waited for them to reach her seat.

"Why are you traveling with a birth certificate?" the man asked, frowning down at the document in Sara's hand.

"I'm from the country," she said, "and this is all I have."

"Take off your shoes," the officer demanded. Sara's heart sank. The only reason he would ask to see her feet was if he suspected she was a guerrilla fighter, as marching for hours in the wet jungle left telltale signs on the guerrillas' feet. Sara slipped off her shoes, and the officer examined her bare feet.

"Why do you have calluses?" he asked, his eyes narrowing.

Sara thought quickly. "Because I'm a peasant," she said. "I work in the country." But the military officer wasn't satisfied.

"Stand up and let me see your back," he said. Carrying guns and heavy bags of ammunition and supplies left calluses on the guerrillas' backs, and the markings were a way to spot a rebel. Sara closed her eyes, reached for the hem of her shirt, and hoped her calluses had had enough time to fade.

Just as she lifted her shirt, there was a commotion next to her. Another officer was inspecting the bag of her seatmate, and he had evidently discovered she was transporting drugs. Both officers turned their full attention to the woman, and Sara slowly lowered her shirt and sat back down. As the minutes passed, Sara realized they'd forgotten her entirely. Once again, she had evaded detection.

ele

MAY 5, 2001

After days of bumping along in the bed of a truck and a terrifying ride on a bus, Sara was finally free. The bus pulled into the station in her hometown, and as Sara set foot on the ground, she saw her older sister running toward her with tears streaming down her face. Sara's younger brother, now so grown up that she didn't recognize him, burst into tears at the sight of his sister who had protected him so many times growing up.

Finally, Sara reunited with her mother at home. In the days that followed, Sara learned that several of her family members had become Christians, and they had prayed for her every day, hoping she'd come home. Sara's family could finally see God answering their prayers.

Sara needed to find a job and sold lottery tickets door-to-door in the crime-ridden, low-income neighborhoods throughout Cúcuta. Whenever she recognized guerrillas—men and women who infiltrated every part of Colombian life as informants and recruiters—she hid her face, hoping they wouldn't recognize her.

But the guerrilla recruiters sometimes *did* recognize her because they knew her or had heard of her. Several pressured her to rejoin the ELN. They were sure their ideas were powerful enough to draw Sara back to the cause. Sara would agree to an appointment time to meet them, then hurry home and lock herself in her house, making a note not to visit those neighborhoods again. When the day of the appointment arrived, she never showed up. And thankfully, none of the recruiters knew where Sara lived, or she would have been shot.

In many ways, life outside of the ELN was still difficult, but Sara found ways to have fun.

At a dance club one night, Sara met the man who would become her husband. Their families had been friends for a long time, but it had been years since Sara and Antonio Gómez had seen each other. "Oh, hi!" Sara said, a huge grin spreading across her face. It was love at first sight. They danced for hours, and at the end of the night, they shared a kiss.

Antonio had already heard bits and pieces of Sara's story, but that week she told him about her past and her experiences as an ELN guerrilla fighter. In the months to come, Sara and Antonio grew closer.

Soon, the two decided to marry. They began their life together on a family farm. Within the year, Sara gave birth to their first child, a beautiful girl they named Veronica.

Sara possessed a knack for administration and was put in charge of the area's community council. Her prominence in the community grew. However, that influence came at a steep price. An ELN guerrilla fighter recognized her and, in retaliation for leaving the group, turned Sara in to the police.

Sara had recently become pregnant with her second child, a boy, when the police brought her in for questioning. "No," Sara protested, "I don't know anything about that life anymore. I'm not involved with the ELN, and I haven't been for a long time." But the police were unrelenting. Sara endured half a day of interrogation so intense that the stress caused her to miscarry.

After the interrogation, Sara and Antonio moved their family— including Sara's mother, her younger siblings, some aunts and uncles, and their two-year-old daughter—thirteen hours south to the capital city of Bogotá where they could avoid the intense scrutiny of the ELN. At least once a week, Sara's grandmother, a devout Christian, pestered Sara about her salvation.

"You are not saved. You have to believe in God!" she insisted.

Reluctantly, Sara and Antonio went to church with her. But in their hearts, they didn't want to be there.

Sara again became pregnant, but scans revealed congenital malformations in the baby's lungs. Desperate, Sara and Antonio decided to go to church, and there they begged God for healing. But when a follow-up ultrasound showed improvement, the couple felt they no longer needed God.

Sara's baby, her second daughter, was born with underdeveloped lungs. The doctors said she would need a life-saving surgery, so once again the couple pleaded with God for healing.

The surgeon who performed the surgery happened to be a Christian. "I'm just a tool from God," he explained to Sara. "He will use my hands, but it's God who does the work." Sara wasn't quite sure how to interpret the doctor's comment. *A tool from God? What does he mean?*

When the surgery was successful, Sara and Antonio knew their baby's life was nothing short of a miracle from God. They surrendered their lives to the One who had healed their daughter. A few years later, Sara gave birth to her third child, a boy. She felt like this son was God's replacement gift to her for the son she'd miscarried. When Sara had a fourth child, a daughter, she and Antonio declared their family was complete.

⁓

As Sara's family grew, so did her faith. Recognizing the couple's dedication and passion for sharing the gospel, their pastor tasked them with greater responsibility. First, Sara and Antonio joined their pastor on his motorcycle trips into the countryside to tell people about Jesus. Between Sara's natural friendliness and Antonio's understanding of the Bible, they made a good team. Then, their pastor commissioned the Gómezes to establish a new church in a nearby red zone. Like other red zones, the area was under guerrilla control, swarming with drugs and violent criminal activity.

In 2015, Sara and Antonio's denomination asked them to plant another church in a red zone—an area plagued with violence, landmines, and roadside bombs—and they were given responsibility over a local church as well. Neither position provided any financial compensation, so to support themselves, the family made *arepas*, a Colombian staple food. By selling the corn cakes on the street, they were able to sustain their ministry and even expand it by striking up conversations with people in the community.

Sara and Antonio rode their motorcycle around the countryside distributing copies of a colorful graphic-novel version of the Bible. They quickly realized this Bible appealed to young people as well as adults who were less literate. Sara liked teaching from it because it made evangelism and discipleship much simpler. Occasionally, guerrilla groups still threatened them. "You're using the Bible to take people away from us," they warned. But Sara continued to evangelize.

In the rural areas where she and Antonio ministered, the visual presentation made understanding the message of Scripture easier and more enjoyable for people. Sara soon discovered that pastors in their area were learning to read with this Bible. Each week, their ministry grew as guerrillas, drug dealers, and coca[1] farmers encountered the gospel and decided to place their trust in Jesus Christ.

But not everyone in the area was pleased by this sudden community transformation. Rebel group leaders grew disgusted as the gospel message spread throughout the villages and rural farmlands, threatening their ideology and the criminal activities that funded their work.

"Your preaching is causing people to go against us," they told Sara and Antonio. "If you're preaching the gospel, people won't harvest drugs, and we need them to."

Sara and Antonio had become the enemy, and the armed groups began looting their church and hindering their evangelistic efforts.

One day, Sara was waiting on the side of the road for a bus to transport her and several boxes of Bibles to an area that needed them. She saw a truck approaching in the distance. As it came closer, she realized it was not a transport truck. The vehicle carried armed rebels from a neighboring town. Sara had seen these men before and knew the guerrillas would seize the Bibles and likely take her as well.

---

1. Leaves from the coca plant are the source of the drug cocaine.

With only seconds to act, Sara flagged down the first truck that came her way. She climbed into the vehicle as relief washed over her. The truck sped away, and Sara watched the vehicle full of rebels grow smaller and smaller in the distance.

While the guerrillas heartily opposed the Bibles Sara and Antonio distributed, the Colombian military, surprisingly, was open to the Gómezes' ministry and allowed them to preach to the enlisted men. While this was good for their efforts to reach members of the armed forces, it further complicated their relationship with the rebels. Talking with the military implied that the couple supported them, even though Sara's intentions were for their souls and not their military objectives. She knew if the guerrillas found out, their threats would only increase.

But Sara and her husband know that sharing the gospel is worth the risk. "Since I fell in love with the Lord," Sara said, "I have felt boldness to preach to the armed groups because I know they have harmed many people, and they make bad decisions. So many people want to leave, just as I did. In my town, I share about what will make them free."

Sara saw herself in the faces of the teenagers she was bringing to Christ. *How different my life would have been*, she pondered, *if someone had told me about Jesus when I was fourteen years old!*

Her oldest daughter, Veronica, also developed a passion to keep young people from joining guerrilla groups. Now a university student, she had been influencing young men and women to go to the city to study. Veronica knew that if young people were in school, they were more likely to stay out of trouble. When students became intrigued by the Communist ideology of Marxism, Veronica encouraged them to expand their perspective with a university education. She also taught them technical and business skills, like how to earn money through baking cakes, which helped keep them away from the rebel groups.

While Sara and Veronica were glad this work kept young people busy and away from the allure of the armed guerrillas, the rebel recruiters were unhappy. Their subtle threats against Veronica slowly escalated.

When Antonio returned home one afternoon in 2019, he saw an unfamiliar truck sitting in front of his home. As he got closer, a group of armed men spilled out of the vehicle and surrounded him. Noticing their rubber boots and that they were traveling in a large group, Antonio knew instantly they were guerrillas.

"Are you Veronica Gómez's father?" one of the men asked.

Antonio nodded.

"She needs to be taught a lesson," he said, glaring at Antonio and spitting on the ground near his shoe. "Maybe we'll kidnap her."

Antonio's legs got weak as he struggled to maintain eye contact with the man.

"Or maybe we'll kill her and slice out her tongue."

Having delivered their message, the rebels returned to their truck. Just before speeding off, the driver turned back to Antonio to make one final threat.

"Don't get involved in things that are none of your business."

When Sara saw Antonio later that day, she knew something was wrong. He told her about the encounter, and Sara realized how serious the threats were against their daughter. They had to get out of town—immediately.

Sara, Antonio, and their younger children moved into a small room, the only place they could find quickly. Infested with drug activity and crime, the neighborhood was so dangerous that the children could not even go outside. Robberies and shootings occurred every day. A ministry friend eventually arranged for them to live on her sister's farm in the countryside, but even there the guerrilla recruiters were active.

After a couple of months, Sara and Antonio's second-oldest daughter, Anita, came to them and confessed that rebels were trying to convince her to join their movement. Anita had never been a strong personality, and she was afraid to say no to the recruiters because they threatened to kill her. She knew her family was in a desperate situation already and that they were out of money with no other place to go. The coronavirus pandemic had just shut down the country, and people were panicking.

Every night, as the couple slept in their small cabin on the farm property, they wondered if it was the night guerrillas would come for their daughter. Every time they heard a motorcycle or a car, Sara and Antonio prayed that if this was the night they were killed, then God would prepare their souls to meet Him.

◦ℓℓ◦

After two weeks of worry, Sara and Antonio relocated their family to Cúcuta. They arrived with nothing and spent several hours looking for a place to live before finding a simple room. They lived there until a Christian worker in Colombia got in contact and arranged for them to rent a house that would fit their family.

The Gómezes were growing accustomed to starting over, but the change didn't discourage them. Each time, they knew God was with them. And at every new location, they trusted that God would provide opportunities for them to share the gospel. "God is involved," Sara said, "and He has a plan."

To earn a living, Antonio repurposed old tires into painted planters and baskets and sold them on the side of the road; Sara made *arepas* as she had before. However, this meager income was never enough to sustain the family. The couple prayed for the Lord's help.

God answered their prayers when Christians heard about Sara and Antonio's need and provided them with a machine to mass produce *arepas*, enough to support their family and ministry.

Starting at 5 a.m., Sara and Antonio begin cooking the corn that has been soaking since the night before. Each of their four children helps with different aspects of the business: grinding corn, cooking the small cakes, or packaging them in the cooler. "With love," Sara said, "we prepare the *arepas*. And every chat is an opportunity to share Christ, to say, 'Jesus loves you and has special things for you.'"

Around 3 p.m., their *arepa* work is through for the day, and the family has time for devotions together before heading out for some sort of outreach. They gather people in a public park to watch a short drama about Jesus, or they visit the local prison to fellowship with inmates.

Since young people are highly susceptible to recruitment by guerrilla groups, Sara and Antonio do everything within their power to point them to a better way—to Jesus Christ.

Loving people and sharing Christ with them are integral to Sara's personality. After leaving the ELN, Sara pursued her nursing degree and is now a registered nurse. Several times a week, she volunteers as a nurse with a refugee camp for Venezuelans who have fled their oppressive government and horrific, government-induced poverty and violence. Many of the women arrive at the refugee camp pregnant due to the sexual violence they experienced while crossing the border with smugglers. Sara's intake exam with each woman allows her one-on-one time to share the gospel.

Sara often thinks back to her former life when she worked as a medic in the jungles of Colombia; she remembers those difficult days of combat, killing, and brainwashing. Sara's life is marked with both blessings and burdens. Even though she can't erase her past, Sara has seen that Jesus Christ can transform anyone's future. "It would have been better for me to start serving Jesus when I was younger," she said. "I repent for not having repented as a young person."

Each day, as she and Antonio deliver *arepas* on their motorcycle, Sara knows the guerrillas might find them. But she does not dwell on it, because she has a bigger mission to accomplish. God has called her and her husband to share His Word and lead others to faith in Him. And Sara can't think of a more fulfilling life. "If you aren't doing anything for God, you aren't doing anything," she said. "We know that God is in our work, and we hope for victory."

In Her Words:
Norine

*Norine Brunson and her husband, Andrew, had served
the Lord in Turkey for more than 20 years when they were
summoned to the police station on October 7, 2016.*

A ndrew and I went to the police station, thinking we were
getting our long-term residence permits. We had planned
out the rest of the day and certainly had no thought of not

coming back home. When the police informed us we were being deported, we were surprised. On one level, we were not shocked—it can happen to missionaries. However, we knew God had us on assignment, preparing for a harvest in Turkey, so being deported didn't fit with that. Besides, we were right in the midst of our assignment.

As the day wore on, it became clear we were not just being told to go home and pack up to leave—we were being arrested. Three months earlier, there had been an attempted coup in Turkey. The country was in a state of emergency, and everything was at a heightened level of tension. People were being rounded up, and tens of thousands were arrested. Their lives were suddenly turned upside down.

The thought going through my mind in those very early days at the detention center was: *Maybe a harvest will start in prison, with these people, and God wants us to be in prison with them.* I was trying to prepare myself and to say, "Lord, if this is what You have for us, I have to submit to it; but it is a struggle."

I was concerned about disappearing into the system and never seeing my kids again. I knew they must be worried. And Andrew and I were afraid of being separated. In this situation, which was so beyond my control, I said, "Okay, Lord, we are suddenly thrust into this ride, and we don't know where we are being taken. I can't do anything to reach my kids. You are going to have to hold them."

It was definitely a struggle, the kind of thing nobody wants to even think about. At the end of the day, we aren't forced to surrender, but that is what the Lord asks of us. When my emotions are screaming *No!*, something that has helped me is to say, "I don't want it, my emotions don't want it, but Norine—in Christ—says, 'Yes,' to everything that You have for me, Lord." Who I am in Christ is who I truly am, so I can say, "Lord, I don't want this, but Norine—in Christ—says, 'Yes.'"

Norine was released after thirteen days, but her husband would spend a total of 735 days imprisoned in Turkey.

Semse

Awaiting the Glorious Reunion

Izmir, Turkey
1994

The bus door opened and twenty-five-year-old Semse looked up from her seat at the stern young man stepping aboard.

She watched him pay his fare and make his way down the crowded aisle, passing by the empty seat next to her without even the slightest hesitation. Semse wasn't surprised that he didn't stop. She knew that any woman would be an unappealing seatmate to a Muslim man, let alone one whose head was uncovered and whose clothes weren't the expected traditional religious garments.

Moments later, though, the young man came back up the aisle toward Semse. The seat next to her was the only available one on the bus. Reluctantly, he sat down.

The noisy bus bumped along the road, and after several minutes the man glanced down at the pocket-sized New Testament open in Semse's lap. He also skimmed the words on the piece of paper in her hand, information about Christianity that she planned to teach to a group of Christian youths later that day. Semse's Christian material often served as a conversation starter during her bus rides, so she always ensured it was visible to her various seatmates.

"Are you a missionary?" the man asked.

Semse immediately knew the deeper meaning hidden behind his question: *Are you the enemy who's here to change the religion and culture of my country?* She paused for a moment before responding.

"If a mailman is supposed to deliver your dad's heritage in a letter and he didn't deliver it to you, what are you going to feel?"

"I would hate that man," he said. "He should deliver my dad's letter and his heritage for me."

"I am like that," Semse said. "I am delivering your Heavenly Father's love letter and your heritage, your salvation. It's in the Bible, and here is your letter," she said, gesturing toward her Bible. "That is why I am a missionary. I am delivering your letter."

The man listened to her for a few moments before speaking again. "Is it Jesus who died," he asked, "or did Judas die in his place?"

After hearing his question, Semse knew this man was going to antagonize and debate her. "The betrayer cannot die in anyone's place," Semse replied. "Jesus came to die for your sin."

"But how can you believe in three Gods?"

"We don't have three Gods," Semse said. "We have one God in three persons for our salvation—the Father, the Son, and the Holy Spirit."

The conversation then turned to Jesus' mother, Mary. "How can God have a wife?" he asked. Semse knew that everything this man had been taught about Christianity was a lie.

As the bus approached the next stop, Semse gathered her things and prepared to disembark. She extended her hand as a farewell gesture, but the man refused to shake it. He wouldn't touch an "infidel" woman.

She scribbled her name and office phone number on a scrap of paper. "Here," she said, handing it to him along with her New Testament. "If you have a question, call me."

It was a risky move. Not only was Semse a woman, but she was a *Christian* woman. If the man interpreted her actions the wrong way—assuming, incorrectly, that this was a flirtatious offer by an indecent young woman—she could end up in a dangerous situation.

Lord, Semse prayed, *if he is not a person You will save, please don't let him connect with me.* She watched the bus drive away. *But if You want to save him, make him read the Bible and return to me.*

Semse began the short walk to her work, a travel agency that offered Christian visitors tours of the Seven Churches mentioned in the book of Revelation. Turkey has a rich Christian history, with its city of Constantinople (Istanbul) serving as the central hub of early Christianity.

But since those early days, Islam had usurped Christianity as the dominant religion of the area. Emperor Constantine's church, the *Hagia Sophia,* was once the largest Christian church in the world until it was defaced by Muslim invaders and converted into a mosque. Though the country was once teeming with Christians, the small church Semse attended had only ten members.

Most Turks gleaned their knowledge of "Christianity" from the movies—films from "Christian" Europe and America that presented everyday life as deeply immoral. *If these countries are immoral,* the Turks surmised, *then their religion must be also.*

For two weeks, Semse prayed for the young man she had encountered on the bus. When he failed to call, she soon forgot about him until three months later when her work telephone rang.

"This is Necati . . ." the voice on the other line said.

Semse paused, speechless.

"The man from the bus," he explained. "I read your Bible, and I have many questions. I want to bring the Quran for you. Would you like to meet to answer my questions, and to compare the Bible and the Quran?"

Semse wondered if it was all a trap. She felt excited by his words, but she was also cautious.

"Okay," she said. "Let's meet in a coffee shop in the old bazaar."

In a large crowd, surely this man couldn't do anything to her. Besides, she was at least five years older than he was. Semse felt like a big sister.

"You bring the Quran," she said, "and we will meet."

ᴄᴇᴇ

Semse was the middle child of nine born to a family that was Christian in name but very much influenced by the Islamic culture around them. Her father, a construction worker who spent most days laboring away from home on the Turkish-Syrian border, returned home just once a week. When he did, he read stories from the Bible to his family, offering praise of the men featured in Scripture but denigrating the women.

Like many of the men in Semse's culture, his perspective affected the family's everyday life as well. While sons were sent to school, and later to university, daughters were treated more like servants in the home. From 9:00 p.m. until 3:00 a.m., Semse scrubbed dirty laundry, a colossal pile collected from all eleven family members. Her small hands ached, and her skin was rubbed raw.

Semse often felt rebellion rising within her. *How could God create me but not value me?* She felt her heart harden toward her father and toward God. In her father's religion, Semse could find no freedom and no peace; she rebelled against her father and her culture.

As she became a teenager, Semse hated men and yet craved love and affirmation from them—sentiments similar to the relationship she had with her father. She'd been taught that her life was valuable only to the extent that she pleased the men in her life.

Even for nominal Christians, life in Semse's village was dangerous. Families carried guns to protect their daughters from being kidnapped by Muslims and forced into marriage. In school, Semse was one of only two Christian students. Muslim classmates would jeer at her, calling out "Crusade coming!" when she walked into class.

By the time she was twenty, Semse felt no purpose to her life, no sense of which way she should go. She awoke every morning envisioning herself on the edge of a cliff, ready to jump. At that time, her sister Janet became a Christian. "I found Jesus," she told their father. "I am now a real Christian."

Their father threw the Bible across the room, fearful of his daughter's new, zealous faith. Still, Janet shared the gospel with Semse. The two young women attended church together, and eventually, they moved to the city.

As time passed, Semse felt tormented by negative thoughts and spiritual oppression. She watched horror movies that filled her mind with dark images. One night, she went to a sleepover at a friend's house, and they played a board game where they asked questions to the spirit world. As they played, Semse grew increasingly fearful. After that night, Semse felt paralyzed by fear and terrified to be alone. When she washed her hair in the shower, shampoo burned her eyes because she was afraid of what she would see if she closed them. She felt like the fear would swallow her whole, like she would lose her mind.

"Call on Jesus," Janet urged.

Janet's advice angered Semse. Since she couldn't see Jesus, she felt like she couldn't rely on Him to help her overcome the fear of being alone. She didn't understand that God is Spirit, and He was powerful to give her victory in this spiritual attack.

Finally, when Semse could bear the overwhelming despair no longer, she followed her sister's advice. One day, Semse needed to go in the dark room to clean the film at the photography studio where she worked. She dreaded the task. In Semse's mind, going in the dark room felt like being buried alive. "Jesus, if You are real," she begged, "please protect me and help me."

In an instant, Semse felt her fear disappear and a calming sense of true peace take its place. In her mind she saw a vision of herself as a five-year-old girl, sitting in the loving lap of her Heavenly Father. Instantly, she knew she'd become a different person.

"Jesus helped me," Semse told her sister. "I am not afraid anymore, and I want to read the Bible for Him." In Christ, Semse found love and a reason to live. She felt like she had found living water in the desert, and she longed to know Him more through studying His Word. Finally, she felt free and valuable. Even her parents could see the radical change in their daughter's life. The rebellious, angry woman had been transformed.

Semse went to her father and sought forgiveness. "Dad," she said, "I am sorry I wasn't a good child for you. I am really sorry for my sins against you." Semse knew God had broken the ice in her father's heart when she saw a flood of love and forgiveness in his tear-filled eyes. Soon, the faith of his two daughters would affect his other children as well, as more of the siblings also chose to place their trust in Jesus Christ.

In the years that followed, Semse felt a tremendous urge to boldly share the gospel. She knew how desperate people were for Jesus, even as they hated Him because they didn't know Him. Semse sensed that the Holy Spirit had given her the spiritual gift of evangelism, and she refused to temper that gift. She rejected the idea that she shouldn't share the gospel with men because she was a woman or because people might take advantage of a young Christian woman. The joy of salvation flowed freely from Semse, and she seized every opportunity to tell others about Jesus Christ.

Five years later, on a bus ride in Izmir, Semse's boldness in sharing the gospel would change her life—and the life of a young Muslim man.

ᴄᴇᴇ

A few days later, after her workday ended, Semse went to the bazaar. Necati met her there, and they ordered coffee. This time, she brought a Bible that included both the Old Testament and New Testament. They sat at a small table as Semse explained the Bible to him, starting from the very beginning in Genesis.

Every week, she and Necati met at the bazaar to talk about Christianity, her faith, and Jesus Christ, who was at the heart of God's Word.

Necati came from a strict Sunni Muslim family with a radical-ized background. His family expected him to become a Muslim leader in the community, a man fully devoted to the worship of Allah and to the spread of Islam. He taught in the mosque and helped young people get serious about Islam.

For all of his early life, Necati lived up to his parents' expecta-tions and eventually even surpassed them.

But after meeting Semse and reading the Bible, Necati began to see Islam for what it really was. He realized that unlike the Bible, the Quran communicates no sure way to salvation. He saw that the Bible was all about how God loves people, not how people must please God to earn His favor.

After six months of weekly meetings at the coffee shop and attending Bible studies with Semse's pastor at her home, Necati finally understood God's grace. He dropped the heavy religious burden of Islam that he'd carried for so long and placed his trust in Jesus Christ.

"I believe in Jesus now," he told Semse one day, sliding into his seat at the coffee shop. Semse could see the transformation God had accomplished in Necati's heart. It was evident on his face. After half a year, God had turned this hardened Muslim man into a follower of His Son.

"Okay, good!" Semse said. Then, pausing, she continued, "You know the way, you know Jesus, and you know His church . . . I guess you don't need me anymore."

They went their separate ways and Necati returned to his home.

Over the days and weeks that followed, Necati's parents and siblings watched in alarm as the young man who once recruited friends to Islam was now reading the Bible; worse, he was telling other people about Jesus Christ. He talked about Jesus and shared Christ's teachings with his family. "Jesus said to love your enemy," he told his parents. Knowing they were about to lose him, they enacted a plan one day.

His older brother held a gun to Necati's head and warned him to stop following Christ. "We don't want to kill you," he said. "If you continue to walk in this way, I'll just shoot you in the knee so you can't walk to church and meet with Christians."

Terrified, Necati ran to the one person in his life he knew was safe—Semse.

Semse had never seen Necati so afraid. She knew he understood the cost of following Christ and the price he might pay for renouncing his Muslim faith and family.

Necati returned home later that day. He loved his family and couldn't figure out a way to have both his family and Jesus in his life. Semse watched him struggle. As they say in Turkey, it was like he was trying to hold two watermelons in one arm—one of them was bound to fall.

Necati decided to hide his faith by enlisting to fulfill his mandatory military service with the Turkish army. But before he left for duty, Necati arranged one last meeting with Semse.

"Will you marry me?" he asked.

Semse knew she'd begun to fall in love with him from the moment he became a Christian. But she wanted a husband who was committed to his faith, someone who was strong in the Lord.

"I want to see that you're serious," she told him. "Go to the army and show me that you are serious."

Necati left for Cyprus. For eighteen months, he served his country. The decision to join the military allowed him to shroud his Christian faith from his family and avoid dealing with the fallout. Semse and Necati exchanged letters often. She encouraged him to focus on his faith and to continue growing in his walk with Christ. Soon after Semse found a church in Cyprus for Necati, the pastor became Necati's spiritual mentor.

By the time Necati returned to Turkey, he had grown to be a man of strong faith and was ready to marry Semse.

Semse's sisters were not as convinced. "He's a new believer," they warned her. "He cannot handle you. He cannot even handle his family." But Semse knew she loved Necati.

Necati's family was also opposed to the marriage. When he revealed his intent to marry her, they were enraged and called Semse on the phone. "Necati told us he wants to marry you," they said, "but only if you come to Islam. Only if you become a Muslim can you marry him."

"I am in love with a Christian man," Semse replied. "If Necati is not a Christian, then I don't know him, and he shouldn't know me anymore either."

For fifteen days, Semse heard nothing from Necati. No phone calls, letters, or meetings. She prayed for him and placed Necati in God's hands. *It doesn't matter how much I love him. If he doesn't have faith, then I will not marry him. If he is really giving up on Jesus, then I am giving up on him.*

ـcelce

God answered Semse's prayers when Necati decided to choose his faith in Christ over his family. "I cannot live without Jesus," he said.

Necati's family cursed him. They kicked him out of the home and disowned him. "We wish you were dead," they spat. "You are our shame! We would kill you, but that would only hurt us. You don't have a family anymore. You are dead to us!"

On May 7, 1998, in a small church and in front of a dozen friends, Necati and Semse became husband and wife before God. The young couple lived off their wedding money as they searched for new jobs. After forty applications, Necati finally landed a full-time position in a candy factory.

Necati became a fervent evangelist. He shared his faith boldly throughout Izmir—a city called Smyrna by the early church. To the Christians who lived in Smyrna, Jesus himself had delivered a message of encouragement: "Do not fear what you are about to suffer. Behold, the devil is about to throw some of you into prison, that you may be tested, and for ten days you will have tribulation. Be faithful unto death, and I will give you the crown of life" (Revelation 2:10).

As Necati boldly shared his faith, Muslims spat in his face and told him how shameful it was that he left Islam. But their threats didn't stop his efforts. Together, Semse and Necati introduced people to Christ, teaching and discipling them in their home. Necati even played the role of Jesus in an Easter play, which was performed in several Turkish cities. A film crew recorded the popular theater performance and began sharing the movie, *Life of Jesus*, throughout the country. Necati's reputation was drawing the ire of the people of Izmir.

Two years into their marriage, as Semse was six months pregnant with their first child, police arrested Necati while he shared the gospel in a village near Izmir. Semse learned that the police had pressured people in the village to lie about Necati, saying he cursed Islam and the prophet Muhammad, a crime punishable by death.

For a whole month, Necati sat in prison. Semse's family had moved to Europe, leaving her alone. But her main worry during those agonizing weeks was for her husband's faith. *I don't want my pregnancy to make him weak in his faith.* Semse encouraged her husband from afar, writing Necati letters encouraging him to look to Joseph in the Bible and his unfair imprisonment as a source of strength and comfort. Like Joseph, Necati also experienced God's help.

Necati feared for his life in prison. The televisions in the jailhouse reported the false narrative and lies that had led to Necati's arrest. He wondered when the beatings would begin. But there was something unfolding inside the prison that Necati didn't know. Fellow inmates saw the love and compassion on Necati's face every day and realized there was something different about this man.

One day, a group of prisoners encircled Necati. *This is it*, he thought, bracing for the attack. *They're going to beat me now.*

But instead, the inmates inundated him with questions. "Tell us why you left Islam," they kept asking. Necati began to share the story of placing his trust in Christ as he sat among a rough group of thieves and murderers in a Turkish prison.

"God loves you," he told them. "There is forgiveness in Christ." Remarkably, no one beat him, cursed him, or harassed him. The inmates had never witnessed the kind of love and forgiveness this man shared. When Necati asked Semse to bring Christian materials to the prison, she smuggled in gospel tracts to share with the other inmates.

When it came time for Necati's trial, the prosecutor offered him a deal. "Renounce Christ," the judge told him, "and all the charges will be dropped against you."

"My freedom is Jesus, and my lawyer is Jesus. I don't need your freedom and your help," Necati responded without hesitation.

Miraculously, when it came time for the villagers to testify, God changed their hearts, and they recanted their slanderous testimony. One by one, each villager confessed to lying. Necati was released from prison, and he and Semse celebrated God's victory together.

ele

Necati's arrest compelled the couple to question their full-time work. Necati could continue working in the factory, but he and Semse wondered if God was urging them to pursue full-time Christian missionary work. Necati felt that God had called him, anointed him, and given him boldness to share God's love with Muslims.

While Necati still felt the sting of rejection from his family, he continued to pray for them. He composed a letter and mailed it to his family.

"Nobody made me believe in Christ and serve Him," he wrote. "Jesus did this by connecting my vein to Him in a spiritual way. He is in me, and His Spirit is in me . . . This is why I serve Him and love Him." Necati wanted his family to understand that his faith was because of God—not because of a girl and not for

BUSINESS REPLY MAIL
FIRST–CLASS MAIL   PERMIT NO. 311   BARTLESVILLE, OK

POSTAGE WILL BE PAID BY ADDRESSEE

THE VOICE OF THE MARTYRS
1815 SE BISON RD
BARTLESVILLE OK 74006-9901

FREE SUBSCRIPTION OFFER

Subscribe to The Voice of the Martyrs' free monthly magazine to continue being inspired by the stories of Christians who are willing to face persecution for the name of Christ — the same kind of Christians you've met in this book. You'll be challenged and encouraged by their testimonies, learning specific ways to pray for them and practical ways to help them.

☑ **YES!** Please send me inspiring stories of today's persecuted Christians in The Voice of the Martyrs' free monthly magazine.

Name _____

Address 1 _____

Address 2 _____

City/State/ZIP _____

Email _____ Phone _____

money. "I am praying for you," he continued. "I love you and I am waiting for you to put your hatred aside and connect with us."

With two children under two years old in tow, Necati and Semse decided to move to the city of Malatya in eastern Turkey. There, Necati would work for a publisher of Bibles and Christian materials.

Their friends thought the Aydins were crazy for leaving Izmir. "How can you go to that city?" they asked incredulously. "It's so dangerous, and the Muslims there are so conservative! You'll be so lonely!"

But Necati and Semse knew God was calling them to Malatya, and His presence and calling were enough. Through tears, Necati said goodbye to the place where he'd grown up, and he grieved the family that had disowned him.

"Until death we will follow You," the couple prayed. "We will not step back, and we will not slow down."

But the threat to their lives was never far from their minds, particularly Necati's.

"I know there's a knife on my neck because I left Islam."

ele

MALATYA, TURKEY
APRIL 18, 2007

Every morning before leaving for work, Necati spent time with his family—eating breakfast, having coffee, praying together, and reading the Bible.

Necati opened his Bible to 1 Samuel 17 and began reading the story of David and Goliath. Six-year-old Esther and seven-year-old Elisha's eyes widened as they listened to how God had helped David, a small shepherd boy, defeat the giant Philistine warrior, Goliath, with only a sling and a few stones. His kids were still giddy from the previous night, a fun evening spent wrestling with their dad and devouring the chocolate he'd brought them from his recent trip to Germany.

After the Bible reading, Necati led his family in prayer. They asked God for courage and strength, even to death, as they continued to share God's love with the people of Malatya. Semse had missed him so much while he was away on the ten-day trip and felt thankful to have him home once again.

At eight o'clock, Necati dressed for work. He had an appointment with two Muslim men he'd been mentoring, Emre Günaydin and Abuzer Yildirim. They lived in a nearby religious dormitory and had shown up at his publishing house one day and introduced themselves.

"We're living in this dorm," they told Necati, pointing in the direction of their housing, "and we don't believe in anything, but we'd like to know about your faith. We want to know about the gospel and Jesus Christ."

Necati didn't believe they were sincere, but he welcomed them into his office and used the opportunity to talk with them about Christ. He answered their questions and even agreed to meet regularly.

Semse had not met these two men, but she was suspicious. She thought about the threatening letters her husband had recently received. Necati usually kept these letters to himself, wanting to shield his family from worry, but Semse knew all about them.

On one occasion, when Semse was visiting her husband's office, someone she didn't recognize walked into the room. "Shhh!" Necati cautioned, not wanting the stranger to overhear their conversation. *This man must be dangerous*, Semse surmised.

"I know their hearts," Necati said to her back at home. "They are like Judas. I want to give them the same opportunity to know the Savior that God gave me. Jesus didn't run away from His Judas, and I'm not going to run away either."

Semse admired her husband's courage and fearless devotion to Christ, but she didn't trust these men. "Don't meet alone with them at your office," she said.

As Necati finished dressing for work, he slipped on his shoes and walked to the door. Semse wanted to go with him, but he shook his head. "No," he said, "not today."

Necati walked out of the apartment door and down the hallway, pressing the button to retrieve the elevator. Semse watched him, thinking about how her husband didn't like elevators, how he felt suffocated in small, enclosed spaces. Just before he stepped inside, Necati turned around and, for a brief moment, smiled at his wife.

ele

A FEW HOURS LATER

At noon, Semse followed her two children into the soot-covered building and stepped into the elevator to travel up to the landing just outside the family's apartment on the fifth floor. She unlocked the door, and Elisha and Esther darted inside, excited to be home from school. They hurried to their bedrooms to change out of their school uniforms and into play clothes.

The telephone rang.

Semse walked into the living room and answered it.

"There's been an attack at your husband's office," said Ercan, a friend and ministry colleague from Izmir.

"At his office in Izmir?" Semse asked. Ercan worked in the Aydins' former office in Izmir.

"No, Semse, in Malatya," Ercan said. "His office in Malatya." He had learned about the attack on television as broadcasters had begun reporting the news.

Semse hung up the phone and immediately dialed her husband's office at the Zirve Publishing House — a small Christian publisher that distributed Bibles, testimony books, brochures about Christ, and gospel tracts throughout the region. Semse grew worried. She knew her husband had enemies who opposed his work.

The extension rang and rang. When no one picked up, she phoned her husband's colleague, Ugur Yüksel, another Turkish man who, like Necati, converted from Islam to Christianity. The two worked together at the publisher.

No one answered.

Finally, she dialed the extension for the office of Tilmann Geske, a forty-six-year-old German Christian who also had an office at the publishing house.

Semse could hear her children playing, and since they were occupied, she turned on the television and flipped to the local news. There had been an attack in Malatya, and the police were investigating the crime. Semse turned up the volume and watched nervously as an emergency medical team carried a stretcher out of her husband's office building.

On the stretcher lay a partially zipped body bag. A pair of feet were visible outside the black bag.

Semse stared in disbelief at the television screen as a wave of numbness spread throughout her body.

Those are my husband's shoes.

ة

EARLIER THAT DAY

Necati drove to the publishing house and spent the morning going about his usual business. At eleven o'clock, Emre and Abuzer, the two young men he was mentoring, arrived. Necati invited them into his office and served them tea. The three sat in a small living room just off Necati's office and talked about Christ. Necati kept the office door wide open, remembering Semse's advice not to be alone with these men. With Tilmann and Ugur working in neighboring rooms, he felt safe.

Near the end of the conversation, Emre had a request. "We want you to meet our other friends," he said. "They're waiting outside in the car. Will you disciple them too?"

"Okay," Necati agreed, not wanting to hinder his evangelism efforts. In the faces of each of these young Muslim men, Necati saw himself. What if Semse hadn't taken time to meet with him? Where would he have ended up? "I don't have a lot of time now, but later we can meet and I can disciple all of you together."

Emre pulled out his cell phone and walked toward the office door. He pressed a few buttons and made a quick call. Seconds later, outside of Necati's line of sight, the car doors opened, and three men rushed toward the publishing house—Hamit Ceker, Cuma Özdemir, and Salih Gürler. They raced up the stairs to the fifth floor and stormed into Necati's office, slamming the door behind them.

The men grabbed Necati and threw him up against the wall. They smashed his head until he fell to the floor, dizzy and bleeding. One of the men opened a backpack and pulled out two knives, clotheslines, pistols, and plastic gloves. They beat and kicked Necati, then tied him to a chair. These five young Muslim men coordinated an attack and intended to kill him because he was a Christian.

Overhearing the commotion coming from Necati's office, Tilmann and Ugur hurried into the room. The five men immediately attacked them, punching and kicking them until they, too, fell to the floor. Two men bound Tilmann's arms and legs and tied him to a chair beside Necati while two others did the same to Ugur.

For nearly an hour, the young Muslims tortured the three Christians. With knives and guns, they demanded they deny Christ and reject their Christian beliefs. For sixty long minutes, Necati and his colleagues refused.

Tilmann called out to Jesus as he watched one of the men murder Necati. Once the attackers were sure Necati was dead, they turned their attention to the German missionary sitting before them. They threw Tilmann to the floor and stabbed him multiple times before they slit his throat and watched him die.

Ugur watched in terrified silence from the chair where he was bound. Both of his colleagues lay motionless on the floor, pools of blood saturating the rug beneath their lifeless bodies. Neither of them had denied Christ.

"Tell us where the money is!" the men shouted at Ugur.

Ugur didn't understand what they were talking about. Unbeknownst to Ugur, the masterminds behind the massacre—a group of about twenty people that included policemen, university professors, and religious leaders—had encouraged these five men to carry out the attack and get money from the Christians. "Kill them, if necessary," they were instructed.

"Where do you keep the money?" they demanded again. They grabbed Ugur's hand and began slicing his fingers with their knives.

As Ugur suffered inside the office, a missionary couple from Necati's church—Gökhan and his wife, Ozge—arrived at the publishing house. Unaware of the murders happening inside, they walked up to the office and found the door locked. This was unusual. They tried to reach Necati by phone, then Tilmann, but no one answered.

Inside the office, Ugur's phone suddenly rang. One of the attackers handed him the device and forced him to answer. "Tell them you're at the Golden Apricot Hotel," the murderer demanded. The hotel was a fifteen-minute walk from the publishing house.

Ugur did as he was told. "Can you meet us there?" he asked Gökhan.

It didn't make sense to Gökhan and Ozge. Ten days prior, their church had rented a room in the Golden Apricot Hotel to celebrate Easter, but why would Ugur want to meet them there now?

Not knowing what else to do, the young couple agreed to the plan and walked back down the stairs of the publishing house. The tone in Ugur's voice sounded troubled, like he was in distress. When they arrived at the hotel and saw that nobody was there, Gökhan followed his instincts and called the police.

The police arrived at the Zirve Publishing House office within minutes. When the killers heard the police banging on the door, they panicked. One of the men grabbed a knife and stabbed Ugur multiple times. With one final, decisive motion, the assailant slit Ugur's throat.

Just then, the police barged through the door and arrested four of the murderers. All of the men were between the ages of eighteen and twenty-two.

The leader, Emre, escaped through the window and climbed out onto the balcony. He tried to make his way to the ground but fell five stories. Emre would spend weeks in the hospital suffering from brain trauma before being questioned about the crime.

The policemen rushed Ugur, still alive, to the emergency room. After receiving more than fifty units of blood, he died at 6:30 that night.

ele

Semse gasped at the sight of her husband's limp feet hanging from the body bag on the stretcher. Her eyes were fixed on the television screen. Moments later, a second stretcher emerged from the office building. On it was Ugur, Necati's colleague. Semse could see blood pouring from a gash on his neck.

The attackers slit their throats, Semse realized in horror. She let out a piercing scream and dropped to her knees. Her young daughter raced into the room.

"Mom," Esther said, "why are you crying?"

"It's okay," Semse said, struggling to offer her daughter a reassuring smile. "I saw some bad news on the television, but I'll tell you about it a little later." Semse took a deep breath and tried to steady her voice. "Go play with Elisha in the other room."

For hours, Semse waited for word on her husband's condition. She desperately needed to know what happened, but she knew she couldn't take her young children to Necati's office. There was no way she'd be able to hold herself together in front of her kids. As she waited, a strange sensation passed over her. She felt peace and strength. *Am I in shock?*

No, shock cannot give me peace, and it cannot give strength. Semse felt God cover her with His hand, like she was surrounded by a protective bubble. She felt His hand on her heart, and every feeling of despair and sadness disappeared.

From that moment on, Semse felt no hatred for her husband's attackers. She didn't cry, she didn't scream, and she didn't feel lost. Instead, she felt like Necati was still alive, just not on earth.

Semse loved Necati more than she loved herself, and she gave her husband to Jesus. She knew her husband was now alive in heaven with Him.

As news spread in Malatya about the attack at the publishing house, Christian friends arrived at the Aydins' apartment. Throughout the day and well into the evening, more than 500 people came to offer Semse support.

For several hours, Semse didn't know for sure whether her husband was alive or dead. The police didn't call with any updates, nor did any of her Christian associates. Instead, she waited and prayed.

When the newspaper finally arrived, a hush fell over Semse's home. Her eyes scanned the article as her friends and family watched in grave silence. The printed words confirmed what Semse already suspected was true: Necati had been murdered. Tillman was killed as well. Ugur, who had been alive when Semse saw him carried from the office building, died at the hospital from the loss of blood. Semse shared the devastating news of their father's death with her children.

Soon, Semse found herself comforting the Christians who had come to support her. "Why didn't God protect them?" the visitors asked. "Why didn't they protect themselves? Why didn't they carry a gun or have security cameras?" Even in those early moments following Necati's death, Semse knew that the most important thing was for her to help protect their faith.

Less than twenty-four hours after the attack, Tilmann's wife, Susanne Geske, made an astonishing comment about her husband's killers. Her words quickly swept onto the front pages of the country's most prominent newspapers. Instead of calling for vengeance, as the readers might have expected, she shocked all of Turkey with a statement of a different sort: "God, forgive them," Susanne said, "for they know not what they do. I forgive the ones who did this."

When reporters came to Semse's home, she offered the same message. "I forgive them because Jesus forgave me," she said.

"We don't want revenge, and forgiveness is not weakness, but the power of God. It is a gift from above."

It is not me, this forgiveness. It is Jesus in me forgiving the murderers.

A day after the murders, Semse's sister Janet arrived. Together, the two women went to the morgue. Semse walked into the cold room and saw Necati's body lying on a metal table like the abandoned cocoon of a butterfly. She touched his feet and his face. She could see how painfully he died.

But even in death, peace was on his face. *Did they make his face look like this in the morgue?* Semse wondered. *Did they clean it and position it this way to disguise his suffering?*

Semse knew of another believer who died from a heart attack. At his funeral, his grimaced face revealed the pain he felt at the moment of his death.

No, Necati died at peace.

In that moment, God reminded Semse not to fear people who can kill the body because they cannot touch the soul. Death had not touched Necati's soul, and it would not touch hers either.

Back at their apartment, each time the doorbell rang, Semse's children would run, hoping to greet their father. "Daddy!" they shrieked. But each disappointment brought fresh grief, and Semse tried to comfort her little ones as they wilted back into the apartment, like flowers without water.

"Your dad has gone to his real home, to heaven," Semse would remind them. "He's not on earth anymore. He's alive, and he's in heaven."

But the concept of their father's death was difficult for the two children to understand. Once they grasped that he would not be coming home anymore, they were convinced that, perhaps, their father was simply away at work. "Mom, do you think my dad is in his office?" Esther asked. "When is he going to come home?"

"He is in his home with Christ," Semse reminded her daughter.

A week after the killing, the police gave Semse the key to Necati's office. She slowly turned the lock on the door, walked inside, and closed the door quietly behind her. With a meticulous eye, she searched for signs and clues that would reveal something about her husband's final moments on earth.

On the table sat the empty teacup her husband had been drinking from just minutes before his death. Technicians had mopped the men's blood from the floor, but there was blood splattered on the curtain, and in the corner of the room she saw the mop, standing upright. The head had been cleaned, but there was still dried blood on the handle.

They had attempted to erase the crime that had happened in this room. But Semse saw it. There were disturbing signs of violence all around her. Yet even then, all she felt was peace.

~ele~

Shortly after her husband's death, Semse arrived in Izmir for Necati's funeral. Just before the burial, Necati's brother visited Semse in the home where she was staying. She hugged her brother-in-law, but he stood straight like a soldier.

"I came to get Necati's body from you," he said. "Without your permission, they will not give the body to me."

"Why do you want his body?" Semse asked.

"To bury him like a Muslim."

"Why should I give him to you?"

"Because I have his blood in my veins," he replied.

"He is a Christian," Semse said. "A Muslim killed him, and you're asking me to bury him like a Muslim. I cannot give his body to you."

To Semse, Necati's funeral felt more like a wedding celebration. More than 300 Christians gathered to mark Necati's passage from earth to heaven.

Seven-year-old Elisha walked with his mother toward the front of the sanctuary. He wanted to speak, but Semse wasn't sure what he planned to say. When the little boy opened his mouth, though, she was amazed. It seemed like God Himself spoke through her son.

"My dad and Uncle Tilmann and Ugur, they are friends of God, and they died for Jesus," he began. "Because Jesus died for us, we should die for Him too."

When they returned to their seats and began to sing, Esther tried to make sense of her mother's response to the worship music. "Mom, why are you worshiping?" she asked. "Are you happy that my dad died?"

Semse leaned down and looked into her young daughter's eyes. "No, Esther," she said, smiling. "We are celebrating your dad entering heaven. The angels there are celebrating even more than we are here. He is alive, he's just not on this earth. It's like he's just changed his address."

Later, Semse learned that a reporter sitting nearby had witnessed the brief conversation.

"The Christians have hope after death," the reporter said on the television that night. *"This is why they are not miserable at their funerals."*

Semse watched in astonishment as the reporter continued.

"The widows, by forgiving the murderers, accomplished more than missionaries have been able to do in 2,000 years."

ℓ

Christians throughout the city were terrified. Even Semse's church, which had grown substantially in the years since she and

Necati moved to Malatya, shrank to half its size after the murders of Necati, Ugur, and Tilmann. *Who would be the next to die?*

Semse's faith, however, shielded her against the arrows of the enemy. "To suffer with Him and for Him is really worth it," she said. "I didn't lose everything. I gained."

Her friends, Ugur's fiancée and Tilmann's wife, were great comforts. "I am glad my husband died with your husband," Tilmann's widow, Susanne, told her one day. "Otherwise, they would bury the evidence and not go to court."

In the eyes of the government, the life of a Turkish Christian had no value. But because a German brother had been killed, the international attention on the crime was too much for the government to ignore.

As the date of the trial drew near, Semse was asked whether she thought her husband's murderers should be punished with the death penalty.

"No," she said. "I have Jesus' mind, and He would say 'no.' But it's up to the court and the government whether they should be put away for life in prison."

Semse, Ugur's fiancée, and Susanne attended several of the early court sessions, holding out hope that justice would be served. "I kill for Islam," they heard each man confess. "We kill for Islam! We are proud of what we have done, and we will do it again, if needed."

Semse stared silently at the killers, watching them plead their case, one after the other. During a restroom break, Semse and Susanne found themselves face to face with the murderers' mothers. "You have destroyed our children's lives!" one of them said. Semse stayed silent.

Back in the courtroom, when one of the suspects tried to spin the story of his involvement in the murders—claiming to have acted humanely and extolling the fact he placed a towel under

Necati's bleeding head during his torture and murder—Semse could not stay silent any longer. In the eyes of the courtroom, the man looked like a lamb on the outside. But Semse knew that on the inside, he was a wolf, just like Necati had suspected.

"You came to kill," Semse yelled from the gallery, "and then later you act kind? This doesn't make sense." As punishment for her outburst, the judge removed Semse from the courtroom.

ele

Semse worried about her son and daughter. TV news reporters speculated that her children might be kidnapped. She also knew that if something happened to her, her kids would be sent to live with Necati's family.

Each day, Semse brought her children to and from school with police protection. She feared she would be killed so that her Muslim in-laws could take Elisha and Esther and raise them in Islam. To protect them, should anything happen to her, Semse tried to write a will, naming her sister Janet as the guardian of her children. But in Turkey, this was not legal. If Semse died, the court would give the children to her husband's family regardless.

"If the government gives us the children," Necati's family members threatened in news reports, "we will be glad to raise them Muslim."

Semse watched the television broadcast of Necati's sister being interviewed at the courthouse. "I don't believe the Muslims killed my brother," she said. "I believe the *missionary* killed my brother, and Semse made my brother a victim of Christianity. Otherwise, why weren't Semse's brothers killed? Why did my brother die, but not Semse?"

Semse stared at the television, hearing her name broadcast throughout Turkey, listening to her former sister-in-law blindly defend her religion. Semse knew she was now a well-known target. To protect her children, she knew she must flee the country.

Eventually, she was able to secure asylum for her family in the United States. She didn't know how to speak English or how to drive a car, but Semse remembered a conversation she once had with Necati.

"I cannot live without you," she told him, shortly before he was murdered.

"You can, and you will," Necati said. "You can live with Jesus."

∽ℓℓ∾

In 2014, seven years after Necati's torture and murder, and without yet receiving a sentence for their crimes, his killers were temporarily released from prison on the condition that they wear electronic monitoring bracelets. The Turkish court had determined that the length of their detention surpassed the newly adopted maximum limit. The court proceedings would eventually continue, but for the moment, the murderers were free.

When Semse heard the news, she tried to feel frustrated and angry, but the Holy Spirit wouldn't let her. He helped her see the situation from an eternal perspective, and soon Semse made peace with this failure of earthly justice.

It doesn't matter if Necati's killers are in jail or not, she thought. *The only thing that matters is whether they come to Christ. Revenge will come through mercy, not justice.*

Semse prayed for God to pour out His Holy Spirit on these young men to become followers of Christ, just like Necati, Tilmann, and Ugur. *This is the way to glorify God and save their souls.*

In September 2016, in the 115th hearing of the case and nearly a decade after the crime, the court system finally offered some earthly justice against the men who killed Necati. On the charges of "premeditated murder," the court handed down three life sentences to each of the five men. Two other suspects received sentences of multiple years in prison.

In an appalling turn of events, Semse suddenly found herself on the receiving end of her own court case when the offenders began their efforts to clear their names of Islamic terrorism and reclaim the money they'd been ordered to pay the victims' families. In 2016, the court awarded Semse and the other victims' families damages for the crimes committed against Necati and his colleagues. A year later, though, the murderers appealed the ruling. The appeal process and the endless waves of proceedings generated enough stress in Semse that she came down with shingles.

Lord, why is this happening? she begged. *This is unfair. They killed my husband and went to prison. How can they now run the court? This is too much, after all that pain and sacrifice.*

But when she focused her mind on God and His Word, the feelings of anger, hurt, and unfairness went way.

Okay, God, she prayed, *this is* Your *problem. This is* Your *court, more than mine. Yours! Everything is Yours. If You are okay, I will be okay.*

ele

"I didn't work at trying to forgive them," Semse said. "God just gave me a gift."

But the gift of forgiveness didn't eradicate Semse's suffering entirely. "I suffer a lot," she confessed. "I'm going to suffer till the day I die. But I'm not sorry for moving [to Malatya]. This was the best thing that could happen for Necati. He did a miracle; he did a wonderful thing. Necati created a very beautiful scenario of his life."

Semse has prayed for Turkey, for Necati's death to be the seed that brings a new wave of spiritual transformation to the country. "Pray for me to embrace this heritage of Necati's faith," she said.

"Necati left us with that heritage. And that heritage . . . belongs to Turkey, too, and also to his family because we are faithful unto death. We want to be faithful unto death. And even in our loss, even in our trauma, in our aloneness, and in all the difficulties of life, we want to be faithful unto death as Necati's heritage and our story."

With her wedding ring still on her finger, Semse has refused to view herself as a widow. Her husband is alive and well with Jesus in heaven, she knows, and one day she will join him.

But until that day, while she awaits that glorious reunion, Semse confidently trusts that she has everything she needs in this life. She has Jesus to rely on, and "Jesus fills Necati's place."

"We are not victims," Semse boldly declared. "We are victorious in Jesus."

In Her Words:
Alice

In 2011, militant Islamic Fulani attacked Alice's village in Nigeria's Plateau state. Alice and her family were asleep when armed men with covered faces stormed into their home around midnight. After calling out her husband, Bulus, by name, the men shot him as he opened the bedroom door.

We heard their footsteps. Just the sound of their shoes was enough to kill you. The shock and the fear could kill you. We never thought a thing like this would happen to us.

My whole body was weak. Tears were running down my face, but I could not cry out loud. My baby, Jerome, held me tight. He did not cry, but he was wide awake, watching. The sound of gunshots woke the other kids up. They also held on to me as they cried. My husband's mother came out and started wailing.

Bulus had a small phone. When he was shot, I heard his phone ring. I answered the call and said, "Send soldiers, my husband has been shot." The Fulani[1] attackers were still in the village at the time. Bulus was lying on the ground, shouting.

To this day, I do not know who was on the other end of that call.

Fulani attackers were still shooting outside, and hearing the gunshots scared me. I put my infant son down and went to grab wraps.[2] I asked Bulus where he had been shot, and I used the wraps to tie his wounds. The attackers left after shooting sporadically.

I could not leave Bulus, so I shouted for help. The soldiers came and asked if I knew the attackers. I told them I did not see the men, but my husband knew the man who shot him.

Two of the soldiers loaded Bulus into a vehicle to take him to the hospital. He died on the way. We buried him the next day in the community graveyard. The service did not last long in case the Fulani attackers came back.

Bulus was my best friend. I was heartbroken. At some point, I wanted to die and leave the kids. I cried. I could not eat. I asked myself when the crying would end. I prayed to God to take away the tears. God answered. It was not easy, but eventually, I started finding peace and healing. And then the Fulani attacked again.

---

1. The Fulani are a people group that is predominately Muslim. In Nigeria, some Fulani are militant and attack Christians.
2. A piece of fabric wrapped around the waist.

One Saturday, the kids, my mother-in-law, and I had finished our morning devotion. It was a normal day. I started getting ready to go to the farm. I put one-year-old Jerome on my back. I told my kids to make breakfast and eat before I came back, and we would sort out lunch. I said goodbye, leaving them to play and enjoy the morning with their grandmother.

I went outside to meet my neighbors who were also on their way to their farms. But before we could head out, one of my friends ran toward us. She told us she didn't think today would be a good day to go to our farms because she had seen a lot of Fulani there. Immediately, our young boys, including one of my sons, climbed a nearby hill. They saw a bunch of men dressed in black and carrying weapons as they approached the village. As soon as the boys saw the attackers, they told us all to leave. We all started running. I ran with the baby on my back. My children and mother-in-law ran in various directions. Everyone was worried about their own lives. No one remembered family that day.

There's only one bridge in and out of our village. When I got there, I noticed that two of the attackers had circled and run ahead of everyone to the bridge. They wouldn't let anyone escape. But as people ran across the bridge, the attackers seemed to be struggling with their firearms. They couldn't get them to work. I prayed in my heart, and God heard. By His grace, everyone got across before the guns started working again.

I was in shock. I never thought this would happen. No one did. This was the first time something like this had happened in our village. All I could do was stare in disbelief. I couldn't comfort my baby or anyone else.

We all thought we could return to our village. But the soldiers told us there was nothing left. There was no way we could go back. My home was gone. The place I knew and loved was gone.

My heart sank as reality hit me. I was in a strange place with only the clothes on my back. All I could do was cry.

I looked at my situation and asked myself what I could do to take care of my children. My first son has no father and no uncles, which means the duty of raising him to be a man falls on me. And what if I die? The future of my children rests on me. So, I prayed and asked God to give me wisdom. "Is this how I'll continue? Running for the rest of my life?" I asked Him. "I ran and came here. Now I'm running somewhere else? Please, give me strength."

When I prayed, I felt at peace. I felt a burden lift. God gave me strength. Without this strength, I wouldn't have been able to endure hardship after hardship. That's why I keep asking Him to continue giving me strength.

Following Christ hurts—a lot! You have to be ready. I face different challenges every day, but God always saves me. After the suffering is enjoyment. I will follow Christ no matter what. If I were to come back again to do this life all over, I would still choose Christ. It has been worth it. I have not seen any other path that beats the path of Christ. If not for Him, I wouldn't be here. If not for Him, there is no life. Without Him, I would not be alive today.

Alice and her children were displaced for the next two years and found shelter wherever they could, including the small hallway of an elderly woman's home. Eventually, front-line workers helped her settle into a new home and rebuild her life. Though she has experienced immense suffering at the hands of Fulani Islamic militants, she has forgiven those who killed her husband, and she continues to share Christ's love with the Fulani in her community.

Susanna

The Hope That We Have

PETALING JAYA, MALAYSIA
FEBRUARY 13, 2017

Susanna Koh stepped from the car and hurried across the parking lot toward the police station. It was just after 10:00 p.m., and she knew her friend, an attorney, would be arriving shortly. Susanna reached the building and paused to wait for him.

Several officers had congregated outside and stared suspiciously at her.

After Susanna introduced herself and explained why she was there, her friend pulled into the parking lot and rushed over to join her. She felt comforted by his presence as an officer ushered them into a small interior room inside the station. Her son Jonathan was waiting just outside the room.

She'd only been to the police station once before—to file a police report after a thief snatched her purse—and that had been handled in the main hall of the station. *Shouldn't we be in the main hall to file a missing person report as well?* Susanna thought as she lowered herself into a chair. *This is a bit odd.*

63

Her attorney friend settled into the chair next to her, and across the table sat a young officer in plain clothes typing at a computer. From above, blinding lights flooded the room.

When the officer finally looked up from his monitor, Susanna explained to him that she'd come to file a missing person report for her husband, Pastor Raymond Koh.

Her husband had missed a scheduled meeting earlier in the day. Susanna hadn't been able to reach him by phone, and he hadn't come home. Jonathan had spent the evening searching local police stations and hospitals, she said, but he had not been able to find any information about the whereabouts of his father.

After several questions, the officer finally asked Susanna, "Did Pastor Raymond proselytize Muslims? Did he teach Christianity to Malay Muslims?"

A knot formed in the pit of Susanna's stomach. Ethnically, Susanna and her husband are Chinese, who comprise 30 percent of the Malaysian population. About 60 percent of the population is ethnic Malays. The federal constitution requires the Malay people to speak the Malay language, practice the Malay culture, and observe the Malay religion, which is Islam. That makes it illegal for Christians to share their faith with people who are ethnically Malay.

Susanna had a frightening thought. *Have the police arrested Raymond?* She knew one careless response could be devastating. Her answers could jeopardize her husband's safety.

"Did Pastor Raymond proselytize Muslims?" the officer asked again.

"I don't know," Susanna replied. To protect his wife, Raymond shared few details of his work. She explained to the officer how she and her husband spent their days engaged with separate priorities—she had her own jewelry-making business and wasn't involved in her husband's work.

But the officer wasn't satisfied with Susanna's explanation. He asked again, and Susanna gave the same answer. "I don't know."

"Does your husband go to the north to evangelize?" Susanna's heartbeat quickened. *The officer seems to know about Raymond's work and activities!*

"Why does he go to the villages?"

For hours, the officer interrogated Susanna. Instead of focusing on where Raymond might be, where he'd been going that day, or what road he would have taken, the officer was only interested in Raymond's Christian activities and the names of his coworkers.

Each time Susanna answered one of the officer's questions, he paused and typed. Hours into the night, he allowed Susanna one five-minute bathroom break, and when she returned, the interrogation continued. None of the questions was relevant to finding Raymond, and she fought to remain focused.

Susanna looked up at the officer. "I'm not answering any more questions," she finally said, stressed and frustrated by the young officer's lack of concern for finding Raymond. "I have rights," she said, "and I'm going to go look for my husband. The important thing for you to do is to go out there and look for my husband."

Finally, with one *click* of his keyboard, the officer's printer hummed to life. He gathered the pages and slid them across the table to Susanna. "Sign this," he demanded.

Under the piercing lights of the interrogation room, Susanna quickly skimmed the document before her. It was a statement— her statement—but its focus wasn't on Raymond's whereabouts. Instead, the statement centered on Raymond's "illegal" activity. In it, Susanna saw the two questions that concerned her the most: Did Pastor Raymond proselytize Muslims? Did he teach Christianity to Malay Muslims?

Susanna stood from her chair and gathered her purse. It was nearly three o'clock in the morning, and she'd been at the police station for five fruitless hours. The trauma of the evening was taking its toll, and she'd had enough. She walked out the door and headed home.

ᘓᘓ

Susanna was born in Malaysia and raised, along with her siblings, by her devoutly Buddhist grandmother in the city of Kuala Lumpur. Susanna's parents lived in a small village, and her grandmother would take Susanna and her siblings back and forth to visit them.

Growing up, Susanna's daily chore was to place fragrant joss sticks in urns near each Buddhist altar throughout their home. In the living room was a large wooden altar surrounded by red lights where her grandmother placed pictures of the many gods she revered, including prominent Buddhists from history as well as her own ancestors. There, Susanna's grandmother prayed to these men and women from the past who had become deities to her. Even as a young girl, Susanna felt no personal connection to her grandmother's gods. Somehow, she knew none of them was the real God.

Known by her friends as "The Tigress," her grandmother had rigid ideas for how her granddaughter should behave. When she scolded Susanna for some sort of infraction, Susanna scurried up the stairs to her bedroom. As she looked out the window at the sky, she talked to God. "I know that You are the true God," Susanna said. "Not those idols."

One day, a neighbor friend invited Susanna to Sunday school at a nearby church. It was there she first heard about Jesus Christ. Susanna continued to attend church, and by the time she was fifteen, she had professed faith in Christ. She kept her decision secret from her grandmother, confiding only in her Christian friends. But the next year, when Susanna wanted to be baptized, she finally told her grandmother about her new faith. "If you get baptized," her grandmother warned, "don't come back."

Susanna had nowhere else to go, but her desire to express her faith publicly through baptism was overwhelming. She knew the peace she had experienced through Jesus, and she wanted to obey Him. Even though she risked rejection from her family, Susanna followed through with her commitment to be baptized.

Afterward, Susanna snuck back home, certain that her grandmother would chase her away; but, to her surprise, she didn't. However, when Susanna's family learned of her Christian faith, they ridiculed her. Her grandmother and siblings mocked her whenever she prayed to God before meals. "Why are you thanking God? Did God make the food for you?" they asked. But in time, many of Susanna's family members would eventually come to know Christ.

Years later, when Susanna was in Bible college, she traced her family tree and learned that her great-grandfather had been a Christian who heard about Jesus from a missionary visiting his village. When the missionary spoke to the community in their native Hakka language,[1] Susanna's great-grandfather and his family invited their neighbors to come hear the missionary's preaching. Susanna's grandmother and mother heard the gospel then, but they didn't yet understand it.

Generations later, after many years of her great-grandfather's fervent prayers for the salvation of his family, his great-grand-daughter, Susanna, came to believe in Christ. Susanna prayed for her mother for years, and she helped her learn to read by studying the Bible. When her mother finally came to know the Lord, she

---

1. The Hakka dialect is a distinct language spoken by Hakka Chinese. Almost 2 million Hakka Chinese live in Malaysia. Raymond and Susanna are both Hakka Chinese.

shared her faith with her own mother, brother, and sister, along with their children. Susanna realized that, by God's grace, generations of her family had come to know the Lord "backwards."

⁕

When Susanna turned twenty, two missionaries with an organization called Operation Mobilization came to speak at her church. The young men arrived in a big truck, a foreign vehicle with foreign license plates—one unlike any Susanna had ever seen in Malaysia. The strange truck piqued her curiosity, and she was eager to hear what these missionaries had to say. The two men shared at the evening meeting about their experiences trusting God as they drove the truck across the continent—from India all the way through Bangladesh, Burma (Myanmar), and Thailand, to Malaysia—spreading the gospel along the way.

Wow, Susanna thought. *It's so dangerous to make these trips, and God protected them.* The depth of the missionaries' commitment, how they gave up everything in their lives to serve God, challenged Susanna. *I want that type of faith*, Susanna thought. *I want to be part of this.*

When Susanna was told about an upcoming conference in Singapore where she could learn more about Operation Mobilization, she truly sensed the Lord calling her into missions. Susanna's mother had been a Christian for only a few months, but by now she had learned to read the Bible. As Susanna explained her desire to learn more about joining Operation Mobilization, her mother thought of Matthew 28:19: "Go therefore and make disciples of all nations, baptizing them in the name of the Father and of the Son and of the Holy Spirit." Her mother understood Susanna's calling and eventually allowed her daughter to go to the conference.

In the weeks leading up to the conference, God prepared Susanna's heart. She listened to tapes, read books about Christian discipleship, and was reading the devotional *Streams in the Desert* during her daily time with the Lord. Leaders in her church were also supportive of her plan to go. During this time, Susanna realized she yearned for a deeper walk and more intimate relationship with the Lord. She wanted to grow, and she wanted to serve Jesus Christ.

Susanna's life was changed at the conference. She learned about the mission organization's many opportunities, some on land in India and others on a ship at sea. Susanna was scared of snakes, so the thought of going to India—a country full of venomous snakes whose bites are often deadly—was unappealing. Instead, she sought more information about the ship. She attended a second conference, this one in Belgium with young men and women from all over the world. Meeting so many other young people who were also working to serve God was an amazing experience.

When the summer ended, Susanna traveled to London to work among immigrants. Despite the culture shock, she learned how to share her testimony by going door-to-door to evangelize— sometimes having the door slammed in her face.

During her second month in England, Susanna was asked to be the girls' team leader. It was an unexpected request, and she felt inadequate for the task. But God gave her grace, and she depended on Him more and more for wisdom.

When her time in England drew to a close, Susanna sensed God was calling her to join Operation Mobilization's ship, *Logos*. On board, Susanna was given the job of pantry boss, working each day from 5:00 a.m. until midnight. From the *Logos*, Susanna soon transferred to the *Doulos*.

She and the team worked twelve-hour days, tirelessly cleaning the ship. Despite the grueling schedule, Susanna was content. *I*

am so satisfied and so happy, she prayed. *This is what I came to do—to serve.*

Susanna's hands eventually became dry and shriveled from the harsh cleansers. Looking down at her wrinkled skin, she prayed, *These hands and feet are for You, Lord.* When she awoke the next morning, she was shocked to see her hands again looked young, like the skin of a newborn baby. For Susanna, it was a reminder of how good God is, and how much He cares for even the little things in life.

On board the *Doulos*, Susanna worked with a team of twenty-five young people from different countries. She was again given responsibility for the pantry, and she coordinated with the ship's temperamental Norwegian cook to help feed the 300 people on board.

One evening, a man approached Susanna as she worked in the pantry long after dinner had ended. She knew he was one of the ship's engineers, a welder, and she glanced down at his grease-stained overalls. He had just come from working in the ship's smokestack, and his face was blackened from the ship's exhaust.

"Do you have any food?" he asked.

Susanna was annoyed. *He should know the leftovers are kept in the walk-in refrigerator at the bottom of the ship. He should have gone to the mess hall for the engineers.* The ship's engineers were known for being workaholics, pulling sixteen-hour workdays.

"I'm sorry," she said coldly, eager for the man to leave her alone. "We don't keep the leftover food here."

The man stormed off in search of a late-night meal, and Susanna returned to her evening work. Little did she know that she would, years later, meet the man again.

ele

Work aboard the *Doulos* was strenuous, but the team felt like a family and enjoyed having devotional time together each day. The crew prayed, worshiped, and engaged in evangelism together at each port. They became more comfortable sharing their faith, and they committed to reading through the entire Bible. Susanna grew in her relationship with the Lord. It was a time that would lay a foundation for the rest of her life.

A year later, after completing the discipleship program onboard the *Doulos*, Susanna was ready to take the next step of her journey with Operation Mobilization. She transferred to a team on land and began traveling across Europe and Asia.

Susanna and a dozen other young women climbed into the back of a box truck with only one small window, and the convoy of missionaries began their journey. Each night, in the back of the truck, they spread out their sleeping bags on top of the stacks of boxes of Christian literature, suitcases of warm clothing, and other equipment. Their intended destination was the rat- and snake-infested country of India—the one place Susanna didn't want to go.

The journey took months. They sometimes stopped to cook their meals in fields, opening canned food or spreading peanut butter and jelly on bread they'd purchased from local bakers. As they drove through warmer climates, the truck was sweltering; and as they traveled through colder regions, the young women shivered. When the convoy passed through dangerous regions, the missionaries memorized Psalm 91 to squelch their fears.

The team traveled through Iran during the country's revolution. Susanna peeked through the small window to see a crowd of citizens toppling a statue of the shah of Iran. Smoke and flames spilled from shops and banks, and soldiers lined the roads as the missionaries passed through.

When they traveled through Afghanistan, the young women walked across sand dunes to find privacy to use the bathroom.

Back in the truck, their leader—a man who served as a missionary in Afghanistan and was familiar with the area—cautioned Susanna that the area they would pass through next was known as Robber Strip. "It's a very dangerous strip," he warned as he sat in the driver's seat next to his wife. "Since we're traveling in a foreign vehicle, they'll come and stop us, for sure."

Moments later, the team heard a pummeling sound on the roof of the truck. Susanna's heart raced. *Are we under attack?*

"Praise the Lord!" their leader exclaimed. "It's raining! It's now a bad day for robbers." In the unlikely desert of Afghanistan, God had provided rain to give the team safe passage.

Finally, Susanna and the others arrived in Calcutta. Homeless people with leprosy slept on pieces of cardboard lining the streets. For the first seven months, she tried to adjust to the culture shock of living in such an impoverished, crowded city.

One day, as she helped wash dishes, Susanna learned that she would, again, be given the responsibility of serving as team leader over the girls, a group of young Indian women. "No, no, no," Susanna protested. "I just arrived, and I don't know anything about India." But the decision had already been made. *Wow, God,* Susanna prayed. *You've thrown me in the deep end of the pool again. Why?*

And it wasn't long before Susanna encountered the snakes she'd feared. As she and a group of girls walked into their bedroom, one of them yelled, "Oh my goodness, there's a snake in the room!"

Susanna was surprised to discover she wasn't the first to flee. "Be quiet," she said. "Walk out slowly, one by one . . ."

When a man came in to decapitate the petrified snake, Susanna recognized God's provision. She had dreaded the snakes for so long, but she saw God take care of her in the experience. She had confidence that His grace would be sufficient in any situation they encountered.

Susanna's ministry routine also consisted of door-to-door evangelism and ten-day breaks during which she and the other young women studied. They sold Bibles and Christian books to fund their living expenses, but sometimes it wasn't enough. However, God always provided.

Often, leaders from the organization came to their missions building and offered teaching and training. When they finished, they gave Susanna's team boxes filled with books, Bibles, and tracts and drove the young women to nearby villages to sell the books.

On one occasion, the missionaries had arranged to meet a local person for a picnic the next day. However, as the women gathered in their missions building the evening before, they discovered they had no money for the needed train tickets. As the group prayed, they heard movement downstairs. It was well after 11:00 p.m.

Someone is trying to rob us!

Eventually, one of the young women mustered the courage to call out. "What do you want?" she asked.

"I want to buy a Bible," came the surprising reply.

The missionaries hurried downstairs and found a man searching for truth. They shared the gospel with him, and he placed his trust in Christ.

The Bible he wanted to purchase was an expensive one, and once the transaction was complete, the young women tallied the funds. They were delighted to discover that the money was enough to cover train tickets for all twelve of them, along with the food for the picnic. At nearly midnight, God had answered their prayer.

Snakes weren't the only danger Susanna encountered in India. One afternoon, she decided to disregard the cultural prohibitions against women speaking in public in order to share her faith. She walked to a nearby market and began to boldly speak about the gospel.

From the corner of her eye, Susanna saw a Hindu man barreling toward her. Clearly, he was furious, and Susanna was certain she was about to be attacked. Would he strike her face? Would she be too injured to walk back to the missions building? She braced for the impact.

At the last moment, though, something miraculous happened. Just before he reached her, the man turned and walked away.

With her heart still pounding, Susanna exhaled a prayer of amazement and gratitude: "God, You protected me!"

⁓

Susanna spent two years in India before returning to Malaysia. There, she continued to work with Operation Mobilization, and it wasn't long before she reconnected with the man she'd first met years before aboard the *Doulos*—the welder with the greasy overalls. Susanna remembered keeping her distance from the man, aside from one unpleasant interaction about leftover food.

In Malaysia, though, the man served as the country leader for the organization, and Susanna was to work for him providing administrative support. His name was Raymond Koh.

As Raymond and Susanna worked together, he learned that she had failed her driving test three times, so he offered to teach her. Early each morning, before the sun became too hot, he arrived at Susanna's home to begin her lesson. As she learned to drive, she also learned that Raymond was a gentle and patient man. With each passing lesson, Susanna's feelings for Raymond blossomed into something more than friendship.

Her colleagues at work noticed the growing relationship between the two. "Hey, I think he likes you," her colleagues would whisper. "He's always looking at you."

Soon, the day arrived for Susanna to take her fourth driving test, but she failed again. As she stared down at the rejection letter, aware that all her effort had once again been in vain, Raymond walked up and gently took her by the hand.

"It's okay," he said, comforting his friend. He paused for just a moment before saying, "I like you."

Susanna looked up from the letter and smiled. "I like you too."

With the blessing of Operation Mobilization, Susanna and Raymond began a year-long courtship. They talked about ministry and the great risks associated with sharing Christ's love with the unreached. "Are you willing to go to jail if you marry me?" he asked.

Susanna nodded. "I'm willing to accept that, if it's the Lord's will." She knew if it was God's will for them to be married, then He would take care of them. If she went to prison with Raymond, God would give her grace to deal with the situation, just as He'd given her grace in India to deal with the rats and snakes.

ele

Susanna and Raymond married, and their first child, a son they named Jonathan, arrived a year later. Soon, their daughters, Elizabeth and Esther, would join the growing family. They moved to New Zealand, where they lived for more than three years while Raymond and Susanna attended a Bible college. After graduation, Raymond knew the Lord was specifically telling him to return to Malaysia, as He had an unfinished task for Raymond to do.

Upon their return to Malaysia, the Kohs began planting churches. It was a passion that would continue for thirteen years. At the same time, Susanna started a kindergarten, and through both of these avenues, Susanna and Raymond began to bring people to the Lord. In Raymond's free time, he had another passion: to share Christ's love with the unreached.

After a devastating tsunami just after Christmas in 2004, the Kohs began a charity to help meet the needs of their community. They provided groceries to single mothers and taught them to earn an income through sewing, baking, and making jewelry. The couple began several reading centers, one in Kuala Lumpur where impoverished children came for literacy classes. They worked with the poor, marginalized, and needy, including people living with HIV/AIDS, and they named their charity *Harapan Komuniti*, or Hope Community. Susanna and Raymond knew that in order to be the hands and feet of Christ, they needed to be where the people were. With acts of kindness, they could touch people's lives and meet the needs of the whole person, not just the soul.

In August 2011, during the Muslim observance of Ramadan, Susanna and Raymond gathered in a church that allowed them to host a celebration dinner to thank their supporters of Harapan Komuniti. Around 150 friends from different ethnicities and religions were among those who supported their charity and attended the event.

Suddenly, there was a commotion just outside the door. The attendees fell silent as at least fifty men poured into the room. Quickly, Susanna noticed that some of the men were wearing orange vests affixed with the emblem of the religious authorities. The others, she surmised, must be police.

All of the guests were in shock. Never before had a church building in Malaysia been raided. Susanna stood and quickly ushered the men back out of the room, closing the door behind her.

"Do you have a warrant to come into the building?" she asked. "You need a warrant."

"We don't need a warrant!" one of the men replied. "Are Muslims here?"

They were in search of Muslims.

"This is a closed meeting," she told them, "and you do not have an invitation." Susanna then explained the nature of the gathering, that it was a celebration dinner and not a Christian worship service. They weren't even meeting in the church sanctuary. But the authorities were unrelenting. Susanna knew that even if this wasn't a formal church service, the religious authorities would fear that Muslims in attendance might be persuaded to leave Islam for Christianity by simply being in a church building.

Inside, Raymond formulated a plan of escape. Instead of identifying and handing the Muslims in attendance over to the authorities, the group would form a united front in hopes of confusing the officers. In solidarity, perhaps they could walk from the room to safety.

One by one, they stood. An Indian man took hold of a Chinese man's hand, and he in turn grasped the arm of a Malay.

As Susanna continued talking to the officers outside the room, the door opened. She turned around and watched as people streamed from the room in one long, connected procession.

Unfortunately, Pastor Raymond's plan only delayed the inevitable. The religious authorities plucked twelve people who appeared to be Muslim from the line, and the police took them away for questioning. From there, some would be sent for "re-education" in a prison camp, an intense process of enduring Muslim propaganda and, oftentimes, torture in hopes of forcing them to adhere to the tenets of Islam.

The next morning, Susanna and Raymond woke to newspaper headlines condemning the raid. "*Church leaders slam raid by state Islamic department*," one headline read. In the days that followed, religious authorities threatened to prosecute the Muslims under sharia.[2] Eventually, the sultan of Malaysia, the constitutional

---

2. Sharia law is Islamic law applied to Muslims.

head of state, was drawn into the situation. In an effort to squelch the public uprisings and restore peace to the nation, he decreed that no one would be prosecuted. Finally, the Muslims who had attended the celebration dinner were released from further action.

The raid began a series of threats. Soon after, the Kohs received a strange package in the mail. They opened it to find two bullets and a bag of white powder marked "anthrax." A note, written menacingly in red, warned, "We know what you're doing, and we want to kill you."

Pastor Raymond reported the death threat to the police, but nothing came from the investigation.

Frantic, Susanna wanted to leave the country. A colleague encouraged Raymond to take a brief break, so he and Susanna packed their suitcases and boarded a plane to Australia.

Raymond was encouraged to stay in Australia, but he couldn't be persuaded. "God didn't say the task in Malaysia is finished," he told Susanna.

Susanna agreed. Even at the risk of losing their lives, they returned to Malaysia and continued their work.

By 2016, Susanna began to notice subtle changes in her husband's activities. Raymond went for long prayer walks around the neighborhood, and he spent time memorizing large passages of Scripture. "I just finished memorizing 1 Corinthians 13," he told his wife one day.

Susanna also noticed a sense of urgency in her husband to preach the gospel. "I might only have five years left," he told her. And as the months went on, Pastor Raymond's urgency increased. He seemed to feel that his time was limited, that God was preparing him for something to come. "Maybe I only have a year and a half left."

Whoa, Susanna thought. *What's going on here?*

Soon, she would know.

⟳

Susanna moved throughout her friend's kitchen and cleaned up the remains of breakfast as the two children in her care rested nearby. Just days earlier, the children's sister had an operation to remove a malignant brain tumor, and Susanna was happy to babysit while her friends took their daughter to her post-op appointment at the hospital.

As she finished in the kitchen, Susanna remembered she had left a packet of shrimp paste, a staple ingredient in Malaysian cooking, sitting in the trunk of her car. The shrimp paste was a gift for a friend who had been staying in their charity's guest house and who was scheduled to return home to Indonesia that morning. Susanna had forgotten to give Raymond the parcel when he left for an important meeting that afternoon.

When she couldn't find her cell phone, Susanna realized she must have left it charging at the guest house. She used a cell phone her friend had loaned her to call Raymond. Minutes later, her husband arrived at the apartment to retrieve the shrimp paste from his wife's car. With the gift safely in hand, he told Susanna "goodbye," and then drove away in his white Honda Accord.

As soon as he left, Susanna remembered she had forgotten to mention her cell phone. The guest house wasn't far away, and she wanted to catch Raymond before he dropped off the shrimp paste. She quickly dialed Raymond once more and asked him to retrieve her phone when he delivered the gift. With a satisfied sigh, Susanna could now concentrate all her attention on the children.

⟳

Raymond turned his car off the highway and onto a quiet, palm-lined residential street. It was just before 11:00 a.m., long after the rush-hour traffic subsided, and he was headed to drop off the shrimp paste at the church's guest house.

Behind Pastor Raymond, three large, black SUVs also exited the highway. Two sedans and two motorbikes traveled with them.

Suddenly, in one swift, choreographed motion, the SUVs surrounded Pastor Raymond's car—one in front, one behind him, and one on his right, blocking the driver's side—and forced him to an abrupt stop.[3] A metal traffic barrier barricaded the passenger side of his car.

Eight men dressed in black, their faces covered by black balaclava masks, leapt from the SUVs. Several were armed.

The men rushed at Pastor Raymond and encircled his car. The Honda surged forward as Raymond tried to escape, but there was nowhere to go. He was trapped on all sides. One of the men smashed the window next to Raymond, and the masked operatives muscled him from the vehicle.

Another man darted from one of the accompanying sedans, his video camera fixed on the scene. The two men on motorbikes stood guard.

A green hatchback approached from behind, its driver unaware of the scene unfolding before him. Hooded men from the two sedans rushed toward the vehicle and waved him away. There could be no witnesses. The driver of the hatchback threw his car into reverse and hurried backwards down the street. One of the motorbikes followed him, ensuring he stayed far enough away so as not to interfere.

Pastor Raymond struggled with his aggressors, but the masked men easily overpowered him and threw him into an SUV. One of

---

3. Driving in Malaysia is on the left side of the road.

the men jumped into the driver's seat of Raymond's Honda and thrust the car into gear.

In one smooth, synchronized movement, the vehicles glided forward and evacuated the street. The only evidence left at the scene were shards of broken glass and the license plate from Pastor Raymond's Honda.

In all, seven vehicles and at least fifteen men were involved in the operation.

The abduction of Pastor Raymond Koh took only forty-two seconds.

ele

Susanna's friends returned home that afternoon from a successful appointment at the hospital. Their daughter was well on the road to recovery, and Susanna was thrilled. She gathered her purse and began the short drive back home.

Back in her apartment, she dialed Raymond's number. The call went straight to voicemail. She tried a couple more times, but the only response was an automated outgoing message. *It's a bit strange that he isn't answering*, Susanna thought, feeling apprehension creep into her heart. She walked into the kitchen, prepared dinner, and waited for Raymond to return her call.

Later that evening, Jonathan came home with his mother's cell phone in hand. When Susanna saw the many missed calls on the screen, her heart raced. She called Raymond's colleague, the man with whom he'd been scheduled to meet.

Raymond never made it to the meeting.

Susanna panicked. Her husband was consistent and punctual. If he said he would be somewhere, then he'd be there. But dinner time had now come and gone with no sign of Raymond. Susanna phoned several friends, first a pastor and then a lawyer. When the lawyer didn't answer, she called the pastor back. "Go and file a missing person report at the police station," he said. Minutes later, the lawyer called back with the same advice.

Susanna hurried to the police station.

⁓ℓℓ⁓

SIX HOURS LATER

Susanna and her son returned home from the police station utterly exhausted and frustrated by the police's unwillingness to find Raymond. Before taking a much-needed shower, Susanna texted some Christian friends and asked them to pray. It wasn't long before the guard at their apartment called on the intercom. A detective had arrived and wanted to speak to Susanna.

"You saw me just now at the police station," the man said. "Can I come up?"

Have the police followed me home? Susanna wondered, terrified. In case the man had come from the police department and planned to search her home, she tried to stall and told him she needed to consult her lawyer.

The detective was livid. "You are wasting my time!" he scolded, frustration evident in his voice. Upset, the detective left.

Rushing around her apartment, Susanna took piles of gospel tracts and threw them in the garbage outside and ferried all of the Bibles to Christian neighbors for safekeeping, sanitizing her home of anything that could be considered incriminating. It had been more than twenty-four hours since she had slept, but her racing mind—waves of fear, worry, and stress—kept her awake.

Just a few hours later, the police again called in Susanna for questioning. This time, she was told to go to the police headquarters, and a specially trained, elite branch of the police took over. By now, Susanna knew something horrible had happened to her husband. When she arrived, police again bombarded her with the same questions as before, then allowed her to return home once more.

ele

Word spread quickly of Pastor Raymond's disappearance, and by the next day, major newspapers were contacting Susanna's lawyer to interview her.

Susanna believed the police had taken her husband in secret, but now Susanna wanted to tell the world. "Okay," she said. "I'll do it."

The news reports immediately went viral, and as she watched them on television, she learned the first bit of useful information about her husband's disappearance. The man who witnessed Raymond's abduction had filed his own report with the police, and journalists had unearthed the report and included the content in their coverage. Headlines about Raymond's disappearance filled the morning's papers, and finally, Susanna had something to go on: the name of the street where Raymond was kidnapped.

Susanna and her son rushed to the site of Raymond's abduction. They slowly made their way along the road, looking for any evidence of the struggle. When they found shattered glass on the ground, they knew they were close.

Seeing a gas station nearby, Susanna and Jonathan stopped. *They will have good cameras*, she thought. She entered the station and asked the worker about their cameras and the video footage from the other day.

"The police came and told us that we are not allowed to give it to you," the worker replied.

Susanna's heart filled with disappointment.

Jonathan glanced across the street and noticed that many of the homes had security cameras. What if one of them had captured the kidnapping?

Homes lined both sides of the road, and Susanna and her son spent the next few nights going door-to-door in search of security footage. Finally, at the nearby home of a man with two cameras, they found what they'd been looking for: one of his cameras faced the exact spot where Raymond had been taken.

Susanna and Jonathan returned home and divided up the hours of footage among their closest friends. For hours, they all scoured the files. Finally, a friend called and said he'd found the relevant portion of video. He transferred the digital segment to Susanna, and when the video filled her television screen, she couldn't breathe. She watched in horror as the hooded men smashed Raymond's car window and dragged him into the black SUV. Tears welled in her eyes as her husband struggled against his captors.

Susanna quickly alerted the police to the existence of the video. But instead of being grateful for the evidence, the officer was furious. Frustrated by the lack of help from the police, Pastor Raymond's friends released the security footage online. In no time, it went viral on the internet.

ele

The video footage of Pastor Raymond's abduction shocked the nation. "An elderly pastor was abducted while driving alone in PJ,"[4] read the headline of one early article.

Not long after her husband's disappearance and amidst the flurry of news reports about Raymond's abduction, Susanna knew she needed to forgive the kidnappers. "I decided that I needed to make that decision, just like an act of the will," Susanna said. "But, this didn't mean that I was completely there with my emotions

---

4. Petaling Jaya is a suburb of Kuala Lumpur, Malaysia's capital. Locals refer to Petaling Jaya as "PJ."

or feelings. I just didn't want to have any darkness, any shadow, anything that would stop God from working in my life."

While Susanna was at lunch one day, a Christian man she didn't know well approached her and said, "You need to pray for the police." Right away, Susanna knew God was speaking to her. *I have a bad attitude toward the police*, she thought. *This is why He is sending someone to tell me to pray for the police.*

On her way home, Susanna felt convicted, and she wept. She repented of her sentiments about the police and released to the Lord her forgiveness for them. There, driving down the road, Susanna experienced a breakthrough in her feelings.

Shortly thereafter, a whistleblower revealed the identity of the man who had led the operation to kidnap Raymond. When Susanna learned this man—the man likely responsible for her husband's disappearance—had been hospitalized for cancer treatment, she discovered the location of the hospital and decided to take him a fruit basket. It would be a practical, tangible expression of her forgiveness.

Susanna brought along a Muslim friend, knowing the man might possibly agree to accept prayer from a Muslim. "Bless your enemies," Susanna knew. "Pray for them."

But when she and her friend arrived at the hospital reception desk, Susanna's plan was thwarted.

"What is the name?" the receptionist asked. Susanna responded. The woman typed into a computer and then said, "He is not registered."

"Hmm," Susanna said, confused. "Has he been discharged?"

The receptionist searched once more. "No," she said, "he has never been registered here."

Susanna walked back to her car, fruit basket in hand and friend by her side, wondering if the man had lied about his hospitalization in order to avoid the scheduled inquiry by the Human Rights Commission.

Even though she had forgiven the police, Susanna's emotions were a process. Still feeling intense anger toward the men who were involved in the abduction, she experienced moments of bitterness. When she saw any police officers—the men she now knew were responsible for Raymond's disappearance—she wanted to slap their faces or strangle them.

But each time, God restrained her. Soon, Susanna was able to echo Jesus' words in her own heart: *Father, forgive them, for they know not what they do.*

During the weeks that followed, Susanna became acutely aware of police efforts to intimidate her. They photographed her with long-lens cameras and sought information from her acquaintances. Fearing that the police were tracking her through her cell phone, Susanna bought a new phone and changed her number several times. She stopped meeting publicly with her friends and focused on her jewelry business. She had trouble sleeping and began to have panic attacks. "Calm down, calm down," her lawyer would say as Susanna struggled to breathe.

At night, Susanna listened to worship songs on her phone. One song reminded her how God is faithful and strong forever.

Before the kidnapping, Raymond and Susanna had planned to attend a silent retreat in Thailand. Now that their daughter, Elizabeth, had returned home from studying in the United States, Susanna decided they should attend together. It would be a welcome respite from the chaos now engulfing her life.

At the retreat center, nestled within the quiet beauty of God's creation and far away from the hounding reporters and police, Susanna was able to focus on the Lord. She was finally able to experience His peace.

One morning, as she walked the grounds and prayed, Susanna fell to her knees. For nearly an hour, she poured out her heart to God. She thought about the words of a favorite worship song that assured her of the Lord's presence in every tomorrow despite the unknown and how He holds her hand each step of the way.

She also thought back to the passage she'd read that morning, the entirety of the book of Ruth. She had sensed God reminding her, "I am your Kinsman Redeemer." No matter what happened, Susanna knew she could trust her future to Jesus. She felt like God was saying, "I am your husband," and she returned home from the retreat full of hope for the future.

☙

Susanna met with police officers and politicians, eventually making her way up to Malaysia's prime minister. Candlelight prayer vigils sprouted in cities across the country and soon the world. Hundreds of people, and sometimes thousands, gathered in each place to pray for Pastor Raymond. An online petition demanding the Malaysian government explain his disappearance was also created.

Despite these efforts, Susanna was unable to make any headway in her investigation. Following a report by the national Human Rights Commission of Malaysia, she deduced that the police were involved in the disappearance. And at every juncture, Susanna felt like they were working to prevent her success.

Nearly three years after Raymond's disappearance, Susanna was again called in for questioning. The night before, fear welled inside her once more, and she felt a throbbing pain in her head.

Suddenly, though, the words of Isaiah 43:2 came to mind: "When you pass through the waters, I will be with you; and through the rivers, they shall not overwhelm you; when you walk through fire you shall not be burned, and the flame shall not consume you." She thought of Psalm 46:1–2, and also verse 10: "God is our refuge and strength. Be still, and know that I am God." Then came 2 Corinthians 12:9: "My grace is sufficient for you." As Susanna began singing the words of a worship song about lifting up our praise before the Lord in the presence of our enemies, she finally felt her headache subside. With renewed confidence in the Lord, she was able to sleep.

The next day, when the officer began his interrogation, the Holy Spirit enabled her to speak boldly. "All these questions you're asking," she said, "they're irrelevant to finding Raymond. You should be looking for his enemies, the ones who want him dead or locked up." She walked out of the police station assured that God would always be present for her in times of need.

Susanna knew the political and justice systems of Malaysia were riddled with corruption, scandals, and evil, but she worked hard to focus on the bigger picture: God was doing a cleansing in Malaysia, and He had to bring up all that is dark and evil so the light could shine on it. As a Christian, Susanna knew she needed to pray for God's will to prevail in her country, so she prayed for the authorities to know the Lord.

"If there is going to be transformation in Malaysia," she said, "there needs to be transformation in the lives of individuals."

❧

In the years following Raymond's disappearance, thousands of Christians from all over the world wrote letters and sent cards to Susanna and her children.

"This really encouraged us when we were down, especially during the seasons, like Christmas," she said. "God used the Scriptures that they put in the cards to encourage us. I see God working in the lives of these Christians. As they pray, it rises up to

God like incense, like fragrance, an aroma to heaven. I'm really thankful for the prayers of the saints."

But even in the midst of those glimmers of hope and the encouragement from the global body of Christ, Susanna has still felt disheartened at times.

"It has been very difficult for our family to not know what happened to Pastor Raymond and not know where he is, and be frozen in grief. We don't know whether he's dead or alive. But in the process, we hold this in tension: We have a living hope because we believe in Christ. We believe in His resurrection. And therefore, if anything happens to Pastor Raymond, he's with God, and God is with him. And the other part is the hope that we will see him one day. So, we have been trying to cope and be resilient, to learn to accept the situation as it is with the ambiguity, the unknown. And we've experienced God's grace because He promised, 'My grace is sufficient for you, for my power is made perfect in weakness.'[5] And so we call out to God with a contrite heart, and He meets us where we are.

"It is through the strength and grace of God that I am able to get out of bed every morning. It is being in close relationship with God, having my quiet time every morning, reading His Word that spur me on. Also I realize that maybe God has a purpose, although I don't wish this to happen to anyone. This has brought us closer as a family and closer to God and has brought a lot of positive things to the church in Malaysia—unity among the churches— and the spirit of prayer."

As they continue to await news of Raymond's whereabouts, Susanna and her grown children have persisted with helping the poor and the needy through their Harapan Komuniti charity, funneling the resources God has provided into the hands of those

---

5. 2 Corinthians 12:9

who need them most. Susanna also continues selling jewelry to support herself. In the years following Raymond's disappearance, God has continued to take care of her and her children.

"I just want to be in the center of God's will, and if He wants to use me to be a voice for others who do not have that voice and to speak out on injustices, then I would willingly do that for God's namesake and be a vessel that He could use for His glory and honor.

"In the coming days, we will see more people being persecuted, and there will be suffering," Susanna said as she reflected on Revelation 5:9 and 7:9, Raymond's favorite Bible verses. "There will be martyrs. But in the end, we will see people from all tribes, nations, and tongues worshiping God in heaven. That is the hope that we have. All that we sacrifice is for a reason, and I believe that Raymond would count it worthy to suffer for Christ."

In Her Words:
Sabina

On February 29, 1948, Sabina Wurmbrand's husband, Richard, never made it to church. He was abducted off the streets of Bucharest, Romania, by the Communist secret police, who wanted to silence the witness of this bold pastor.

Now we sat silently, waiting for Richard. But he didn't come.

We telephoned all the hospitals. I went around casualty wards, thinking he might have been in a street accident. No sign.

And then began the hours and weeks and years of searching. Of trailing from office to office. Of pushing at any door that might open.

I learned that important prisoners were kept in cells in the Interior Ministry's basements. So many women were seeking arrested husbands, sons, and fathers that an "information office" was opened to handle inquiries. The stairs were crowded with mothers and children. They stood hopelessly, waiting to ask for news.

Each in turn asked her question. The officials pretended to examine lists of typed names. They peered into filing cabinets. But of all those missing men, no trace could they find.

A rumor spread that Richard had been taken to Moscow. But I couldn't believe he'd gone from my life. Evening after evening, I made a meal and sat by the window. *He'll come tonight*, I thought. *He's done nothing. He'll soon be free. The Communists cannot be worse than the fascists, who always let him go after a week or two.*

He didn't come. I put my forehead against the pane and wept. I went to bed late but couldn't sleep. One morning Pastor Magne Solheim, Richard's colleague at the Lutheran church, went with me to ask the help of the Swedish ambassador, our ally in the past, who said he would speak at once to Foreign Minister Ana Pauker.

Pauker's answer was ready: "Our information is that Pastor Wurmbrand has absconded from the country with a suitcase full of dollars entrusted to him for famine relief work. They say he is in Denmark."

The ambassador brought the case up with Prime Minister Petru Groza, who repeated Pauker's version, with a jovial promise: "So Wurmbrand's supposed to be in our jails? If you can prove that, I'll release him!"

The Communists were so sure of themselves. Once in the secret police cells, a man ceased to exist.

No one else could intervene now. The only hope left—which thousands were trying—was bribery. The price of those favors was high. We collected the sum with great difficulty. It was handed over.

Nothing happened.

It was not the first nor the last time we were swindled in this way. There was nothing we could do. I'd met thieves and criminals aplenty, but these professional tricksters were in a class of their own. Some were high-ranking officials. Few were Communist in anything but name.

After some months of wasted effort, a stranger came to the door one evening. The man was unshaven and reeked of plum brandy. He insisted we talk alone.

"I've met your husband," he said. And my heart turned over. "I'm a warder—don't ask what prison. But I take him his food, and he said you'd pay me well for a bit of news."

"It depends . . . how much?" I asked. We'd had so many failures.

"I'm risking my neck, you know."

The sum he named was huge. He would not bargain.

Pastor Solheim was as doubtful as I was. He told the warder, "Bring me a few words in Wurmbrand's writing."

He gave the man a bar of chocolate from the famine relief supplies. "Take this to Wurmbrand and bring back a message with his signature."

Two days later the man returned. He removed his cap. He felt in the lining and handed me the wrapper from the chocolate bar. I read: "My dearest wife—I thank you for your sweetness. I'm well—Richard."

It was his handwriting. Bold and clear, determined and yet troubled. No possibility of mistaking the tempestuous serenity of those lines.

"He's all right," said the warder. "Some can't take it, in solitary. Don't like their own company." He breathed brandy. "He sends you his love."

We agreed to pay the money if he would continue to carry messages. Finally, he said, "All right. But people have gotten twelve years for this. You know, it's not just the cash."

He risked his freedom out of a divided love: he loved the money, loved the drink it bought. And he also loved Richard. Sometimes he slipped him extra bread. He continued to bring us verbal messages.

Solheim and his wife immediately dropped everything else and concentrated on keeping my courage up and rescuing Richard. Pastor Solheim came with me to the Swedish Embassy where we were promptly received by the ambassador. When he saw the scrap of paper with Richard's writing, he quickly drafted a note to the premier:

"You promised to release Pastor Wurmbrand if we could prove he is in a Romanian prison. I now have that proof in my hands."

Groza passed the note on to Ana Pauker at the Foreign Ministry. His joke had misfired. She sent for the ambassador and stormed at him. If she said Wurmbrand had fled to Denmark, then he had. She would not be insulted by the envoy of a minor power who was poking his nose into a purely domestic matter. She was not a liar!

The ambassador was declared persona non grata. His superiors questioned the wisdom of his intervention. Richard was a Romanian national, even if he did work for a foreign mission. The ambassador was recalled to Stockholm and retired from the diplomatic service.

Next, Solheim—who thought of Romania as his second homeland—was obliged to leave the country. He had identified himself with us and his mission station. He could help no more.

But we still had loyal friends, although to be friendly with us was to put oneself in danger.

I wept to think Richard might be at that moment bearing torture. I feared he might break and betray his friends. He had promised that he would die rather than do so, but who can say how much a man can bear? Peter promised that he would not deny Christ.

If Richard died, I knew we would meet in the next life. We had agreed to wait for each other at one of the twelve gates of heaven. We had decided that our rendezvous would be at the Benjamin Gate. Jesus made an appointment like this with His disciples, to meet them after His death, in Galilee. And He kept it.

Sabina would also learn where he was imprisoned, see his face, and communicate with him — all with the help of her friend, Bianca. You can read Sabina's story in the first volume of Hearts of Fire.

Bianca

Jesus, Her Constant Companion

Distributing Bibles to Russian soldiers was risky for any Christian living in Romania—especially females. Russian soldiers were notorious for raping young women, and many of the victims were discovered with their throats slit.

Bianca Rechnitz, a woman in her early twenties, knew it was an especially perilous operation. World War II had just ended, and the Communists, now holding an iron grip on Romania, were proving to be just as brutal as the Nazis had been.

Christians were the next group to be targeted, persecuted, and silenced once all the political opponents were arrested and imprisoned. Some church leaders and laypeople even collaborated with the Communists, becoming secret police informants on their congregation.

Bianca knew the only hope for her country was the message of salvation through Jesus Christ. She was willing to risk her life to share the gospel with Russian troops occupying her country, even if it meant lugging a heavy bag of books into the courtyard of a Russian outpost.

That's why she had traveled by train to Brashov, a beautiful town nestled in the mountains of Transylvania. The bag on her back contained copies of one of the Gospels that her pastor had secretly printed in the Russian language.

As Bianca approached the outpost's main gate, she caught the eye of several soldiers. Seconds later, she understood why so many troops were gathered in one place. She had stumbled upon the regional headquarters of the Soviet Army. One of the soldiers grabbed her by the coat and dragged her through the courtyard and inside a building to be questioned.

The commanding officer stood behind his desk and glared at Bianca. He surveyed the Bibles now scattered across the floor. Was she a spy? He picked up one of the booklets.

"Where did you get these?" he sneered.

If Bianca told him the truth, it would compromise her pastor, who had sent her on this mission. If she disclosed his real name—Pastor Richard Wurmbrand—the government would track him down, imprison him, torture him, execute him, or deport him to the slave labor camps in frigid Siberia.

"These books are from the British Bible Society," she replied.

The officer shook his head. "But who is the leader? What is his name?"

"I'm sorry, I don't know," she replied. "The British Bible Society is in London, not Romania. I've never been to London, so I don't know who the leader of this society is."

"Who's the leader?" the man yelled. "Tell me his name!"

Bianca gave the same answer.

Again and again, the officer shouted at her, his face turning red as he questioned her. Droplets of saliva spewed from his angry lips as he cursed at her. But each time, Bianca refused to disclose any meaningful information that might endanger her pastor and his congregation in Bucharest.

After thirty minutes, the officer finally gave up. "Escort her to the police," he ordered. "Have her interrogated until she confesses."

~elle~

Bianca was born in Bucharest, the capital of Romania, in 1925. At that time, the entire country was plagued with poverty, and Bianca's widowed mother, too ill and poor to care for Bianca, had placed her in an orphanage for Jewish girls. She was only three years old.

The orphanage was strict, with an apathetic staff who barely fulfilled their minimal duties of feeding, clothing, and educating the children. During the early years of her life, Bianca experienced little love or laughter in their care. She was the youngest girl in the orphanage by more than a decade. Lonely and bored, she asked the older girls to teach her to read. Not only did they teach her to read and write, but they also mothered her and helped fill some of the emptiness in her heart.

Wealthy Jewish families living in the countryside financed the orphanage, but they had little direct contact with the children. And without regular oversight, the orphanage staff often stole the food intended for the orphans, taking it home to feed their own families instead.

One day, the president of the orphanage committee visited to investigate a troubling report: the children had been receiving only a small bowl of soup and a cob of corn for dinner. The president questioned the older girls to learn if the report was indeed true. Fearing retaliation, they kept silent, too afraid to tell the truth.

Eight-year-old Bianca, however, tired of being hungry, boldly spoke up.

"Yes, it's true," declared the feisty little girl. While Bianca earned the respect of the other girls, the staff saw her response as a betrayal. They made her life so difficult that at times Bianca would climb into a large wooden chest and hide there, retreating into her box to escape her misery and to find safety.

Bianca was delighted when a younger girl arrived at the orphanage. *Finally, a playmate!* The girl was lovely, and she had a beautiful singing voice. At night, she sang songs about angels with harps in their hands. She sang about a place called heaven that had streets made of pure gold, and about a man named Jesus. Her songs promised a warm, sun-lit place where there was no crying or tears—a place utterly unlike the stark, gray life Bianca had known at the orphanage. The little girl didn't understand the songs she sang, nor did Bianca. But singing them made the girls happy.

A rabbi educated the children at the orphanage. He taught them Jewish traditions and encouraged the children to be proud of their heritage. But when antisemitism flowed into Eastern Europe from Germany, Jewish education was suddenly prohibited. Bianca and the other girls continued their schooling at a nearby Orthodox school. As the Orthodox Church was the predominant faith in Romania, once a week a priest came to the class to teach the Christian religion. But as soon as he arrived, he exempted Bianca and two other Jewish girls from his teaching hour.

"You are not compelled to stay in my class," he told them, "as Christianity is our religion, not yours."

Bianca's friends were happy to have an extra free hour to play outside, but she chose to stay and hear more about Jesus. Her attentiveness caught the old priest's attention.

"Shame on you," he told the Christian children in the class. "She who has another religion is more diligent than you!"

ele

When Bianca turned sixteen, she was required to leave the orphanage and earn her own living. But where was she supposed to go? Even though she was a free, educated young woman, Bianca felt something hollow inside her soul. She knew little of life, of living in a stable family, of belonging and relating to others, so she moved back home to live with her mother, who was still very sick.

Their tiny, single-room home had no heat and only one narrow bed. Bianca slept on the floor. During the harsh, bitter winter, Bianca couldn't even leave the house because she didn't have any warm clothing. Instead, her mother walked through the snow to retrieve hot soup from a local Jewish soup kitchen. By the time she returned, however, the soup was frosty and they couldn't waste their precious fuel to reheat it. The kerosene stove gave off just enough heat to prevent the two of them from freezing to death.

Eventually, Bianca acquired warmer clothes and accompanied her mother on outings. One day, as Bianca joined her for a walk through the city, her mother stopped suddenly and pointed across the street to an old man with a walking stick. "There is your father," she announced.

Bianca was shocked. All this time, she'd believed that her brother's father, a man who had by this time died, was her father. Bianca's mother guided her across the street and introduced the two, but it was a strange and strained meeting. Bianca returned home with a new hurt from the past to further add to her pain and confusion.

One morning, Bianca awoke and was astonished by a strange sight—her mother was kneeling on the floor, praying to Jesus. Bianca's mother was the daughter of strict Jewish parents, but at some point, she had evidently become a Christian.

Not long after, a young Jewish man arrived in their neighborhood and distributed leaflets and New Testaments to all the Jewish families. Bianca and her friends mocked him mercilessly.

"How can a man be Jewish and Christian at the same time?" they taunted. "Surely he must be mentally unstable!"

But when he invited Bianca to take part in a Christmas celebration at a pastor's home, her feelings changed. Her mother, curious about seeing other Jewish people celebrating Christmas, insisted on coming, too.

Inside the home, the pastor—a thin, tall man—opened the Bible and read about the suffering servant of the Lord in Isaiah 53. He spoke about His death and resurrection, and how the nation didn't recognize their own Messiah and Savior.

"Do you know, dear guests," the pastor said, "that Christmas is actually the most beautiful Jewish holy day and should be celebrated by us as such?"

He flipped to the book of John and read. "He came to his own and his own people did not receive him."[1] The pastor hesitated. "The greatest tragedy of our nation," he continued, "is not to have recognized our own Messiah."

After the message, as the people congregated in the house, Bianca turned to a friend and asked, "What's the name of this pastor?"

"That's Richard Wurmbrand," she replied.

Pastor Wurmbrand's preaching and teaching interested Bianca. She wanted to learn more about Jesus, but she also wanted to be free to enjoy the pleasures of life. For three years, she refused to yield to Jesus, even though she continued attending the meetings in Pastor Wurmbrand's home, listening to the truth he preached.

Bianca was learning more and more about Jesus of Nazareth, but years of poverty, hunger, misery, and desperation continued

---

1. John 1:11.

to plague her. One day, the pain became too much to bear, and Bianca decided to end her life. She walked to the edge of a lake and threw herself into the water.

Standing on the opposite shore was a man who had noticed Bianca preparing for the desperate act. He leapt into the water, swam frantically toward the drowning girl, and saved Bianca.

Tragedy struck one afternoon when Bianca was returning home, only to find the structure engulfed in flames. Even more devastating for the young woman, who had known so little of love in her life, was that her mother had burned to death in the fire.

Alone again, Bianca felt helpless. Not even Jesus, she thought, could pull her out of her hopelessness. Slowly, though, as Bianca grieved her mother, she became increasingly grateful for the faith her mother had shared with her. It was a legacy more precious than any other. Her mother had taken her to church and encouraged her to pray.

The next year, Bianca decided she had run away from God long enough. She renounced her worldly, sinful life and was baptized by Pastor Wurmbrand. She decided to devote her time to helping her pastor and his wife, Sabina, in their mission to the Jews, a ministry they had been running for several years.

Bianca was so full of the joy of the Lord that she no longer was conscious of her poverty, nor did she envy others who had more than she did. No longer did she have to carry the heavy burden of loneliness and sadness that had weighed her down most of her life. Finally, she had inner peace and purpose. No longer alone, Bianca knew she was now part of the family of God.

ele

Richard and Sabina Wurmbrand nurtured Bianca in the faith and became her family. In the wake of World War II, the

Wurmbrands also cared for many Jewish children who were orphaned when their parents died in Nazi concentration camps. The Wurmbrands' love for these lonely children touched Bianca profoundly and revealed to her the heart of God.

But Bianca's new faith was put to the test one day as she made her way through the streets of Bucharest. Just ahead she saw her father, weak and sick, hobbling down the street. She glared at him. *Never once has he contacted me, not even on my birthday. I owe him nothing.*

Bianca's first instinct was to walk away, but her heart had now been touched by Jesus. It was telling her to take her father back to the mission and give him a parcel of food, just like she did for other needy people. There, Sabina reminded her that just as she'd been forgiven, she also had to learn to forgive. Her father was amazed that she helped him, and Bianca was even more amazed at the power of God to change her heart.

Then, under the guise of "liberating" Romania from the Nazis, the Russian Army invaded and unleashed a second reign of terror on the impoverished country. Pastor Wurmbrand felt compelled to reach out to these Russian men who lived in the darkness of atheism under a Communist government. He secretly met with a Christian printer to publish thousands of copies of the Gospels in Russian and organized a small group of young people from his church to distribute them to soldiers in the streets. Pastor Wurmbrand trained his young missionaries, preparing them for the dangerous work ahead.

Bianca volunteered for the assignment, even though she feared the savagery and brutality of the Russian Army. All of her prayers were distilled into two requests:

Protect my body against the ruthless soldiers.

Protect the Gospels from the hands of the men who roll their pages into cigarettes.

الحاكم

BRASHOV, ROMANIA
1945

Bianca stood in the police station and awaited instruction from
the commanding officer who now oversaw her future. When he
ordered Bianca to be escorted to Romanian police, she scooped
up her pile of Russian Gospels and shoved them back into her
large bag. It was decided she would be sent to the central city of
Ploiesti, about thirty-five miles north of Bucharest, to be interrogated by the police commissioner.

A soldier escorted Bianca to the train station. Surrounded by
soldiers and terrified by the thought of being interrogated, she
felt the train begin to inch forward. Outside the window, the
Romanian landscape soon became a blur.

The first stop of the journey was a smaller police station. A
soldier ushered Bianca off the train and into the station. He left
Bianca in the lobby while he talked to another soldier on duty.
Bianca struggled to overhear their conversation. Evidently, the
man who was scheduled to relieve his comrade hadn't arrived.

"Sir, I need to go home. It's so hot, and I haven't changed my
shirt or underclothes for two days now." The man sighed. "I'm
so hungry, but how am I supposed to leave while we have this
arrested person here?"

They're talking about me.

"You can still go home," Bianca's soldier said.

"But what if she runs away? This place is so isolated that she
could very easily escape under the cover of darkness."

"I'm telling you, you can go home. I'm sure these people don't
run from responsibility."

These people? Bianca wondered.

"I know them," the man continued. "I've had to deal with them often."

Suddenly, the meaning of the man's words became clear to Bianca. *These people* must mean Christians!

The two men exited the station, leaving Bianca alone. By now the sun had set, and Bianca contemplated her options. She felt an overwhelming urge to run. No one would see her, and she could avoid the unpleasant interrogation to come.

But something stopped her from running. She kept hearing the officer's words: *"These people do not run from responsibility."* He seemed to know other arrested Christians who had left a favorable impression in his mind. How could Bianca ruin that good testimony?

How could I behave so cowardly when the others had been so brave?

Bianca remained in the station until the men returned later that night.

As they continued their journey, the officers cursed her and terrorized her with threats.

"You'll see what will happen to you tomorrow," one of the officers said, a twisted grin spreading across his face. The next morning, once they arrived in Ploiesti, Bianca was scheduled to be interrogated by the police commissioner.

"Not only have you endangered us all and the whole country by your subversive activity among the Soviet Army," the officer continued, "but we also have to disturb our commissioner on his day of rest to come and interrogate you. You really deserve the punishment that's coming."

But Bianca wasn't worried, and for the rest of the journey she felt a supernatural sense of peace. Unable to contain the surge of joy bursting from her heart, she sang hymns throughout the night, comforted by the unmistakable presence of God.

ele

The train finally arrived at Ploiesti on a Saturday night. The next morning, the soldier brought Bianca before the commissioner. She slid her bag of Bibles from her shoulder and placed it beside her feet. Bianca studied the commissioner carefully, wondering how the interrogation would unfold. He was an elderly man, dignified, and seated at a large desk. Around him were a dozen younger officers standing silently at attention.

"Well, young lady," the commissioner finally said, "could you tell me what made you become involved in this kind of activity among the Soviet soldiers? What was your motivation?"

Bianca had never thought of herself as an especially courageous person. But she did feel that God had strengthened her with boldness, even from childhood, and had removed any lingering fear from her heart. Bianca took a deep breath and began to speak.

"Sir," she said, "I believe the Red Army that now occupies our country is not here by coincidence. I believe this was planned by God."

She paused to look at the commissioner's face, but his expression revealed nothing.

"These people," she continued, "kept forcibly in the darkness of atheism for so many years since the Bolshevik Revolution, have now come to our Christian country to receive the light of the gospel through us for their salvation. Christ died for their sins, too."

The commissioner looked at Bianca, and she held her breath. Slowly, a small smile creased his face. He turned his eyes toward his young officers. "Listen, gentlemen," he began. "I am convinced that if our country had more people of this kind, then our country would have been spared a lot of trouble."

He turned back to Bianca. "Now go, young lady. You are free!"

Wide-eyed and in disbelief, Bianca quickly snatched her heavy bag of Gospels and rushed out of the office. She burst out into the sunlight, letting out a long sigh of relief, and retraced her steps to the train station to board a carriage for home.

From that moment on, whenever she was caught and arrested by the Russian soldiers in that area, the police commissioner made a phone call and gave orders for Bianca's release.

On one occasion, Bianca was detained in a resort town high in the mountains of Transylvania. As she waited in the police station, the telephone rang.

When the officer on duty hung up the phone, he looked at Bianca and smiled. "You are free to go now. But please, tell me, how do you know our commissioner?"

Naively, Bianca replied, "Oh, he knows me from previous times when I was arrested by the Russians."

The officer smiled again and then made a surprising request: "Would you please do me a favor before you leave? Kindly help me wash my socks. It's so hot today, and I haven't been home to change them for several days."

Bianca fumed. *How dare this fool ask me to do such a humiliating thing! Especially now that he's seen the high protector I have— his own boss!*

Immediately, though, the Lord spoke to Bianca: *"Didn't I also wash the dusty feet of My disciples? Are you greater than your Master?"* Bianca felt so ashamed of her prideful attitude that she took the man's smelly socks, washed them, and hung them outside to dry before politely scurrying from the police station.

Years later, long after she left Romania, Bianca met a preacher from Romania who knew the police commissioner from Ploiesti.

"Was that man a secret believer?" Bianca asked.

"Of course," said the man. "I knew him well. He was Inspector Marinescu, and his sister was a member of my church."

It had taken thirty years for Bianca to discover the identity of her protector. The commissioner helped many Jews hide from their Nazi pursuers and aided Christians who were persecuted by the Communist regime. Whenever a Christian was brought before him for "illegal and subversive activities," the commissioner would ask to be left alone with the subject for "interrogation." He locked the door of his office, took a Bible from his desk drawer, and said, "I'm a Christian also. Let's study the Word of God and pray together."

The commissioner was eventually arrested by the Russians and jailed for twelve years.

ele

The Lord granted Bianca the two requests she'd prayed for when she began her evangelistic work. Though she was caught many times distributing those Gospels—and though Soviet soldiers arrested her, threatened her, and cursed her—God protected her body. Jesus continued to provide "angels with human faces," people who appeared just at the right moment to rescue Bianca from evil hands.

Also, the huge bag of Gospel booklets she carried through the years was never confiscated. It was as if God blinded the Russians' eyes to the presence of Bianca's bag. After a day or two, the soldiers always released her with the bag still full of Russian Gospels, ready to be distributed to those in need of the Good News of Jesus Christ.

As she stood outside the mission house one day, distributing tracts and inviting people in the street to repent and come to Jesus, she spotted a familiar face. It was the man who had rescued her from drowning and taking her own life. He recognized Bianca immediately.

Bianca held out a tract to the man. "I'm very grateful to you, because you saved my life here on this earth. Now, I want to see you saved for eternity." The man happily took her Christian material, and as the two parted ways, he pondered the "coincidence" of encountering Bianca on the street.

Often, Bianca employed creative strategies to get her copies of the Russian Gospels into the hands of the soldiers. She knew a KGB guard always traveled in the front of the trains carrying Russian troops, so she waited on the train platform near the last carriage. The very moment the train started to move, she threw the Gospels through the open windows, hurling them right into the laps of the Russian soldiers. The men snatched them up and hid them under their uniforms. By the time the guard at the front became aware of what was happening, it was too late for him to do anything. All he could do was shake his fist at Bianca and curse her as the train left the station.

God had done a powerful work in Bianca's heart. She'd spent so many years at the orphanage looking for safety, hiding in the wooden chest so the world couldn't hurt her. But now, for Bianca, Jesus was her refuge. And in His arms, she felt safe.

ele

Bianca, who still had much to learn about love, was greatly challenged by Richard and Sabina Wurmbrand.

When the Russian Army first invaded Romania after World War II, any German troops left behind during the Nazi retreat had to fend for themselves. Those who weren't arrested found themselves in a troubling and desperate situation. Forgotten by those they had served, and hated by the Romanian people they had persecuted, there was nowhere safe for them to go.

One night, three young German soldiers were on the run, still wearing their Nazi uniforms. The men hid from their Communist pursuers in a shed in the Wurmbrands' courtyard. When Richard and Sabina discovered the frightened men, they quietly fed them and washed their clothes.

At the same time, Soviet soldiers secretly visited the Wurmbrands' home to ask about God. These men were beginning to question communism and wanted to know about Christianity.

When the Wurmbrands' close friends realized there were fugitive Nazis hiding in the shed while Russian soldiers met in the house, they panicked. *What if they discovered each other? Didn't the Wurmbrands realize the terrible risks they were taking?* They could be betrayed and shot without warning.

But Richard was unperturbed. "God has commanded that we love our enemies, so I will continue to do so," he said, calmly. "Keeping the Germans and the Russians apart is up to God."

How could I not believe in a Savior who enables His followers to forgive and help even those who harmed them? Bianca thought. She had observed a new kind of love and was forever changed.

Life was tough and challenging as Bianca and fellow Christians daily took risks in reaching out to help each other physically, emotionally, and spiritually. If they couldn't keep their faith alive and meet together for mutual encouragement, then all hope would be gone. But soon, Bianca's hope would be put to the test.

ele

On Sunday, February 29, 1948, Bianca went to church as usual. When she walked in, she was surprised to find that Pastor Wurmbrand hadn't yet arrived. It was his habit to go to church early to pray and prepare himself for the service, but nobody knew where he was.

How strange, Bianca thought.

Pastor Wurmbrand didn't appear that entire day or any of the following days. It was as if he had completely vanished from the face of the earth.

Soon, the Christians in Pastor Wurmbrand's congregation realized what his disappearance meant. He must have been kidnapped by the Communist secret police on his way to church. Bianca had heard of others mysteriously vanishing, being sent to be "re-educated" or killed by the Russian "liberators" in their slave labor camps.

Six months passed with no news of Richard's whereabouts. Sabina searched endlessly for information. She was even swindled by imposters who pretended to have government contacts but were really preying on the vulnerability of brokenhearted wives and mothers. Sadly, she didn't discover any clues to help locate her missing husband.

One day, the pastor's colleague, Magne Solheim, approached Bianca. "I'm very much afraid that our Richard is dead by now. Or, if he's alive, he must have been deported to Siberia. In all my years of living in this country, it's always been possible to bribe a guard to deliver a message to a prisoner, or even to smuggle one out, but these guards are too scared to get involved."

"Pastor Solheim," Bianca said, "my conviction is that Richard is not only alive, but that he's here in Bucharest somewhere, hidden from our eyes, probably in the hands of the secret police."

Shortly after, a rumor spread throughout the city. Twice a week, relatives of missing people could go to a government office where information would be provided on their missing loved ones. Sabina, who by now didn't have the courage to confront yet another false hope, asked Bianca if she would be willing to present herself at the office on behalf of her "brother," Richard.

After writing a petition, Bianca made her way to the Ministry of Internal Affairs. What she didn't realize was that building was also the headquarters of the secret police.

Bianca waited in the courtyard outside the office with a large group of women, each desperately seeking information on her loved one. One by one, the women entered the building and spoke with an officer holding a list of names.

Quietly striking up a conversation with the lady next to her, Bianca looked around the courtyard while the woman faced the building. As the two women whispered back and forth, the woman suddenly drew Bianca's attention to one of the small windows of the government building, a basement window just above ground level.

"Look there," she whispered, "at that window, but be careful not to be observed. It seems a man is there, and he's pointing toward you. It's as if he wants to pass a message to you."

Bianca turned slowly so as not to draw the attention of watching officers. The hot August sun shone brightly in Bianca's eyes, but gradually she was able to distinguish the face of a man standing in the darkened window. She could see that he was emaciated, like a skeleton, and unshaven with dark, sunken eyes. Bianca rubbed her own eyes to see him better.

Yes, it's him! Richard is alive!

Knowing that Bianca couldn't let on that she recognized him, Richard quickly raised one hand in a fleeting wave and smiled at her. That was all. That was enough.

When it was finally Bianca's turn to enter, she was certain the officer on duty would confirm what she already knew to be true — Richard Wurmbrand was alive and imprisoned here in this very building in Bucharest.

"Wurmbrand . . . Wurmbrand . . ." the man murmured, scanning his list of names. "No, he's not on our list. That means he's not with us, and we don't know his whereabouts."

Instantly, Bianca understood that this supposed inquiry was nothing more than another Communist trick to deceive and mock the anguished families. Confronted with such a blatant lie, Bianca was livid.

"If this country had fewer liars, it would be a much better place!" she shouted, slamming the door as she left the office. Bianca returned home, realizing how utterly foolish her reaction had been. It was a miracle she wasn't arrested on the spot.

From that day on, Sabina presented herself twice a week, petition in hand, presumably to "inquire about her missing husband." In reality, these visits allowed her to see her husband, to secretly communicate with him, and to make sure he was still alive. They were so grateful the Lord had shown them, yet again, that He is mighty and able to preserve life, regardless of the evil plans of His enemies.

The church kept this great secret for many weeks until Richard was finally transferred to another prison. Bianca and the others learned that he was "Prisoner Number One," targeted because of his outspoken Christian witness, underground work with the church, and absolute refusal to deny his faith in God. Failure to break him had infuriated his Communist captors and prompted them to inflict greater punishment and torture.

The first months of Richard's imprisonment caused a revival among the young people in his church. Until then, they had listened to his sermons without being fully committed to Christ and His work; but now, they dedicated themselves wholly. If this Jesus could inspire such courage, strength, and loyalty in His followers, and cause their pastor not only to live for Him but also

be ready to die for Him, then He must be the true Savior and the Messiah.

ᴇᴇᴇ

As Bianca distributed Russian copies of the Gospels throughout Romania, she also worked as a typist at the State Bank. Her salary was low, and if she needed to buy a pair of shoes or a blouse, she would have no money left for food. Each day, she received a coupon for a small loaf of bread.

Bianca sometimes was forced to work sixteen hours a day— overtime hours the comrades called "voluntary hours," for which the workers received no pay. Those who refused were fired and designated as "undesirable elements." Her bank, like other businesses, had a representative of the Communist Party whose job was to report on employees to their superiors. Bianca was often summoned to the representative's office and accused of spreading religious propaganda among her colleagues. If she didn't cease her "missionary propaganda," he warned, there were other ways of convincing her. Bianca understood these thinly veiled threats of arrest.

On one occasion when Bianca was called to his office, the man immediately rebuked her.

"Your Bible is full of injustices!" he said. When Bianca asked him to show her where, he pointed to Matthew 25:29: "For to everyone who has will more be given, and he will have an abundance. But from the one who has not, even what he has will be taken away."

"Is that social justice, comrade?" he demanded. The man waited for Bianca's reaction.

Silently, she asked the Lord to give her the right reply.

"I will explain to you what the Lord Jesus meant by these words," Bianca said. "For example, our branch of the bank has been recently promoted, hasn't it? And with that promotion, everybody received a higher salary. Even our director received it, although he already had the highest salary of all of us. He deserved it, for he is indeed a very honest and conscientious director. But, on the other hand, just imagine that one of the cleaners was a drunkard and a lazy person. Instead of coming in on time, he came in late and sometimes did not come at all. And when he was here, he quarreled with the other cleaners and was dishonest in everything. Despite the fact he had the lowest salary of us all, he would have eventually been fired, wouldn't he? And very rightly so. Well, that is what the Bible means by these words."

Bianca stopped speaking and looked at the Communist representative, hoping her illustration had clearly communicated the message of the verse. But, the man seemed confused and stared at her in silence. Finally, he waved Bianca out of his office.

As she walked back to her workspace, Bianca knew the significance of this meeting: the Communist Party was trying to invent a reason to fire her . . . or, perhaps, a reason to do something even worse.

⁓

In the summer of 1950, when Pastor Wurmbrand had been in prison for two years, some of Bianca's close friends began urging her to emigrate to the new State of Israel with them.[2] "It's now time for all Jews to go to Israel," they said. "This is the fulfillment of God's own promise to our nation!"

But the idea of leaving Romania for Israel upset Bianca. She didn't want to leave the country right now, mainly because the people she loved most, the Wurmbrands, had been left without any source of income. When they arrested Richard, the Communists

---

2. On May 14, 1948, the State of Israel was established.

punished his entire family by denying them a right to a job. Even though her wages didn't spread very far, Bianca felt like she was the only one who could help the family.

One Sunday evening after the church service, Bianca went to Sabina for advice. "What should I do?" she asked. "Should I prepare myself to go to Israel, or should I stay here?"

"I suggest we pray about it," Sabina said. "Let's ask the Lord to show you His will within three days. He will surely give us a sign if we ask Him."

Three days passed, and on the fourth day, Bianca went as usual to her job at the bank. The minute she stepped through the door, the director summoned her to his office and thrust a letter in her hand he'd received from the Communist Party leadership. Bianca read the first few sentences and realized she was to be fired immediately.

This must be a sign from the Lord that I should go to Israel. Bianca was overwhelmed with sadness. *Why did I ask the Lord to show me His will?* she lamented. *If I hadn't prayed that prayer, I would still have the liberty to choose my own way . . . and my will isn't to go to Israel!*

Bianca dragged herself home. Weeping, she fell to her knees and prayed. *Oh, Lord, in the Bible, Gideon asked You for more than one sign, and You weren't angry with him. You gave him a second sign. I promise that if I open my Bible and You show me a Scripture that tells me clearly and unequivocally that You want me to go to Israel, I won't bother You anymore, and I will obey.*

Bianca stood, desperately hoping that no such message existed in the Bible. She picked up her Bible, squinted her eyes, sucked in a breath, and allowed the book to fall open on the bed. She looked down at the page and saw Ezekiel 3:4–5, which says, "And he said to me: Son of man, go to the house of Israel and speak with my words to them. For you are not sent to a people of foreign speech and a hard language, but to the house of Israel."

Bianca closed her Bible, and the next day, she went to the government authorities to present her application for emigration to Israel. Sabina collected some clothing for Bianca from various Christian friends and helped her young friend pack her luggage.

Three days before Bianca's departure, Sabina, too, was arrested by the secret police. Now, with the two people she loved most in prison, Bianca felt as if she had lost everything, and there was no reason to stay. Feeling fearful and alone once more, Bianca, at age twenty-five, left her home country to begin a new life in a new land.

ele

Bianca arrived in Israel just two years after the War of Independence—a complicated conflict involving first a civil war between Palestine's Arabs and Jews, then a declaration by the United Nations partitioning the country into separate Jewish and Arab states, and finally the invasion of the newly formed State of Israel by five different Arab armies. The State of Israel was in turmoil. Although the U.N., including Russia and the United States, officially recognized the new state, all the surrounding Arab neighbors worked hard to strangle the new entity from its very inception.

Bianca soon learned that life was hard for everyone in Israel. The Jews who emigrated exchanged one type of poverty for another. Jews came from so many different countries that over ninety languages were spoken, and unemployment was widespread for those who couldn't speak Hebrew. Bianca settled in Haifa, and for years she did various kinds of hard, manual work. Eventually, Bianca enrolled in nursing school and began to study Hebrew.

Wanting to succeed in her new life, Bianca became too busy for God. At that time, she began receiving letters from a German man living in Romania, a man for whom she had prayed. His letters, written in rudimentary Romanian, warned Bianca against having a worldly spirit and being lukewarm in her faith, but she paid little attention to them. Only later did Bianca realize the Lord was using those letters to help her, to make her aware that she was drifting spiritually and to remind her how much she still needed God.

Years into her schooling, Bianca met a man named Tom Adler, one of the instructors who was also a physician in the psychiatric ward of the state hospital. After her graduation, Bianca took a job in the ward where Tom worked. Soon, the two fell in love and married, a relationship that provided much healing from the pain they had both experienced in their pasts.

On Bianca's birthday, Tom came home with a beautiful red rose. "This is what my father used to give my mother on her birthday," he said, smiling at his new bride. Each year, Bianca looked forward to the precious tradition.

Tom was a Holocaust survivor and an atheist. He had lost nearly his entire family in Auschwitz and was himself a slave in the Nazi labor camps for almost three years.

"Where was God when so many Jews and rabbis called on Him to be rescued from Hitler's ovens?" Tom asked.

Many of his patients at the hospital were also Holocaust survivors. A great number were bedridden, and most struggled to recover from the psychological damage inflicted by their Nazi captors. The mind, Bianca learned, takes much longer to heal than the body, and the work of healing wasn't easy.

Several months into their marriage, Tom and Bianca both recognized that he wasn't well. Tom's symptoms of depression were evident, and as his illness worsened, he became unable to continue his psychiatric work. The hospital director, an elderly German Jew, understood the young doctor's plight and gave him a leave of absence. His job would be waiting for him once he recovered.

Bianca knew Tom needed some space to finally confront the pain of the past and the God he blamed for the circumstances he'd experienced. Tom had been helping others deal with their hurts; now, it was time to address his own. Until he found his own peace, he couldn't expect to pass it on to someone else. The doctor had become the patient.

During one of his restless nights, as Tom tossed in bed and battled the thoughts tormenting his mind, he blurted out, "Can you help me find any relief from this depression?"

"Have you tried the medication that you prescribe for your patients?" Bianca asked.

"Of course! I've tried them all, but nothing is working."

"In that case," she said, "I know of only one doctor who can help you. He's healed me and some of my friends, and I'm sure He can help you, too."

"Really?" Tom asked, skeptically. "And who is this doctor I know nothing about?"

"His name is Yeshua Ha-Mashiah, Jesus Christ, and our Messiah. And He promised His followers that whatever they ask God the Father—the God of Abraham, Isaac, and Jacob, the God of our forefathers—in His name shall be given to them."

Bianca paused and knelt beside the bed. "Let's pray right now," she said. "This will also be your chance to see if what God said is true."

Tom joined his wife and repeated the words she prayed. When they stood again, Bianca looked up at him. His eyes had become clear and serene again. The tormented look on his face was completely gone and he appeared more peaceful than she had seen him in a long time.

"Do you know what happened during that prayer, Bianca?" Tom later asked. "I feel as if that terrible burden on my heart that has oppressed me for these long months has disappeared. It's as if an iceberg started melting—slowly at first until it melted away completely." Tom's excitement was palpable. "Now, I feel like I am free again, really free!"

Over the coming days, Tom and Bianca repeated the process each night. When Tom's depression settled in, they prayed, and they witnessed God respond to their need. Bianca was overjoyed. Tom's heart had thawed, and he felt for the first time the warmth of God's healing love.

Bianca knew she was still drifting spiritually. But when she saw how God used her to bring Tom to faith in Christ, she repented of her ungrateful heart and, with tears streaming down her face, asked for forgiveness.

Tom never found out why such cruel atrocities occurred during the Holocaust. There were no easy answers. But with God's help, he discovered how to move on to a new life filled with hope and happiness. At the same time, Bianca rejoiced that she finally belonged, that she was loved and had her own family where God was Father and Counselor. It was a fresh start for the couple, and they wondered what the future would hold.

ele

In 1966, Tom decided to travel overseas to further his studies and gain experience in other hospitals. He and Bianca arrived in England where Tom spent twelve months working in a psychiatric hospital.

Not long after they arrived, Tom and Bianca received an incredible surprise. Pastor Wurmbrand and Sabina came to visit. Richard had been released from prison in 1964 through a general amnesty after spending a total of fourteen years in confinement.

Sabina endured three years in prison, including long months in a labor camp. Realizing the likelihood and danger of a third imprisonment, a group of Christians in Norway negotiated the family's emigration from Romania. Romania's Communist government had begun "selling" political prisoners. The government demanded $10,000 for Pastor Wurmbrand—more than five times the standard price for a political prisoner.

How special it was for Bianca to be reunited with the Wurmbrands, and to know that finally their suffering under the Communists was over! Tom and Bianca translated into Hebrew the Wurmbrands' books, *Tortured for Christ* and *The Pastor's Wife*, and Bianca then translated the second title into Romanian as well.

When their year in England was up, Bianca and Tom returned to Israel, where they resumed their work. Years later, Tom became discouraged with the practice of psychiatry. Early in his career, he was helping Holocaust victims in their recovery. But now, he was receiving more private patients seeking a psychiatric excuse for wrongdoing. Soon after Tom and Bianca prayed for direction, a friend from Finland offered Tom a place to study at a Bible school to prepare himself for ministry. The couple moved to Finland, where Tom obtained a degree in missiology.

During the last three weeks of Tom's studies, he and Bianca once again asked the Lord for direction. Restrictions and opposition to Christian witness prevented them from returning as missionaries to Israel. A recent law in Israel prohibited certain kinds of Christian missionary activity, and the state viewed Christian missionaries with a large measure of skepticism.

But early one morning, while the two were still in their pajamas, the doorbell rang. A telegram had arrived from New Zealand.

"Dear Tom and Bianca, please prepare your luggage and be ready, for you are to be here on 20 December. Letter follows. John."

How curious! Bianca thought.

Days later, a letter arrived that explained the mysterious telegram. Their friend, John Heasman, worked as the director of a Wurmbrand mission[3] in New Zealand that shared the plight of persecuted Christians in Communist lands. Bianca and Tom had met John a few years earlier when he visited them in Israel on his way to Germany to attend a conference for Wurmbrand missions. John felt it was time to return home to Australia but couldn't find anyone in New Zealand qualified to lead the mission.

John had concluded that the new leader of the mission could be no one but Tom Adler. Tom had escaped the Holocaust, and Bianca herself had been led to the Lord and discipled by the Wurmbrands.

At age fifty-five, Bianca, along with her husband, departed for Auckland, New Zealand. They both carried Israeli passports, and all flights from London to Auckland went through Arab countries. Tom and Bianca were worried they'd be seen as a risk and prevented from traveling. When their flight stopped in Dubai, they remained on the plane. No one suspected they were Jews or asked to see their passports.

When they arrived in New Zealand, they got to work. They spoke in churches, sharing the message of persecuted Christians. The couple invited other Christians to pray in their home, interceding for their brothers and sisters suffering in Communist prisons.

Tom worked hard, even in the midst of frequent illness. After his experience in the Holocaust, he never regained good health; and while he didn't talk about it to others, Bianca saw how often he was unwell.

---

3. Originally named Jesus to the Communist World, many of the Wurmbrand missions would later change their name to The Voice of the Martyrs, which was the name of the missions' monthly publication that was distributed by the various Wurmbrand missions worldwide.

For three years, Tom and Bianca labored together in New Zealand until one day, in September 1983, the Lord took Tom to his eternal home in heaven. He was just fifty-nine years old.

For two months after Tom's death, Bianca couldn't pray at all. She held prayer meetings in her home, but she couldn't utter a single word. She was spiritually mute. After a while, she found a small flat nearby to rent—a modest unit of two rooms and a living area where she continued to hold intercessory prayer meetings.

Soon after Tom's death, two verses began to press on Bianca's mind. "The Lord spoke to Joshua, saying, 'Moses my servant is dead. Now, therefore arise . . .'" Again and again, the verses played in her mind.

Various friends tried to draw her attention to the fact that now, since her husband was gone, shouldn't she replace him as a leader? But Bianca wouldn't hear of it. She had been her husband's secretary, but never the one in charge. To be a director of a mission? She was trying to deal with her grief and felt totally inadequate for the role.

How on earth could I accept that great responsibility?

Nevertheless, Bianca couldn't shake the feeling that God was speaking to her. She flipped open a Bible to Joshua 1:1–2 to see exactly what the verses meant.

"The Lord said to Joshua . . . , 'Moses my servant is dead. Now therefore arise . . .'" Bianca froze in shock. Just after the phrase were three extra words in brackets, words that she had never seen before: *"'Take his place.'"*[4]

After reading those words, Bianca knew what she must do. She fought against her doubts, fear, and the tremendous weight of the great responsibility, and she agreed to become the new director of the Wurmbrands' work in New Zealand.

---

4. The Bible translation Bianca used had "to take his place" in brackets.

One afternoon, while she was alone at home, a sudden cry burst forth from the depths of her soul, and with it came a flood of tears. Bianca recognized this outburst as a cry of repentance to the Lord. She knew the real reason she'd been unable to pray. She was angry at God for taking her husband from her so unexpectedly. The man she'd loved and who had loved her. The one with whom she'd worked and shared, who had supported and encouraged her.

Tom was gone. And once more, Bianca felt completely alone.

ele

Several months later, it was Bianca's birthday, the first one since Tom died. As she sat remembering past birthdays with her husband, Bianca came to a sad realization. This would be the first year without a red rose from Tom. A tradition that had lasted more than thirty years was now over. Feeling the weight of the day, Bianca left the room to begin her work.

After a while, she returned to the room and opened the window to enjoy the beautiful day outside. Suddenly, a flash of red caught her attention. She leaned forward to get a better view.

Bianca couldn't believe her eyes. A thin branch was climbing up toward the window, and at the end of the branch was a little red rose. The petals were so close that she could have reached out and snipped the bud with a pair of scissors. Bianca rushed outside to see where the rose was coming from. The tiny branch was growing in her neighbor's yard. It had somehow pushed through their fence, climbing up to reach her window.

In that moment, Bianca remembered Isaiah 54:5: "For your Maker is your husband, the Lord of hosts is his name; and the Holy One of Israel is your Redeemer, the God of the whole earth he is called."

ممم

Over the years, Bianca visited Romania several times. Her first visit was in 1970 when Romania was still under communism. She witnessed the great poverty and misery brought about by this regime that had promised so much and delivered so little. Romania was in ruins, and the poor were even poorer than before.

But even in the darkness, Bianca saw beams of God's love shining brightly through the Christians of Romania. Many were her friends who had endured long years in prisons and slave labor camps because of their love for and loyalty to the Lord.

In 1989, after nearly half a century of oppression rooted in compulsive atheism, communism fell after the dictator Nicolae Ceausescu and his wife, Elena, were removed from leadership and executed. Hundreds of thousands of Romanians knelt in the center of the public square in Bucharest and prayed the Lord's Prayer: *"Our Father, who art in heaven . . ."* Then they sang a popular hymn, a song of victory composed years earlier by a Romanian Christian poet who had been brought to the Lord through the Wurmbrands' ministry.[5]

In 1991, the Wurmbrand mission opened the first Christian bookstore and print shop in Romania after the Communist era. When the organization needed a larger warehouse to store all its books, city council allotted the group more space—a space where Richard was formerly imprisoned.

Ceausescu had built his palace over what had been the underground prison where Richard was held in solitary confinement— the place where Richard had dreamed of one day distributing Christian books. At the time, the dream felt impossible. Now, decades later, Richard and Sabina visited the new Christian print

---

5. The hymn is called "There Is a God" by Costache Ioanid.

shop and danced for joy inside its walls. The place of death and despair had been transformed into a place of life and hope.

What a tremendous victory over atheistic communism, Bianca thought. *God is still in control, and in His time, prayers are answered.*

"I was alone at the beginning of my life," Bianca said, "and have been alone again since Tom's death. But Jesus is my constant companion. I know without a doubt that I am complete in Him. The climbing rose that God sent so many years ago to comfort and encourage me is really a picture of my life. I often struggled with weakness, but like that fragile flower, I grew, pushed through barriers, climbed walls, and blossomed. I am humbled to have been used as a witness to others in my years of ministry to my fellow Jews and persecuted believers."

Bianca continued serving with The Voice of the Martyrs in New Zealand until she retired. After a brief illness, she went to be with the Lord on January 29, 2012, at age 87. Bianca's obituary offered special thanks to the "angels with human faces" who cared for her in her final days.

In Her Words:
Aida

A bold Christian witness in the Soviet Union, Aida Skripnikova was first arrested and imprisoned from 1965 to 1966. She was arrested again and sentenced to a labor camp from 1968 to 1971. She shares how God sent His comfort and encouragement through His Word and fellow believers during these difficult times.

My arrest on April 12, 1968, was a complete surprise. Although outwardly I remained calm, I had a storm in my soul. It seemed to me that God had left me. When I was locked in a cell, I could not even pray. I tried several times but could not. I had only one question: "Why? Why, Lord, did this happen right now?"

I walked around the small cell from corner to corner for quite a long time. All the walls in the cell were covered with scribbles, mostly curses and swearing. Suddenly, I saw words clearly written on the wall. I was surprised I had not noticed them before.

"THE WAYS OF THE LORD ARE PAST FINDING OUT"
(Romans 11:33).[1]

That was my answer.

Often, the appropriate verse from the Bible came to mind at the right time. Later, I found out that those words were written by a sister from my church who was held in that cell because she led Bible studies for children. After a year and a half of my imprisonment, a New Testament was secretly given to me.

You can read Aida's full story in the first volume of Hearts of Fire.

---

1. The King James Version uses this phrase in the verse.

Gracia

We Must Run

MAY 27, 2001
PALAWAN, PHILIPPINES

Gracia Burnham slept soundly beside her husband, Martin, lulled by the waves that lapped lazily outside their overwater bungalow. Their anniversary trip to the Dos Palmas Resort was an extravagant, romantic getaway for the couple, a luxury experience unlike anything they'd had during their eighteen years of marriage.

After dinner, the couple had watched the sun dip beneath the tropical horizon and then drifted off to sleep.

Gracia was startled awake during the night by someone banging on the wooden door of their cabin.

Ugh—they want us to move to the next cabin, she thought. At dinner, a member of the resort staff had said something about wanting the Burnhams to change rooms.

"It's too early to move!" Gracia called out from the bed.

But the pounding continued. This time, Martin chimed in. "What?" he yelled.

133

"It's a guard," came the reply.

"I think the guard is drunk," Gracia said.

"No, I think something's wrong," Martin responded, rising to his feet.

Martin grabbed a pair of khaki cargo shorts from beside the bed as Gracia sat up and reached for her clothes—a pair of shorts and the gray T-shirt she'd worn the night before.

Just as Martin reached the door, it burst open as three men carrying M16 military rifles charged into the room. The men were young—a teenager and two others in their early twenties wearing long-sleeved black shirts and camouflage pants.

Two of the men swept Martin out the door.

"Go, go, go!" the third man ordered Gracia.

"No, no, no!" she said, clutching the bed sheet around her body. "I'm not dressed." She hoped the man spoke English. Hands shaking, she pulled on her shorts and quickly slipped her shirt over her head. The man dug through their belongings until he located the couple's camera and cell phone.

"Move, move, move!" he commanded.

There wasn't time for Gracia to find her purse, but she managed to grab two pairs of flip-flops before hurrying outside. She felt a sharp pain as the man jabbed her in the back with the barrel of his gun, and she fumed. *I am not going to run.* He ushered her toward the dock where Gracia saw a long speedboat—equipped with three, powerful outboard engines—the kind used for drug running. Her husband was already sitting on the floor of the boat, along with several other frightened hostages.

"Oh, I'm so glad to see you," Martin said, breathing a sigh of relief. He was still shirtless and wasn't wearing his contact lenses. Sitting down beside him, Gracia handed him the flip-flops. Neither of them spoke as others were marched down to the boat from various cabins while dawn brightened the eastern sky.

Gracia glanced down at the wedding ring on her finger. *These guys are not going to get my ring!* she thought. When no one was looking, she slipped the ring from her hand into the pocket of her shorts.

In addition to being an anniversary celebration, the Dos Palmas trip was the celebration of the end of a chapter in Martin and Gracia's ministry lives. Martin had been promoted to serve as chief pilot with New Tribes Mission.[1] In the months to come, the Burnham family—Martin, Gracia, and their three children—was scheduled to move to Arizona to take up his new role.

In their seventeen years serving in the Philippines with New Tribes—Martin as a missionary pilot and Gracia as "mission control" managing the radio and charting Martin's flights—the Burnhams had faced many challenges. Storms that tossed Martin's red-and-white Cessna to and fro like a toy, as well as sicknesses, loneliness, and other challenges all caused upheaval at various times. But none of those were like the challenge they faced now.

As the engines powered up and the boat pulled away from the dock, Gracia counted the number of hostages. Twenty. A few of the kidnappers spoke English, she discovered, and at least one other language she didn't recognize. The fifteen or so captors pumped their fists in the air, chanting in unison, "*Allah akbar! Allah akbar!*"—Arabic for "Allah is the greatest."

Instantly, Gracia knew with whom they were dealing: the dreaded Muslim terrorist group Abu Sayyaf.

"We're in big trouble," she whispered to Martin.

⁓ele⁓

Gracia, the fifth child of six siblings, was raised in a Christian family. Her father, a pastor who helped start a Bible college, made sure she was in church every time the doors were open—for Sunday

---

1. New Tribes Mission is now called Ethnos360.

school, morning and evening worship, midweek prayer services, plus any additional special events that always seemed to arise.

When she was seven or eight, a Sunday school teacher explained to Gracia the importance of committing her life to Jesus Christ, and shortly thereafter, she begged to be baptized. Reading became one of Gracia's most treasured hobbies. Over the years, she devoured biographies of brave Christian women like Amy Carmichael, the young Irish woman who moved to India to help children; and Mary Slessor, the courageous missionary to Africa who stood against witchcraft and cannibalism.

In her late teenage years, Gracia applied to several colleges but eventually decided to enroll in Calvary Bible College in Kansas City, where her father had served on faculty as a professor. During her final year of college, Gracia's friend Elizabeth was dating a cute guy named Doug Burnham, a quiet "missionary kid" from the Philippines.

"Did you know that Doug's older brother is transferring here for the second semester?" Elizabeth asked. Gracia was intrigued. "He'll be a junior," Elizabeth continued. "Want to meet him?"

His name was Martin, Gracia learned. He was a pilot who would be taking classes at Calvary Bible College while also teaching in the school's aviation department. Martin was easy-going, with a strong sense of humor and a warm smile. As they began spending time together, their friendship blossomed, and Martin invited Gracia to attend one of the plays performed by the school's missionary student group.

Eventually, Martin asked her on a date. "The fall concert is coming up," he said. "I wonder if you'd like to go with me." But Gracia didn't give him an immediate answer.

"Hey, guess who just asked me out?" she bubbled to her friends. "Martin Burnham! Should I do this?"

"Of course!"

As their relationship grew, Gracia learned about Martin's childhood in the Philippines where his family members were missionaries. He learned how to fly in Wichita, Kansas, so he could become a missionary pilot. Gracia soon found herself falling in love. She felt God calling her to be with Martin, to follow this man wherever God would lead.

During spring break of 1983, Martin pulled a tiny ring box from his pocket. "Gracia . . . would you marry me?" he asked. A few months later, in a simple ceremony and surrounded by friends and family, the two became husband and wife. They honeymooned in Branson, Missouri, and spent several months crop-dusting to further hone Martin's piloting skills. In Mississippi, they completed a year of "boot camp" training with New Tribes Mission, the first step in their journey to becoming missionaries. Part of the training included a grueling, six-week period of "jungle camp," during which they learned how to survive in the woods.

When the year of boot camp ended, Gracia was devastated. She had bonded with the eighteen others in their class, and saying goodbye tore out her heart. She sobbed and grieved until a stark truth struck her: *Girl, your whole life is going to be a series of goodbyes. You've got to get your act together if you're going to survive.* She determined never again to let goodbyes shatter her that way.

With boot camp completed, Gracia and Martin were certified to move to the next level of missionary training—flight training in Arizona—before they would be assigned to the country where they would serve as missionaries.

"Please send us anywhere except the Philippines," Martin requested of New Tribes Mission leadership. He didn't dislike the country, but he had grown up there and wondered if the seasoned missionaries who remembered him as a child would be willing to climb into an airplane and entrust their lives to him.

Gracia, on the other hand, didn't care where she and Martin went. She knew she'd be happy anywhere as long as they were together.

One day, the New Tribes Mission leadership called the couple in for another meeting. "You know, they really do need a replacement pilot in the Philippines," they said. "Martin, you know the culture and you partly know the language. It's kind of ridiculous to send you somewhere else. Would you be willing to go back?"

Without hesitation, Martin agreed, and he and Gracia made preparations to move to the Philippines. Just like she'd committed, Gracia handled her goodbyes at the airport well. But when she boarded the Philippine Airlines flight at Los Angeles International Airport and heard the flight attendants greeting passengers in Tagalog instead of English, tears began streaming down her face. She was truly leaving home, and she didn't know when or if she would ever live in the U.S. again.

ele

Gracia and Martin spent their first few days at the New Tribes Mission guesthouse in the capital city of Manila, securing Philippine driver's licenses and being fingerprinted at immigration. Soon, though, they were on their way north into the interior of Luzon Island, a seven-hour bus ride to a mission compound with an airstrip at Aritao.

The compound was located in a beautiful area, and Gracia loved her new home. It was built on stilts, and she was delighted to discover it even had an indoor bathroom and cold running water. On the veranda was a porch swing Gracia pictured herself sitting on, enjoying the beauty of the mountains and the view of the farmers plowing rice fields with their water buffalo.

Martin was in the air almost immediately, tending to the needs of several missionary families who worked with different remote tribes on Luzon. Martin delivered everything from powdered milk to eggs, meat, and fuel for refrigerators and stoves.

Gracia hardly had time to unpack in their little house before she took over responsibilities for the radio. Twice a day—once at 7:00 a.m. and again at 3:30 p.m.—she went through roll call and talked with each tribal station. If anyone had "traffic," which she learned meant messages for anyone else, she made a list and then began matching up the parties like an old-time telephone operator. By radio, she took orders for groceries and medicine, requests for appointments, and flight needs.

The other component of Gracia's radio work was to "flight follow" Martin whenever he was in the air. He called her every ten minutes with a position report, which she recorded in case of an emergency so she'd know his last location. She also had to keep track of the weather by checking with the person at the destination. When Martin was in the air, Gracia sat by her radio and didn't leave.

The Burnhams loved missionary life in the Philippines. They shared the gospel with unreached people and supported other missionaries in the island nation. Martin navigated his tiny Cessna toward primitive landing strips of remote villages, maneuvering his wings over the jungles and landing a fully loaded plane on a 300-meter[2] airstrip with trees crowding in on each side. When he hopped out of the cockpit, the missionaries on the ground soon recognized his heart for both the tribal people and for them. Martin greeted each family with a warm, friendly smile, knowing the front-line missionaries—who hadn't spoken to another English speaker in weeks—just needed someone to hold a cup of coffee and listen.

Before long, Martin knew everything about every missionary—who was struggling financially, who was discouraged by

---

2.   984 feet, roughly

language study progressing more slowly than expected, who was having marriage difficulties. He held their newborn babies and congratulated missionary kids on their homeschool projects. He was always eager to meet villagers who had recently become followers of Jesus Christ. Martin had a heart for everyone he came into contact with, and everyone who knew him loved him.

Back at their home, Gracia witnessed the Lord provide for the couple's needs. There were times when she and Martin didn't have enough money to eat very well, or they had to walk instead of taking Martin's motorcycle in order to save money on fuel, but they always had what they needed.

Beginning just six months after the Burnhams arrived in Aritao, their first child, Jeffrey, joined the family. Jeff was still just a tiny baby when a delegation of missionaries from the southern island of Mindanao came to visit the Burnhams. "We really, really need a flight program on our island," they said. "There are eight families altogether—more than you have here on Luzon. Would you consider coming down and putting something together?"

Soon, Martin and Gracia packed up their small family and moved to Malaybalay, a small city in the mountains of Mindanao, where Mindy and Zachary were added to their family. The Burnhams would spend the next eight years in Malaybalay before returning to Luzon. As her children grew, Gracia spent much of her time homeschooling them, along with welcoming traveling missionaries into their home for brief periods of respite. The Burnham family served the Lord in the Philippines until one spring day when a trip to the coast changed the course of their lives forever.

MAY 27, 2001
EARLY MORNING

The speedboat bounced fiercely in the open water as the white bungalows of Dos Palmas grew tiny on the receding horizon. Gracia forced herself to stay calm. She thought back to a course in her training that prepared future missionaries for hostage situations.

"The first few moments, when everyone is being rounded up," the instructor had said, "is when the captors are the most trigger-happy. So do what you're told. But soon after that, begin to make eye contact with your kidnappers. Start to become a real person to them, not just an item. Go ahead and let them know what your needs are. That helps establish your individuality in their minds."

What else had he said? Gracia couldn't remember. It had been hard to pay full attention that day in training. At the time, kidnapping felt like something that happened to other people, not to Gracia and Martin. But she decided to put into practice the part she remembered and asked for a restroom. One of the other hostages volunteered to hold up a *malong*, a large wraparound skirt, to give the women a bit of privacy. One after the other, they took turns squatting on the boat.

About an hour into the trip, an older Abu Sayyaf leader leaned over to Martin. Looking down at Martin's hand, he announced, "I want that ring." Martin could do nothing but hand over his wedding band.

Gracia was crestfallen, wishing she'd tucked Martin's ring safely in her pocket with her own. She thought back to the day so many years earlier when she'd paid just fifty dollars for his simple gold band. *It's just a gold ring. A ring can be replaced.* She gripped Martin's hand tightly.

Occasionally, other boats came into view on the horizon. When this happened, the captors herded their hostages together and covered them with a tarp. During one of these times, Gracia heard the engines throttle back and another boat come alongside. When the second boat left, she noticed the terrorists had received some sort of food package. Gracia had not realized how hungry and thirsty she was until they began to pass around bits of *cassava*. She'd never eaten *cassava* before—a hard paste made from pounding the fibrous root vegetable, mixing it with water, and then steaming it in banana leaves—and she hoped it was safe to consume.

As the day progressed, the sun grew hotter. Gracia and Martin studied the faces of their captors, trying to figure out their names and who the bosses were. Around two or three o'clock in the afternoon, a man named Solaiman walked over with a yellow legal pad.

"We're the Abu Sayyaf. Some people call us terrorists. We want you to know, we're not terrorists. We are simply people whom the Philippine government has robbed of our homeland, and we just want it back. No one in the government will listen to us, and so we have to do things like this to gain notice."

One by one, he asked the captives their names and occupations, writing them down. Except for a man named Guillermo, a tall Californian whom Gracia remembered from the resort dinner the night before, Gracia and Martin were the only Americans. The other hostages were all Philippine citizens, wealthy enough to afford a vacation at a place like Dos Palmas.

"We're American missionaries with a group called New Tribes Mission," Martin told Solaiman. "We try to help the tribal people."

A cloud of disappointment suddenly darkened Solaiman's face. Gracia could see that he had hoped Martin would be a wealthy businessman whose company would readily pay a ransom. But mission groups, on the other hand, were poor organizations with known policies against ever paying ransoms.

"Yours will be a political ransom," Solaiman said. "We will make demands, and we will deal with you last."

Uh-oh, Gracia thought. *We're going to be in this a long time.*

As the boat powered through the water, Gracia's thoughts settled on her three children. Jeff was now fourteen, Mindy was eleven, and Zach, ten. In situations like this, the mission protocol was to evacuate the kids out of the country. But she kept wondering if they knew about the kidnapping yet. *Who would have told them? Are they on a flight yet?* Her heart ached as she thought about the fear and confusion they'd be experiencing, but she tried to reassure herself with more optimistic thoughts. *Worst-case scenario, we'll spend the summer with these guys and be out by the time the kids go back to school.*

At sundown, the speedboat approached a larger fishing boat. Aboard were another ten to twenty Abu Sayyaf, along with the fishing crew. Gracia, Martin, and the other hostages were ushered across a narrow, bamboo boardwalk onto the fishing boat. Together, they sat down on the deck as their captors began their evening prayers. *I can't believe this is happening*, Gracia thought.

"Do you think people know yet that we've been captured?" she asked Martin, as the darkness enveloped them.

"It's hard to tell," Martin said. "But don't worry, Gracia, we're going to be okay."

A song she'd heard the previous week began playing in Gracia's mind. As Martin drifted to sleep, she quietly sang the chorus.

Be strong, be strong, be strong in the Lord,
And be of good courage for He is your guide.
Be strong, be strong, be strong in the Lord,
And rejoice for the victory is yours.[3]

~ele~

On board the fishing boat, the hostages began taking care of each other's needs. One man gave Martin a sleeveless shirt to wear. A woman passed Gracia a long piece of lace to cover her head, and someone else tossed her a malong. Her bare arms were still showing, but at least she was somewhat more modest, which was important to the Muslim men aboard the boat.

At some point during the day, a man named Sabaya handed Martin a satellite phone and instructed him to make a statement to Radyo Agong, a radio station friendly to Abu Sayyaf and willing to air their messages.

"I, Martin Burnham, along with my wife, Gracia, who have lived in the Philippines for fifteen years, members of New Tribes Mission, have been taken hostage by the Abu Sayyaf . . . We appeal to the American and Philippine governments to work to bring this situation to a peaceful end very soon."

"You did a good job, honey," Gracia said as Martin walked back to her. "You always do."

That evening, the religious diversity of those on the boat was noticeable. The Muslims conducted their ritual of bowing and praying as they faced west toward Mecca. The Catholics removed their rosary beads and prayed. One of the hostages asked Martin to pray aloud for the group.

---

3. *Be Strong in the Lord*
   Words: Linda Lee Johnson
   © 1979 Hope Publishing Company, www.hopepublishing.com. All rights reserved. Used by permission.

"Lord, all of this doesn't surprise You. You know where we are, even though we don't. We know that people are worried about us. But You hold us in Your hands. Give us the grace to go through this trial. We are depending on You. Amen."

A peace washed over Gracia's heart as she listened to her husband's prayer. It calmed her, as it did the other hostages who came to regard Martin as the unofficial chaplain of the group.

For days, the hostages stayed aboard the fishing boat. At night, as the temperature dropped and they tried to sleep, they squeezed themselves along the narrow sides of the deck with their feet hanging out over the ocean. The vessel was much too small for the number of passengers it now held.

When the drinking water ran out, the hostages had no choice but to drink the melted runoff from the ice that had cooled the boat's fish before it was hijacked. Somewhere along the way, one of the captors gave Martin another shirt to wear, and Gracia was relieved he wouldn't be so cold at night.

Finally, after five days and four nights at sea, the kidnappers arrived at their destination and docked the boat at the Philippine island of Basilan, a well-known stronghold of the Abu Sayyaf.

Because the shoreline was rocky, the fishing vessel couldn't reach the coast, so the passengers were forced to wade through chest-deep water to reach land. More Abu Sayyaf greeted the group with cries of "Allah Akbar!" The kidnappers marched their hostages up a hill. Martin had lost his flip-flops in the boat and was now barefoot. It was just as well because Gracia's flip-flops kept sliding around on the steep trail. She finally took them off and carried them with her.

At the top of the hill, the group arrived at a small shelter built for converting coconut husks into charcoal. The structure was twelve feet square and elevated about a foot off the ground. The hostages climbed inside and slept on the split-bamboo floor for the night.

When daylight broke, the group learned they would be taken to the river, a few at a time, to bathe in the cold water. The first few hostages had just begun bathing when gunfire suddenly erupted. Gracia was petrified, her heart thumping through her chest.

"Drop!" someone yelled.

Gracia hit the jungle ground, crawling on her stomach back to the coconut shelter. The Abu Sayyaf returned fire, charging into the forest. Within just a few hours of landing on shore, the Armed Forces of the Philippines (AFP)—the military of the Philippine government—had found the terrorist holdout.

As the shots rang out, Sabaya entered the coconut shelter looking for a hostage named Tess. "Come with us," he said. "We want you to call the radio station and give a message to President Arroyo. You tell her to call off the troops on Basilan and stop the indiscriminate shooting at the Abu Sayyaf, because they're going to injure innocent hostages."

For the first time in nearly a week, Gracia and Martin knew their location.

After ten minutes the shooting stopped. Amazingly, no one had been injured. The group soon pressed farther into the jungle, the terrain becoming much rougher. When they sat to rest, they were attacked by a swarm of bees, plunging their morale deeper into despair. Everywhere the hostages turned, things were getting worse.

As darkness fell, the Abu Sayyaf roped their captives' wrists together to keep them from running away. For hours the hostages plodded single file through the jungle, Martin still barefoot and Gracia wearing her flimsy flip-flops. Eventually, they reached a jeepney, a minibus-like vehicle that is a popular means of public transportation in the Philippines. Not everyone could fit inside the jeepney, so three of the hostages were left behind. Later, Gracia and Martin learned that all three were instantly beheaded.

The crowded truck bounced along the jungle trail until it reached a small, one-story hospital. Gracia's heart sank. *This is the last thing this place needs! Patients are already sick and trying to get well—and here in the middle of the night comes a bunch of terrorists with their captives. Now even more lives are going to be endangered.*

Three of the captors began bashing out the windows with the butts of their rifles. Martin and Gracia soon realized the Abu Sayyaf were taking refuge in the hospital because the Geneva Convention prohibited the government from attacking hospitals. But their plan was soon thwarted when gunfire erupted once again. The government troops blasted the hospital, with the Abu Sayyaf quickly returning fire. The fighting dragged on into the late hours of the night. To avoid the bullets, Gracia, Martin, and the other hostages moved from room to room, keeping away from the windows.

The AFP had cut off the hospital's electricity and phone service, which infuriated the terrorists who had hoped to use the phones to call the press and give interviews. Martin was summoned to the courtyard the next morning to make another call on the satellite phone. Gracia was terrified for him to leave her side, but he had no choice.

"Call your mission in Manila," said Sabaya. "Tell them to call the American Embassy and have *them* call President Arroyo."

As Martin stood outside, phone pressed to his ear, he could hear the voice of his friend, Bob Meisel, on the other end of the line. At first, Bob didn't recognize Martin's voice. It took a while to convince him, but Martin was able to relay his message before the phone battery died.

Gracia's constant stress soon affected her digestive system, and she ran desperately to an unoccupied patient room to relieve herself. "If I don't come back within a couple of minutes," she said to Martin, "you need to come looking for me, okay?"

Back outside, the gunfire was unrelenting. The Abu Sayyaf brought their wounded into the hospital, dropping them on the floor before rushing back outside to fight. When the roar of shelling increased, someone yelled "Drop!" and Gracia fell to the floor once more, her gaze riveted on the bloodied, writhing face of one of the terrorists. It was almost more than she could bear. *Is this what it's like to watch someone die?* Gracia felt her mind cloud over. She could no longer think straight and was slipping into shock. *Oh, God, help me! Calm me down, please. Keep us safe, and keep us sane.*

Somehow, in all the confusion of the gunfire, the Abu Sayyaf received word that the ransom money for two of the captives had arrived. They also released R.J., the young son of one of the hostages.

The shooting continued late into the afternoon, and Gracia's emotions were drained. She couldn't help but feel as if the hospital would be their tomb. "They're just going to gun us all down," she said to Martin. "We're all going to die here."

"It's all going to end soon," Martin said, reassuring as always.

Half an hour later, the Abu Sayyaf had a new plan. "Everybody, start packing up! We're leaving!" Gracia grabbed a nearby sheet and made a makeshift knapsack for Martin's extra shirt, their shared toothbrush, and a few scraps of extra food.

Just as soon as she stepped into the courtyard, Gracia saw the flash of a grenade detonate over her shoulder.

"I'm hit! I'm hit!" shouted Guillermo.

Martin felt a sharp pain in his back. He'd been hit by fragments.

"Let's go!" a terrorist shouted. The only option was to jump up and run. At the edge of town, the group finally slowed to a walking pace. Every hour or so, they stopped to rest. Each time, Gracia was so exhausted she sank down on the ground and instantly fell asleep.

Oddly, the AFP didn't pursue them. The kidnappers explained that they'd used the earlier ransom money to pay off the Philippine military.

That night, Gracia, Martin, and the others lay down beneath a tree, the first of many nights they would spend on the cold, hard ground. One of the other hostages, a woman named Angie, had become hysterical, in such bad shape that Gracia leaned over to Martin and said, "Maybe I ought to sleep beside her tonight, just to help her through." Martin nodded. The two women scooted close together, and Gracia kept her arm around Angie through the rest of the night.

The next morning, Gracia woke up to find Martin shivering. "I just about froze during the night," he admitted. Gracia was devastated. *He needed me, and I wasn't there for him.* She cried and cried as she thought about her husband lying all alone, shivering in the cold. *From this moment on, I will never leave his side when it's time to sleep, no matter what the circumstances.*

‍⁂

As the group of hostages and terrorists made their way through the island, they looked out for each other as best they could. When one of Gracia's flip-flops was swept away as she forged a brook, Sabaya offered her a pair of tattered blue rain boots to wear. Someone else in the group had given Martin a pair of rubber sandals, an enormous relief for his bare feet.

Several nights after leaving the hospital, just as the group was settling in for the night, Gracia heard someone shout "Soldiers! Soldiers!" The Philippine army was coming once again, and the hostages scurried to collect their belongings for another dash into the woods. Gracia suddenly noticed that Martin's sandals were missing, and she was instantly upset. *Who would have stolen his shoes?*

"Don't worry about it," Martin said. "I'm sure they'll turn up."

"What do you mean?" she retorted. "We're going to have to go into the forest again, and you don't have anything to wear on your feet!" Gracia approached a man named Musab, who seemed to be a leader within the Abu Sayyaf, and with little attempt to restrain her anger, demanded, "Martin needs his shoes."

Musab glanced around casually and shrugged. This infuriated Gracia. "Martin can't walk through the forest in bare feet! This is ridiculous. He's going to get injured, and you have to do something about it!"

Musab's face clouded at being reprimanded by a woman, and he turned and walked away. Solaiman appeared by Gracia's side and said, "Gracia, you need to calm down. This will all work out." At that moment, she saw Musab's brother, another of the terrorists, walking up the hill from where he'd been bathing. On his feet were Martin's sandals, and he'd broken one of them. Without a word of explanation, he smiled and handed them back to Martin.

Rage boiled within Gracia, but gradually, she settled down. *If I want to get out alive and see my kids again, I'd better get a grip on my temper.*

Ten weeks into their captivity, after countless periods of hope followed by deep pits of despair, Gracia felt herself slip into an unfamiliar emotional place. Several of the other hostages had been released, their ransoms successfully negotiated by their families. While Gracia was thrilled for these men and women, she began to feel abandoned by God. She knew God was all-powerful, but she could no longer understand how, if God loved her, He would allow her to stay in these horrifying circumstances.

As she sat on a rock next to the river one afternoon, she felt the weight of her depression, which had begun to spill over into her relationships with the others, making her terribly difficult to get along with. She stared at the water and watched a leaf break free from its branch and float down the river. *Why can't I go down the river with it and be free?* In the constant rush of the river, Gracia felt like she could hear Satan taunting her: "You trust in the Lord—but you're still here." She found herself beginning to believe Satan's lies.

Martin sat down next to her. "Gracia," he said, "it's so sad to see you giving up your faith."

"I'm not giving up my faith," she said. "I still believe that God made everything and Jesus died for our sins. I'm just choosing not to believe the part about God loving me. Because God's not coming through."

Gently, as always, Martin said, "Oh, it seems to me that either you believe it all, or you don't believe it at all. You need to decide what you believe." After being spiritually tormented for several days, Gracia felt miserable. Whether she was at the river or in the house, she was crying.

One day, as she sat by the river, she began thinking about what Martin said. *Okay, Scripture tells me that God loves me.* She began to think through all of the verses about love. *Maybe I'm not feeling it right now, but God's Word says that He loves me.* Gracia knew she had a choice—she could give in to her resentment and allow it to dig her into a deeper and deeper emotional hole, or she could choose to believe what God's Word says to be true, whether she felt it or not. For Gracia, that had to be enough. *I'm going to take God's Word for what it is, and I'm going to believe it. I'm going to hang on to it with everything I have, because I'm in a really bad place, and I can't help myself. I may as well let God do it.*

There, deep in the jungles of the Philippines, Gracia prayed for God to help her trust His love. She couldn't trust her captors, and she couldn't trust herself, but she could trust the Lord. She looked up from the river and realized she felt different. It was as if God were saying, "If you're going to believe that I died for you, why not believe that I love you? Why don't you let Me put My arms around you and love you?"

So she did. Gracia finally gave in and handed all her pain and anger over to the Lord. From that day on, the Lord let her know in her spirit that He was still faithful. One of her favorite hymns, "How Great Thou Art," became even more significant, especially the second and third verses, and she sang it often.

When through the woods and forest glades I wander
And hear the birds sing sweetly in the trees,
When I look down from lofty mountain grandeur
And hear the brook and feel the gentle breeze,

And when I think that God, His Son not sparing,
Sent Him to die, I scarce can take it in;
That on the cross, my burden gladly bearing,
He bled and died to take away my sin.

Then sings my soul, my Savior God, to thee:
How great Thou art! How great Thou art![4]

Whenever Gracia or the hostages would sing, the Abu Sayyaf would oftentimes hiss at them. But they never reprimanded

---

4. *How Great Thou Art*
   Words: Stuart K. Hine
   Music: Swedish folk melody/adapt. and arr. Stuart K. Hine
   © 1949, 1953 The Stuart Hine Trust CIO. All rights in the USA its territories and possessions, except print rights, administered by Capitol CMB Publishing. USA, North and Central American print rights and all Canadian and South American rights administered by Hope Publishing Company. All other North and Central American rights administered by The Stuart Hine Trust CIO. Rest of the world rights administered by Integrity Music Europe. All rights reserved. Used by permission.

Gracia when she sang "How Great Thou Art," because they found the song so beautiful. More than once, Martin told her, "Maybe God has us here just to praise Him in this very dark place."

As the months passed, Gracia continued to realize in a new and deeper way what a truly wonderful man her husband was. She'd always known what a strong Christian he was, but under the immense pressure of their circumstances, she saw new depth to his character and Christlikeness.

Together, she and Martin prayed for their captors. They prayed for them to have compassion on their hostages and to reject Islam and turn, instead, to follow Jesus Christ. In the long stretches of time between attacks, when the group sat and waited to begin moving once more, Gracia and Martin sought out moments when they could share the gospel with the Muslim terrorists.

Solaiman was especially interested in talking about religion, and he sought to convince the Burnhams that Islam is a religion of justice. "We are trying to get justice for everything bad that has ever happened to us," he explained.

"Well," Martin said, "I guess Christianity is a little different. Jesus told us not only to love our neighbors but also our enemies."

Solaiman sneered. "Where's the justice in that?"

Gracia chimed in. "I, for one, don't want justice, because I am a sinner. I believe Jesus is God and came to earth to die for my sins. I don't have to pay for my sin, because it is already paid for."

Solaiman shook his head. "I don't want anybody paying for my sin. I'll do my own paying."

Later that afternoon, when Martin and Gracia were alone, Martin said, "You know, that's exactly what Solaiman is going to do. Someday when he stands before God, he's going to pay for his own sin, and it's not going to be pretty." Gracia and Martin had already been praying daily for their captors, but now they felt an even greater urgency to pray for their salvation.

In the jungles of the Philippines, prayer was often their only lifeline, their only hope. And often, Gracia knew she and Martin weren't praying alone. One day, as they traipsed through a waist-high swamp, exhausted and with the Abu Sayyaf dragging their wounded behind them, Gracia felt an overwhelming certainty that people were praying for her and for Martin. That knowledge gave her the strength to keep moving forward.

ele

Over the twelve months that followed, Gracia saw the pattern repeat itself over and over. When the military attacked, a furious battle ensued, killing and injuring Abu Sayyaf terrorists and hostages alike before the group retreated, once more, deep into the jungle. For days, or even weeks, the group stayed still in their new locale before the military discovered them again. In all, the Burnhams would face seventeen clashes between the AFP and the Abu Sayyaf.

The number of Abu Sayyaf members holding the hostages captive had once grown to eighty men. But many of them were killed by the military, and others deserted due to low morale; the captors eventually shrunk to just fourteen men. The number of hostages diminished too, as the Abu Sayyaf negotiated ransoms for their release.

As the months wore on, Gracia and Martin, along with the other hostages, experienced insufferable hardships. There was never enough food, clean water, or medical care, and they lived under the constant stress of impending attacks from the government and threats from the terrorists. Their days oscillated between mobilizing to the point of exhaustion as they ran for their lives and sitting with absolutely nothing to do, bored and stressed.

The Abu Sayyaf employed various means to secure food for themselves and their hostages. Once, they planned to stop any jeepney that drove by and take whatever food was on board. The first to drive by was loaded on top with sacks of rice and filled with civilian passengers. A CAFGU, a civilian deputized by the Philippine government to maintain peace in a particular territory, sat on top of the jeepney holding a gun.

When the Abu Sayyaf stepped from the woods to stop the jeepney, the peace officer raised his weapon. The terrorists opened fire on the vehicle, mowing down not only the CAFGU but also the civilians inside.

The Abu Sayyaf gathered close to a dozen bags of rice—the ones not covered in blood—and looted the passengers' purses and bags. In one, they were excited to find a large can of milk. In another one that looked like a diaper bag, they pulled out clothing for a little girl. All the spoils were brought back to the camp.

Martin and Gracia sat in shock that night when one of the captors brought them hot milk with sugar. They were so starved they felt they needed to drink it, but their hearts ached, knowing the massacre that had produced the milk.

"Lord," Martin prayed, "we don't know at what cost this food has come our way. We just pray that you would have mercy and give strength to the families of these people who have died."

Gracia stared down into her cup of milk, wondering if the little girl whose milk she now held had survived. A few days later, she had her answer. The child had been killed, and to make matters worse, she had been the niece of one of the Abu Sayyaf raiders. The man had helped gun down his own sister-in-law and niece.

ell

Life in the jungle was unrelenting, and the Abu Sayyaf never seemed to have a real plan. Whenever the order came to pack up, a deathly silence fell upon the camp. Gracia's heart would begin to pound, and she would shake so uncontrollably that she could hardly pack her things—a few meager personal hygiene items, some pieces of food, and the letters she and Martin had written to their children. If they finished packing before the Abu Sayyaf leaders decided which direction was safest to move in, Gracia would sit terrified that a barrage of bullets would come flying at any second.

One night, after the group had been walking for hours, they finally came to a banana grove to rest for the night. Gracia was too exhausted to even remove her boots.

"Martin," she said, "what's going to become of us?" Hot tears streamed down her face. Martin's calm assurance comforted her as they held hands, prayed, and then fell asleep.

The next night, the group mobilized again, soon coming upon a river. As they waded through the chest-deep, frigid water in the dark, Gracia fell farther and farther behind. She reached the other side soaking wet and shivering. *Oh God*, she prayed, tears running down her cheeks, *how much longer can this go on? Is there a certain line that we need to cross, a breaking point where You say I've suffered enough? Where is it?*

Gracia and Martin knew the only hope for rescue was negotiation, and for the Abu Sayyaf, negotiation meant one thing: money. One day, after numerous rounds of discussion with President Arroyo's chief negotiator, Gracia heard Sabaya on the satellite phone. This time, he was speaking with the president herself. Evidently, someone from Malaysia had requested permission to mediate the hostage situation and attempt to negotiate the hostages' release.

"Madam President," he said, "it does not seem that you are getting the picture. We have three Americans. We need a million dollars for Martin. If we get that, we'll let him go free, and his companion, too." But when the president demanded the terrorists' unconditional surrender, Sabaya spewed, "If you don't let

Malaysia in here to mediate within seventy-two hours, we're going to kill one of the whites!"

Gracia was horrified. *If Martin, Guillermo, or I are killed, it won't be with a simple bullet to the chest.* Gracia knew it would be by beheading with the wide, curved blade of a bolo knife.

Three days later, Sabaya kept his word. Guillermo's decapitated body was left lying on a hillside, marked only by his raised head atop a bamboo pole.

✐

JUNE 7, 2002

For more than a year, Martin and Gracia had been held in captivity deep in the jungles of the Philippines. When they heard from the Abu Sayyaf that several shiploads of soldiers had landed nearby, it was clear the noose was tightening around the terrorist group. The kidnappers had been hustling their few remaining hostages through the jungle, again trying to evade capture. But the weary captives had finished the last of their rice and for a week and a half had resorted to eating leaves.

"Pack up! Pack up!" came the order.

For what felt like the five hundredth time, Gracia turned to Martin and said, "I just don't think I can keep doing this much longer. I can't take this anymore."

Like he'd done so many times before, Martin said, "You know, Gracia, I just think we're going to get out of here soon. I think this is all going to work out. After we're home, this is going to seem like such a short time to us. Let's just hold steady." It was difficult, though. Ransom negotiations for the captives had continued; now, only three hostages remained.

Around noon, the group stopped to rest on the steep slope of a mountain ridge. It started to rain, and Gracia and Martin slipped into their hammock beneath a tarp.

"I really don't know why this has happened to us," Martin said. Gracia could sense he was in a reflective mood. "I've been thinking a lot lately about Psalm 100—what it says about serving the Lord with gladness. This may not seem much like serving the Lord, but that's what we're doing, you know? We may not leave this jungle alive, but we can leave this world serving the Lord with gladness."

The two prayed together, thanking the Lord for keeping them safe, and again begging Him to get them home and back to their children. "We want to keep serving You with gladness," they prayed.

Just as they closed their eyes to sleep, gunfire rang out from the crest of the nearby mountain. After sixteen previous battles, Gracia knew to drop to the ground immediately. She flipped her feet around to get out of the hammock, but before she hit the ground, she felt the sharp *zing* of a bullet hit her right leg.

She rolled down the steep hill, dazed. When she saw Martin on the ground, she quickly crawled to his side. His torso was twisted with his legs underneath his body, and his eyes were closed.

Gracia saw blood soaking through his shirt from his upper left chest. Martin's breathing was heavy, almost a soft snore. Gracia lay next to him and tried to look dead.

Every so often, Martin moaned softly as the shooting continued. Gracia was sure each moment would be their last. The terror in her heart was even more severe than the pain in her leg. She forced herself to remain still. *If the Abu Sayyaf see that I'm wounded but still alive, they'll drag me down the hill.* They would force her to leave Martin and continue walking on her wounded leg.

Several minutes passed until, without warning, Gracia felt Martin's body become heavy and sag against her. *Is he dead? Maybe he just passed out.*

Finally, the shooting ceased. Knowing she might get shot if she made a sudden movement, Gracia slowly moved her hands around to signal she was still alive. Two AFP soldiers spotted her and lifted her from the ground by her arms and her throbbing legs. She looked back at where Martin still lay. The red spot on his shirt was larger now, and his complexion was pasty white. At that moment, Gracia knew—the man she loved more than anyone in the world was gone.

She wanted to stop the world in that moment, to reflect on her dreadful loss, to mourn the senseless death of her wonderful husband. But unfortunately, Gracia's circumstances demanded otherwise. "Go get that bag!" she insisted, pointing toward the sack she and Martin had carried through the jungle. The soldiers looked at her like she'd lost her mind, but Gracia insisted. "Go get that bag! It has letters from Martin to our children. It will be the only thing they have left from their dad. You have to get it!" Finally, they agreed.

The rain prevented rescue helicopters from attempting a landing. While they waited for the weather to clear, the AFP soldiers tried to make peace with the knowledge they had shot all three hostages during their rescue attempt.

I can't go to sleep and I can't fall apart here, Gracia told herself. *I've made it this far.* She tried to remember Martin's words from so many times before: "You can do this, Gracia. You've got to go home whole."

Eventually, the lieutenant in charge came to talk to Gracia. "Mrs. Burnham," he said, "I know that you're probably very angry with us, but we were just doing our job."

"I know," Gracia replied. "We never forgot who the bad guys were and who the good guys were." Not long after, she heard the *chop-chop-chop* of a helicopter rotor. A small patch of blue sky was peeking through the clouds.

Soon, the AFP soldiers were carrying Gracia toward the waiting Black Hawk helicopter. *Wait! What about Martin's body? Am I just going to be whisked away and leave my husband on this soggy hillside? This can't be . . .* Gracia leaned back and sadly realized that in her physical condition, she had no other choice. The helicopter lifted off into the sky, leaving her best friend lying in the rain below.

ele

In less than half an hour, the Black Hawk set down at an airport in Zamboanga City, and Gracia's world instantly changed from rugged jungle to the once-familiar amenities of modern life. The helicopter door slid open to reveal American troops and an ambulance waiting on the other side. The EMTs maneuvered Gracia onto their stretcher, loaded her into the back of the ambulance, and within minutes, she was on her way to the U.S. military's Camp Navarro General Hospital.

The bullet that struck Gracia's leg hadn't broken any bones or sliced any arteries. It had passed through her flesh from the back of her thigh out the front, and she would need a simple surgical procedure to close the entry and exit wounds.

When she awoke from anesthesia, Gracia's leg was engulfed in a thick wrapping from her hip down to her knee. The surgeon deemed her well enough to leave, and Major Reika Stroh, an American servicewoman tasked with liaising for Gracia, explained that Gracia would return to Manila aboard a C-130 military transport plane.

"The whole mission of this plane and its crew has been to sit on the tarmac and wait for you and Martin to come out of the jungle," Major Stroh said. "They'll finally get to finish their mission." Gracia was overwhelmed with relief to learn that Martin's body had been recovered from the jungle and flown aboard a U.S. military plane to an air base in Japan.

In Manila, Gracia was ushered to the U.S. Embassy where, finally, she was able to call home.

"Hello," she said as her mother-in-law answered the phone. "This is Gracia, calling from Manila. I just wanted you to know that I'm fine." She was desperate to speak to her children, but she was terribly disappointed to learn that since school had let out, her children were visiting her parents. She would have to wait just a bit longer to hear their voices.

Before she hung up with her in-laws, Gracia knew she needed to broach the painful subject of Martin's death.

"I'm so sorry that Martin didn't make it out," Gracia said.

"We're sorry, too, but we're glad you're okay," her mother-in-law replied. Not wanting them to hear the information from the press, Gracia relayed the details surrounding their son's death. Like she'd done so many times during the past year, she tried to focus only on the next second, the next minute, and make it through the terrible task at hand.

As she hung up the phone, Gracia realized how exhausted she was. A nurse arrived and cleaned her up a bit. The clean, warm water on her skin was such a soothing treat. Gracia looked at the waiting bed, with its spotless sheets and comfortable mattress, and thought, *No hammock tonight. And no one is going to chain Martin ever again.*

As she tried to sleep, Gracia found herself reliving the scene of Martin's death. *What if I had spoken to him and tried to wake him up? What if I'd rolled him over so the bleeding wouldn't have filled up his lungs so fast? Would he still be alive?* She berated herself for not doing something, anything—but deep inside, she knew that no matter what she might have tried, the outcome would have been the same. Finally, she nodded off. It would be the first of an endless string of such nights to come.

Just as Gracia drifted to sleep, the sound of gunfire erupted. She bolted upright in her bed and screamed. Her heart pounded in her chest, and she knew she needed to drop to the ground, but with her injured leg, she couldn't get out of the bed.

The nurse came running.

"Who is shooting?" Gracia demanded, sweat pouring from her brow.

The nurse looked at her sympathetically. "There was no shooting," she assured her. "You're fine. Trust me—there was nothing."

Through the haze of sleep, Gracia realized the attack had been a dream. She was safe, no longer running for her life. The nurse sat with her as she regained her bearings and, finally, fell back to sleep.

ele

Days later, Gracia was back in the United States. She wasn't even out of the jetway when she got her first glimpse of Zach, pacing back and forth. She stretched up her arms from her wheelchair to squeeze him. As she reached for Jeff, then Mindy, she exclaimed, "Oh, thank You, God! We're back together! I didn't know if I would ever hug you again."

When the day of Martin's funeral arrived, Gracia was pleased to see the funeral home had put together a beautiful video tribute to her husband—with pictures from boyhood to his college days, their early years in the Philippines, and photos with his children and his airplanes.

As she looked in the casket at her husband's lifeless body, Gracia was shocked at how thin Martin looked—only 125 pounds, they said—and how old. *Poor Martin*, she thought, as she raised her hand from her wheelchair and laid it on his hard chest. *You went through so much. You were so brave, and you kept me going so I could return home. I'll always love you.*

During the service, as TV trucks waited outside for their broadcast signal, friends from various seasons of the Burnhams' life spoke about Martin.

"We haven't 'lost' Martin," one pastor observed. "We know where he is. And someday, because of the promise of God and the sacrifice of Jesus Christ on the cross, we can join him and be reunited."

Finally, a pastor named Clay Bowlin stood up to speak. He and Martin had been close friends in college two decades earlier, working together in the student missionary group and performing the plays that Gracia had attended in her early days of friendship with Martin. Gracia knew Martin would want Clay to preach the sermon at his funeral. As their friend walked toward the podium, she leaned forward, not wanting to miss a word.

For more than half an hour, Clay held the rapt attention of the room, honoring Martin's life and work and presenting, for a listening world, the gospel for which Martin had given his life. "Gracia was rescued from the jungle by a helicopter," he said. "Martin was rescued from the jungle on angels' wings."

∽∾

In the weeks following her release, Gracia learned specific details about the way the body of Christ had prayed for her and Martin during their year in captivity. She was amazed to learn that in one instance, a moment of peril when she had felt certain that people were praying for them, Christian radio stations across the

United States had called for prayer at that very moment, urging the body of Christ to come together on behalf of the Burnhams.

There were other wonderful discoveries Gracia made as she readjusted to life back in the U.S., particularly relating to her three children. As she settled back home, Gracia didn't know what to expect from Jeff, Mindy, and Zach. She watched them carefully, trying to discern how their father's death and their mother's long absence had affected them.

"I saw that they were the same kids," she said. "They were just a year older, and they seemed so well adjusted." *How can this be?* she wondered.

Then, she began noticing all the people that God surrounded them with: their Christian teachers at school, their youth pastor, their pastor at church, and their grandma and grandpa. Through these people of great faith, God had cared for her children.

"I think my kids doing well has just been God's special gift to me somehow," Gracia said. "I don't take any credit for that. I think that it was God's special favor on me."

Not only did God care for her children, He also cared for Gracia's physical ailments. Her leg wounds healed quickly, and within a few weeks, she no longer needed crutches to get around. She was able to walk normally again. Her biggest health challenge was her gut health. During her jungle experience, tropical amoebas had made a home in her digestive tract.

Gracia knew her in-laws would happily allow her and her three children to live with them forever, but she knew that one day she and her children would need a home of their own. *Maybe we can afford a modest trailer*, she thought.

Then God gave her another special gift. She received a letter in the mail from a local man who wanted to build a home for Gracia in Martin's honor. She was overwhelmed by his act of kindness. Soon, other blessings began flowing in. Gracia was inundated with speaking requests from churches, seminaries, military veterans' organizations, jails, universities, and countless other groups. She had never considered public speaking to be one of her gifts, but she accepted the invitations, trusting that God would give her words.

"My husband died at age forty-two," she often said. "None of us knows the length of the race we are running. We aren't told at the starting line. We only know that we must run. We see the ongoing tension between the West and the Muslim world, and we wonder if it will ever end. God has a solution for this problem. What is it? You and me! God gave *us* the job of caring for the world and bringing people to love Christ."

Gracia was constantly on the lookout for ways to continue her ministry. On the advice of wise friends, she founded the Martin & Gracia Burnham Foundation, using the many financial gifts she'd received from caring people after her release from captivity. Through the foundation, Gracia was able to fund the causes she and Martin had pursued: ministry to Muslims, missionary aviation, persecuted Christians, and tribal missions.

In the summer of 2004, the U.S. State Department asked Gracia to return to the Philippines to testify in a court trial against eight of the Abu Sayyaf terrorists. The court proceedings took several years, but eventually, twenty-three of the men were sentenced to life in prison. Gracia began communicating with some of her captors, and so far, four of them have placed their trust in Christ.

"The Abu Sayyaf were dirty rats," Gracia said, "and they still are. But Jesus died for dirty rats, and we are all the same. We ourselves are awful sinners in need of God's grace.

"Had we known that *any* of them would become believers in Jesus because of our experience," she said, "the days would have been easier to bear during that long year. God can take any situation and make it turn out well."

Gracia expected to tell her story for a few months before interest waned, but that didn't happen. Over the next two decades, she continued to travel and speak, encouraging others to follow God.

"People have said to me, 'I thought God wanted me to be a missionary when I was young, but it just never happened . . .' Following God is never going to 'just happen.' You will have to deliberately give up your will and follow God's will. You might have a 'good life' following your dreams and your passions, because God is good and loves to bless His children. But if you really want to be a good disciple, you deny yourself. You take up your cross, not your dream, and you follow God no matter the cost.

"Following God and being a good disciple are going to be costly. You will get scars. But you will also one day hear, 'Well done, good and faithful servant.'"

~

At times, Gracia thinks back to that anniversary trip she'd planned for her husband. She can't help but speculate as to what might have happened if she had not booked their anniversary stay at the Dos Palmas resort.

Would Martin have never been kidnapped?

"I often think of that, and I'm kind of glad that I didn't get to choose. We would still be in the Philippines. Martin would still be flying for the New Tribes Mission, and I would still be sitting by that crazy radio. I am glad the Lord didn't come to me in a dream or something and say, 'Gracia, do you want to be taken hostage, or do you want to grow old with Martin?' Because I would have chosen to grow old with Martin in a heartbeat.

"It's good that we don't get to choose. God calls us to certain things, and He causes us to react in certain ways in certain situations to work all things together for good and for His glory. I think that is what happened. I think that things have worked for good in our story, and I think that God has gotten glory. I guess that is the point, right? The point isn't to grow old with your husband. The point is to glorify God with what we have been given down here.

"There cannot be a harvest without seed planters. And the seed we planted in the jungle did not die. All these years later, we are watching God do something awesome, and we are amazed."

In Her Words:
Rashin

On Dec. 3, 1990, Rashin Soodmand learned that the Iranian government had executed her father for leaving Islam and placing his trust in Christ, a decision he had made at age 17. Rashin reflects on the spiritual legacy her father left her.

My father had a vision to establish a church in the city of Mashhad. He established a small church in the basement of our house, and the church was growing. Iranian people desire an intimacy with God they can't find in Islam.

We were the only Christian family in the neighborhood, and I always felt there were differences between us and others. Even at school, I was the only Christian. When teachers would ask about my father's job and I replied, "My father is a pastor," they didn't understand.

I remember one day when religious police came to our house, and they told my father to close down the church. After that, they constantly called him to the police station for questioning. My parents were very careful about what they shared with us. When they would speak secretly to each other at times, we realized something was going on. They told us not to talk with our friends about the people who came to our house. We didn't know how serious it was.

I was playing outside with my siblings one day when a group came and arrested my father. "Where are you going?" I asked him. "Don't worry," he replied. "I will come back." He was gone for a month, and we couldn't see him. When they released him, they told him not to leave Mashhad, and they would be monitoring everything he was doing.

Eventually, they gave him an ultimatum. "This is your last chance," they told him. They showed him a paper sentencing him to death and gave him two weeks to respond. My father traveled to Tehran and shared the news with other pastors who offered to help our family escape to a safer place. But my father refused and made a formal statement to the church:

I am a follower of the Great Shepherd of the sheep, our Lord Jesus Christ, and I am ready to sacrifice my soul for my sheep. For me to escape from this persecution would cause the hearts of my flock to become cold and weak, and I never want to be a bad example for them. So, I am ready to go to prison again, and, if necessary, to give my life.

While my father was in Tehran, authorities called my mother and told her to send my father to them when he returned. So, my father immediately returned and reported to authorities. We didn't hear anything for two weeks, but then we were allowed to visit him. We waited for hours. When I finally saw him, I was very excited. He didn't say anything about what had happened to him. He just hugged us and encouraged us to study and look after my mom. When we were about to leave the prison, he stood close to the door and started to cry. We never saw him again.

For weeks there was no news about him. A pastor from Tehran came to Mashhad to see what happened. He learned that my father was executed two weeks prior because of his faith and his ministry. They buried him in a deserted, dusty place, with no sign of his grave. They broke a simple stone to mark his gravesite.

During the two weeks before we were allowed to visit my dad in prison, a man came to our house and told us to come with him immediately to see my father. We went and waited for hours, but we never saw him. After my father's martyrdom, someone from the religion office told us that though we didn't see my father, he could see us from afar. They showed us to him for the last time and told him, "This is your family. This is your wife who is blind, and this is your chance. Choose Jesus or your family."

I had a very close relationship with my dad. I always told him, "I love you more than God." And he always tried to teach me that, "You need to love God before everyone and everything." I would tell myself, "Rashin, you can't survive without your dad." But the day I heard about his martyrdom, I felt the presence of God. He embraced me. I couldn't survive without His presence, His love, His grace, and His mercy.

If I had the chance to see my father again, I would tell him how much I love him and that I am proud of him. I'm proud of the choice he made. I can't deny the difficulties we went through after his death, but we are happy, and we are proud of him that he chose Christ. He taught us a big lesson; he showed us that Christianity is not just a religion, it's reality. It's the truth.

Three days after his martyrdom, I wrote a letter to God, and I promised Him to follow in my father's footsteps. Although I was really sad about losing my dad, writing that letter helped me to survive, and it helped me to understand that my father is alive. Although he's not with me, he's with the Lord. God called me to carry this torch. I have decided to follow his footsteps.

Today, Rashin reaches Iranians inside and outside of Iran.

Tamara

"We Are Not Going to Leave"

ISFARA, TAJIKISTAN
JANUARY 12, 2004

Tamara Bessarab was preparing for bed in the small home she shared with her husband, Sergei, in northern Tajikistan. The streets were empty as people rushed home to take advantage of the two hours of daily electricity allotted by the city.

All afternoon, Tamara had suffered from the sharp, familiar pain of an ear infection. After slipping on her nightgown, she squeezed a few drops of medication into her ears, stuffed them with cotton, and stretched out across the colorful *kurpacha* mat on the concrete floor. She hoped to be free of the throbbing pain and fast asleep soon.

Even through the cotton in her ears, Tamara could hear the calm and rhythmic voice wafting from the front room as her husband worshiped God with his guitar. Sergei was the pastor of the only Christian congregation in a city of 126 mosques, and the front room of their home served as the sanctuary for the small church Tamara and her husband had planted together.

Sergei devoted himself daily to reading the Bible, praying, strumming his guitar, and singing to God. He had learned his favorite worship songs in prison, and he sang them beautifully. Tamara was amazed by her husband's unfailing devotion to the Lord, and she knew Sergei cherished his time alone with God. It was a sacred and essential part of his daily routine, and he honored it faithfully.

Rustam—a military veteran who had served in the war between the Soviet Union and Afghanistan—and his wife were getting ready for bed in an adjacent room. Sergei and Tamara had welcomed the couple into their home and had mentored them in the ministry.

Suddenly, Tamara heard noises that sounded like fireworks. *Maybe people are still celebrating?* she mused, as it wasn't long after the New Year holiday.

Tamara removed the cotton from her ears and heard Sergei crying out from the other room. That's when she realized it wasn't fireworks but gunfire. She reached for clothes to cover her nightgown as a bullet whizzed by her head, just missing her. She jerked back, gasped, then eased her head past the bedroom doorframe, trying to lay eyes on her husband.

He was lying on the floor, wounded, but she couldn't see all of him. The gunfire had come through the window and reached its intended target. The first bullet struck Sergei's hand. A second bullet hit his leg.

There was nothing Tamara could do to help him.

⁓

From the beginning, Tamara's life was fraught with pain. When her mother died at thirty-nine after years of breathing coal dust in the brick factory where she worked, thirteen-year-old Tamara was left to navigate life with her sisters and father, an abusive drunk.

She began drinking, smoking, and trying to make sense of her painful existence.

Who are we? she and her younger sister wondered. Her mother was Russian and a nominal Orthodox Christian, and her father was Tajik and a Muslim. *Are we Tajiks? Should we live our lives according to Islamic law? Or are we Orthodox?* Neither parent had taken the time to instill their beliefs into their children, and Tamara was left floundering.

When her father remarried just months after his wife's death, he soon began to beat his new wife the same way he'd beaten Tamara's mother. One day, after drinking tea with her stepmother, Tamara walked into the bedroom and discovered her father had hanged himself. She returned to the other room, sat down at the table with her stepmother and stepsister, and told them what had happened. Rushing from the table, her stepmother and stepsister pulled him down from his noose. While her father skirted death that day, Tamara wished he would have died.

The violent instability of her life caused Tamara to realize she was the only one she could rely on, so she worked hard to support herself and her siblings. Her first job was as a hospital orderly— bathing, changing, and attending to the patients in her care. Then she worked in an orphanage, an experience even more troubling. Employees laid baby bottles on the chests of the abandoned infants, and if the bottle rolled off, Tamara realized in horror that no one came to put it back. Instead, the babies were left hungry, crying for nourishment.

Like the babies in her care, Tamara felt unloved, and she fought hard to protect herself and her sisters. She was a wild wolf cub learning to make her way in the unsafe world.

Tamara was admitted to university to study Russian language and literature, and she flourished. She loved learning, and her studies came easy to her. Tamara worked during the day, attended classes in the evening, and then studied at the university late into the night. Without any money for bus fare, she would walk from work to the university, and then from the university home, arriving long after the rest of the family had gone to sleep.

The disruptive rhythm of Tamara's schedule eventually proved too much for her family. Three years into her studies, her stepmother complained to her father; to Tamara's chagrin, they soon forced her to drop out.

Without her studies to occupy her time, Tamara found a group of peers: difficult teenagers like herself who lived a rogue life on the streets. She became convinced that she was more like her father than her mother.

She spent her nights with different men, just like so many other women her age. She became pregnant twice—first with a daughter she named Nadia, then later with her son, Seryozha. While Tamara was pregnant with her daughter, she lived in an apartment with her father, stepmother, and siblings. Five months after Tamara gave birth, her stepmother grew tired of the inevitable complications of living in a home with a troubled young woman and an infant. She gave her husband an ultimatum: choose me, or choose Tamara and the baby.

Tamara's father chose his wife.

"Go wherever you want," her father said as he packed her belongings. "Just get out of here, because I'm not going to quarrel with my wife."

Tamara had nowhere to go, and her baby was very ill with a fever. Tamara herself was nursing a black eye, the tragic aftermath of a nasty encounter with Nadia's father a few days earlier. Dragging her belongings out of the house and carrying her daughter, she walked to a park nearby. There, as a homeless single mother, she cried out to God with her first prayer.

"Who are you?" Tamara screamed. "Why does it hurt so much? Why did You take my mom, the only one who loved us?"

She wept as she lashed out at God. She was hungry, thirsty, and desperately needed to feed her baby. Once she'd calmed, Tamara looked over at a vending machine and prayed a second prayer. *Lord, send me three kopeks[1] so I can at least buy a soda.*

To her shock, she looked down and found three *kopeks* lying on the ground. *What a fool I am,* Tamara thought. *Why didn't I ask for at least a ruble so I could buy a bun?* Thus began Tamara's search for a God she didn't yet know or understand.

Tamara desperately needed to find work, but she also knew it would be impossible to find a job without someone to care for Nadia. She needed a break—just a small window of time where she could get back on her feet. So, she came to the only conclusion that seemed to offer any possibility of hope: Tamara would leave Nadia at an orphanage. *Just for a year or so,* she thought; surely that would give her enough time to forge some kind of future for the little girl.

Tamara left the park with Nadia and walked to the orphanage where she'd worked during the summer holidays. She entered the rambling building and found the manager. Tamara could tell that the woman had noticed her black eye.

"How are you living?" the manager asked kindly.

"I'm on the street," Tamara said. The woman nodded as Tamara explained her difficult situation.

"Who beat you up?"

Tamara told her about Nadia's father, how he drank alcohol and became violent. "He's disappeared now."

Just then, a nurse rushed in carrying a swaddled baby. "A woman just came and abandoned him," she explained breathlessly to her supervisor. "She laid him on a table and then left."

---

1. A kopek is a cent in Russian currency also used during the Soviet Union. There are 100 kopeks per ruble.

The two women ran from the room, and Tamara followed. They opened the front door and yelled for the mother to come back. "You'll regret it!" the nurse shouted. "Come take him back!" The woman kept walking and soon faded into the distance.

The nurse turned to Tamara. "No matter how hard it is for you, don't do that—ever."

Tamara left the orphanage with Nadia and returned to the park, even more distressed.

That night, a police officer approached Tamara and asked why she was there. Needing a convincing explanation that would allow her to stay, Tamara gestured toward an apartment building across the street. "The baby was crying," she lied, "so I came outside to the park." Satisfied that she wasn't a drunk making mischief, the officer wished her well and walked away. Tamara spent the night in the park once more, but she knew it was only a temporary solution. The only option she could think of was to relinquish Nadia to the care of the orphanage.

In a final, desperate effort, she decided to visit the parents of Nadia's father the day before she surrendered her daughter. "I'm leaving tomorrow to find work," she explained. "I have nowhere to live, and I'm going to leave my daughter at an orphanage." As Tamara explained her plan to Nadia's grandmother, she felt her heart wrenching. *How am I going to leave my child?* Tamara searched the woman's eyes for any sign of support, but without the unlikely consent of her husband, the older woman knew she had nothing to offer.

"Yes, I understand," she told Tamara, reluctantly. "This is probably the only way out."

Suddenly, the woman's husband spoke. "These are two women talking about my granddaughter!" he said. "No orphanage!" Tamara couldn't believe her ears. Was this a way out? "Come and live here," the man said.

His wife nodded. "Yes, yes," she said. "Here, come in! Grandfather has allowed it." Tamara moved in with Nadia's grandparents, relieved she didn't have to give up her daughter.

ele

Slowly, Tamara got back on her feet and was able to afford her own small apartment.

She had an old copy of the Bible that Christians had given her when she was a student and when her country was under communism as part of the Soviet Union. She wanted to sell it. At that time, a Bible was a rare commodity, and Tamara knew she could exchange it for at least enough money to buy groceries. But something stopped her. She remembered the words of the Christian who had given it to her: "If you don't need it," he told her, "give it away the same way you got it." Tamara decided she would never sell the Bible.

For a long time, the Bible sat unopened in her home, like a relic that was revered but not touched. But soon, her country was embroiled in a civil war just as Tamara was at war within herself. She was dying of drunkenness, of debauchery, of poverty, of starvation. Her daughter had dark circles under her eyes from hunger; her son, whom she'd given birth to several years after Nadia, had rickets. Twice, Tamara considered suicide, but her desperation to help her children survive was enough to keep her alive.

As the civil unrest in her city intensified, though, and as violent massacres filled the streets, Tamara became more and more desperate. She was working as an accountant in a large factory, but there was no food in the country. She cried each night, knowing that in the morning there would be nothing to feed her children. Often she roamed the bazaar, and what fell from the meager vegetable stands she would pick up from the ground and bring home. Sometimes she returned with one potato, or maybe a carrot, and it would have to serve as a full meal.

Eventually, Tamara opened her Bible. "*Lord, if You exist . . .*" she'd say, and then she would start reading.

One day, she opened the Bible and read about how the disciples were sitting together, and Jesus crossed to the other shore of the sea by boat. When His disciples found Him there, His first question was, "Children, do you have any food?" Tamara whispered their response: "No, Lord." She saw that He immediately made them dinner and fed them. Tamara closed the Bible. *It was good for you*, she scoffed at Jesus' disciples. *Jesus was with you. Who's with me? Who's going to feed me?*

The next morning, Tamara arrived at work to find half a jar of sauerkraut, a little oil, and two potatoes placed near her desk. She looked around, but no one else had arrived yet. When a coworker walked in, Tamara asked her about the food.

"This is for you," the woman said.

How could this be? Tamara knew her friend was also starving.

"What do you mean that it's for me?" she asked.

The woman explained that after her family had finished their meal the night before, they were still hungry. There were a few more ingredients left, but she did not cook them. "God said to me, 'You will now take this to Tamara and put it near her table.'"

Tamara was overwhelmed. She had just read the passage of Scripture and had doubted God; but now, for the first time, she saw Him as a living God. He had heard her cry.

Tamara raced back home to cook the food for her hungry children. She told them of the miracle that had occurred that morning. "God did it," she said.

After experiencing God's provision for her family and seeing that He is the God who will never leave, Tamara eventually surrendered to the Lord at age thirty-five.

The first thing she did when she turned to Christ was make this request: *Give me abstinence,* she prayed. *I don't want to live such an ugly life anymore.* Tamara had dreamed of having a husband and wearing a white wedding dress; but now, she thought she would never be a bride. She gave up hope of ever having a husband and surrendered her deep-seated desire to God. No longer did she ask for, or expect, a spouse. Now, God was sufficient.

Finally, Tamara felt like someone truly cared for her. She felt God shouldering her burdens. He provided the security and stability she'd sought for, and she wanted to tell others about Him. So Tamara joined a group of Christians to minister to imprisoned criminals.

∽℮℮∾

Tamara and her ministry group visited many prisons, including a correctional facility in Dushanbe. Like so many other prisons throughout Tajikistan, this facility was in the midst of a paralyzing food shortage, and more than a hundred prisoners were dying of tuberculosis and starvation each day. Mountains of corpses stacked like firewood filled the prison yard.

Inside the prison, Tamara and her colleagues served tea and flatbread while telling the hungry prisoners about Christ. They held worship services and ferried letters between family members and their imprisoned loved ones. One Christian prisoner, a man named Sergei Bessarab, was a frequent recipient of their ministry work.

Tamara witnessed Sergei's leadership within the prison. He spoke little, preferring instead to listen, but when he did speak, he asked profound questions about Scripture. She learned about Sergei's life before he came to Christ. He grew up on the streets with an older brother who was a seasoned criminal. After Sergei broke his leg in an accident, his brother passed along some of the drugs he was dealing to relieve his pain. Eventually, Sergei became addicted.

Sergei was a leader in Tajikistan's organized crime underworld and managed the organization's dirty money. It was a life he was ashamed of now, and he preferred not talking about it. Because of his criminal activity, Sergei had been sent to prison for a total of eighteen years. His brother had been imprisoned as well.

Sergei arrived in prison in tremendous pain because his leg was still broken. His mother had starved herself so she could afford parcels for her two incarcerated sons. When Sergei had received each package, he bartered everything in it to buy drugs.

At some point, Sergei began thinking about God. He wanted to know the truth, but he wasn't sure where to find it. He met a fellow inmate named Sergey Gavrilov, who had trusted Christ in prison after he was given a Bible. In the prison prayer room, Sergey explained the gospel to Sergei, and he, too, placed his faith in Jesus Christ. In the presence of fellow prisoners, he promised never to take drugs again and gave up his long-time habit of smoking. Now a new creature in Christ, Sergei turned his sharp mind toward studying God's Word in the prison prayer room for hours each day.

When Sergey Gavrilov was released from prison, Sergei took his place as the leader of the prayer room. Sergei influenced others in the prison. Firmly and calmly, he spoke truth into the lives of his fellow Christian inmates and challenged them to live in a manner consistent with their faith. Through his life and testimony of drastic transformation, Sergei led many men to faith in Christ.

When the prison ran out of food, life inside was unbearable, but God was present with Sergei even during these immense trials.

"There was nothing to eat," Sergei told Tamara, "so I prayed and went to bed, and I dreamed of a feast. I ate it all and couldn't get enough. When I woke up, I felt like I was so full, as if I really ate it all."

Shortly after this conversation, Sergei's leg became swollen and turned black, the painful repercussions of a previous injury, and the guards sent him to the prison hospital. Tamara visited him in the ward and, with a sly glance, slid her hand into her pocket. When it reemerged, she was holding five small chocolate candies. She quietly slipped them to Sergei. "These are for you," she whispered.

Sergei knew he couldn't keep all five, not when he was surrounded by such devastating hunger. Instead, he gave four away and kept one for himself. Once he had distributed the candy, he leaned back in his hospital bed and devised a plan to enjoy his chocolate.

When the hospital ward had quieted down, he prepared a steaming cup of tea and reached for the chocolate treasure in his pocket, imagining the candy melting slowly on his tongue and quieting his growling stomach. Just then, a man walked up to his bed.

"Sergei," the prisoner said, "I'm so hungry. Do you have a piece of bread?"

"I have nothing," Sergei said, concealing the candy in his closed palm. "I can't help you." The man nodded, his weary face etched with disappointment, and he walked away, resigned to go to bed hungry once more.

Immediately, Sergei knew the Holy Spirit was quietly correcting him to go and exchange his candy for a piece of bread, find the man, and give him the bread.

"No, Lord," Sergei begged. "*Not that, please.*" He couldn't bear the thought of surrendering his last chocolate. But he knew God was right. Sergei hobbled on his throbbing leg into the prison common area, bartered his precious candy for a single ration of bread, and gave the man the food.

In prison, Sergei had become a new man. Tamara knew that only God could perform a transformation as complete as his.

ⅇⅇ

After Sergei was released from prison in 2001, he joined Tamara's team in their prison ministry. During a phone call one day, Tamara told Sergei, "I've seen how brothers who are freed from prison have fallen, just because they do not have a soul mate. They begin to search and end up going back into the world. You need to look for a person who will be next to you."

"I already found this person," Sergei said. "It's you. I prayed, and God pointed me to you. Do you understand? We are walking in the same Spirit. We are ministers, and we will complement each other."

Tamara was shocked by Sergei's proposal. *How am I going to explain getting married to my children?* She never thought marriage was a possibility for her. Besides, she had surrendered her desire for a husband to the Lord. But Tamara soon realized that she was attracted to Sergei. She wanted to be with him. She had been alone all her life and was ready for the protection he would provide her, a shoulder next to hers. She felt safe and secure with Sergei. She knew that a husband would allow her to participate in ministry opportunities not afforded to single women in Tajikistan's extremely conservative culture. He would be a man with whom she could share her life and her work.

That summer, Sergei and Tamara were married.

Tamara continued her prison ministry, now with Sergei by her side. They often traveled days by train to minister to incarcerated prisoners in cities far away. Two imperfect people had become perfect partners for the work God called them to do.

ⅇⅇ

Toward the end of 2002, Sergei and Tamara moved to Isfara to help the church grow and to share the miraculous transformation Jesus Christ had made in their lives with the people of the city. Tamara had left her teenaged son back home to live with a caregiver and finish school.

Tamara struggled with the move to Isfara. Her daughter, now an adult and living on her own, and her son were in different cities, each several hours from Isfara, and they saw each other only occasionally. Tamara also felt the spiritual darkness of Isfara, a city dominated by Islam. Two mosques stood on each street, and women covered themselves from head to toe. There wasn't a single Christian church in the entire city. Tamara wanted to leave but resolved to stay.

The Bessarabs' home was a hut purchased for $1,000 in U.S. currency. There were no doors, no glass in the windows, no electricity, no water, and no toilet. Sergei and Tamara moved to Isfara in December. The temperature inched just above freezing during the day before dipping back down overnight. They placed waterproofed cloth over the openings of their new home to keep out the biting wind.

Their home had a large front room where their fledgling Christian congregation could gather for worship services.

Immediately, Tamara and Sergei got to work. Sergei settled into a routine of studying his Bible, visiting and evangelizing, praying, and leading worship. He quietly and wisely counseled people who came to him with problems. Together, he and his wife served the community.

Shortly after the Bessarabs arrived in Isfara, a delegation of Muslim women came to visit Tamara. She welcomed them into their home, and they sat on the benches Sergei had set up for worship services. Almost immediately, Tamara realized the visit was not a friendly one.

"Get out of here," the women warned Tamara. "There is not enough room for you! Only Islam will be allowed here. Don't you understand that it's dangerous for you here?"

Tamara took a deep breath. "You know, we're not going to leave, because when God opens a door, only He can close it. Not Islam, nor Buddhism, nor fanaticism; only He can." She smiled at the women, trying to convey the love of Christ through her words. "In the future, you will understand that having Christians as neighbors will be a great blessing for you. For the city where Jesus comes, a living faith in the living God begins. It will only be a blessing for you."

At that moment, Tamara did not fully understand the danger she and her husband were in.

Not long after Sergei and Tamara had arrived, someone burned a large Quran in a prominent mosque. Word spread throughout Isfara that the Bessarabs were responsible. Tamara brushed off the rumor. *Who could believe such a thing?* A short time later, several important Muslim leaders were murdered. Tamara wondered if this, too, would be blamed on them.

One day, a group of men called Sergei out of church and threatened him for quite some time. It had happened before, and Sergei always tried to protect his wife from knowing about these sorts of threats, but this time, she overheard.

"You'll be in trouble if you don't leave," they warned.

When Tamara later asked Sergei about the encounter, he reassured her. "Never be afraid of anything," he said. "We will not be abandoned by God."

Soon after, Sergei and Tamara traveled to the *hukumat,* a bureaucratic office in town, to register their church. There, a government agent delivered another warning. "As long as I am sitting here," he said, "there will be no Christianity here, and there will be no church. Get your things and get out."

"Wait," Tamara said, "my father is Tajik, and my mother is Russian. My father observed the laws of Islam, and my mother was a Christian. What was I supposed to do? I chose Jesus." Tamara eyed the man as he listened. "You understand that I am the person who did not belong to any religion. Jesus, Muhammad—they weren't important to me. I didn't know Christian teachings or Islamic ones. But when I saw how Jesus worked in my life, He freed me from drinking and many other vices. He gave me new thoughts, a new heart, and most importantly, He gave me hope. I am not here to offend Islam. You can follow Islam if that is what you choose to do. But my husband and I came to this city to tell about Jesus' wonders."

The official remained silent, so Tamara continued. "Our religion, as you call it, is very peaceful. We do not bring evil. Faith in Jesus makes a person different. It converts a drug addict into a normal person. People are supernaturally freed. No one could change me and him," she said, pointing at Sergei. "No one could change him. Only faith in Jesus supernaturally transforms a person."

She and Sergei shared the gospel with the official. "Choose this blessing," they said. "Choose life."

Finally, when Sergei and Tamara finished, the man narrowed his eyes and spoke. "I'll do everything possible for you not to be here in this city."

Days later, Tamara opened the local newspaper to find an article written about her, Sergei, and their new church.

New people came to the city, and they are very dangerous to our society, the author claimed. *One is a criminal, and the other one, it's not even clear who she is.* Tamara's heart pounded in her chest as she read. The author of the article had dug up Sergei's criminal records and listed his offenses, one by one. The article said they were sent from Uzbekistan—a country embroiled, at the time, in tense relations with Tajikistan—and that the Bessarabs were paid good money.

Now, the journalist claimed, *these people have come to dominate the power in our city. They act on people's minds, using black magic. Like zombies, people go to their place, and these criminals drug them with something.*

Tamara's blood boiled and she felt her ears ringing. She couldn't stand seeing these lies in print, but she kept reading. Moments later, she was shocked to see the address of their church, the building where she and Sergei lived, printed in the article.

Don't go to this address, the article warned. *You will be lured into their web.* Tamara's nostrils flared. The newspaper creased in her tightening grip. *You notice,* the article continued, *that with their arrival, respected people were killed.*

Who will free the city of Isfara of these people?

Tamara was livid. *How dare they defame us like this! How dare they misrepresent the good work Sergei and I are doing! Where did the author get these fabrications?* All she and Sergei had done was help the people of Isfara.

Tamara stormed over to her husband and jabbed her finger at the article as she struggled not to shout.

"Let's go to where this was printed," she pleaded, "and we will demand to know on what basis they printed this!"

"No," Sergei said, his voice calm and measured. "Let's pray for him."

That night, Tamara overheard her husband as he knelt in the front room praying. "Lord," he said, "bless this scribbler, the one who wrote all of that."

Soon after the article was published, people from all over the city flocked to Sergei and Tamara's home, not realizing it also served as their church. Some were curious to see this couple for themselves, but most were in search of help.

"Can you heal me?" the people asked. "The article said you could." Sergei and Tamara explained who they were, the work they were doing, and about Jesus. As people came, the Bessarabs worked with them to know the saving power of Jesus Christ.

Their church grew, and Tamara couldn't help but chuckle. God had used the libelous efforts of the local newspaper as the best ministry advertisement she and Sergei ever could have imagined.

It wouldn't be long, though, before Tamara's smile faded. About two weeks later, after the first article, a second one appeared in the local newspaper. She read furiously, her eyes widening in disbelief. A single, terrifying line jolted her and sent a chill down her spine:

"What's going to be done about Sergei Bessarab?"

ele

A YEAR LATER

For ten minutes, the shooters pelted the home with rifle bullets. Tamara remained motionless on the floor, trying to avoid the bullets flying past her.

In the next room, Rustam threw his wife to the ground and covered her with their bedding. "Keep your head down!" Bullets punctured a water pipe, and frigid water sprayed the room. Rustam crawled on his elbows toward Sergei, who was wounded, as bullets pierced a window above his head.

The guns' deafening explosions continued outside, but Tamara knew she needed to get help. The moment the gunfire ceased, she bolted for the door, barefoot and still in her nightgown.

Knowing her neighbors had a telephone, Tamara hurried along the path and banged her fist against her neighbor's door. "My husband is wounded!" Tamara screamed. "Call an ambulance!"

Still in shock, she ran back to her home.

The mayor of Isfara lived across the street, so police were always nearby. By the time Tamara got back home, they had arrived, along with an ambulance. A crowd of onlookers had gathered, and Sergei's killers casually walked through them, calm and composed, toward a waiting car at the end of the lane.

Next to Sergei on the floor were his open Bible and a songbook. His eyes stared blankly ahead, his lifeless hands still clutching his blood-splattered guitar. Horrified, Tamara realized her husband was dead.

Sergei had been shot four times. The first bullet pierced his hand and splintered his guitar. The second shot landed in his leg. The final two bullets—the fatal shots—struck Sergei right in the heart.

Rustam checked Sergei's pockets and found a bit of cash. He handed Tamara the money. *How am I going to bury my husband with only this?*

She stood nearby as the police examined Sergei's body, but it soon became too much. She walked away and sat down. The next thing she knew, an officer held her shoulder as she felt the sharp sting of a needle pierce her arm.

Within seconds, Tamara's mind went numb as she slipped into a drug-induced stupor.

ele

"Get dressed," the officer said. In a haze, Tamara stumbled back to the bedroom, slipped out of her nightgown, and put on some clothes. The police escorted her to their car and then loaded Sergei's body into the back of the vehicle. Tamara could see Sergei's white Volkswagen parked on the street, riddled with bullet holes.

When they arrived at the prosecutor's office, officers led Tamara to a small interrogation room. Three men sat across from her. Even drugged, Tamara realized she was their prime suspect.

"We know that you had him killed," the first interrogator said. "We know you ordered his murder." Though it was a brazen lie, Tamara knew it was useless to justify herself to these men who were skillfully trained to extract information. With the full effects of the drug in her system, Tamara didn't trust herself to speak.

"How much were you paid?" another interrogator asked. She stayed silent, stubborn in her resolve. "We know it was a lot. You were sent in from Uzbekistan, and we know you are the mastermind of the murder."

The questions continued for an hour, one after another. Still, Tamara didn't speak. "If you're going to be silent," an interrogator said, "then we can play that game too." He slid a piece of paper in front of her. Tamara looked down at the prepared confession. "If you don't sign this right now and tell us the whole truth, we'll take you down to the basement." The man sneered menacingly. "In the basement, you'll tell us everything."

Tamara's eyes widened. She thought about Sergei, his body resting on a cold metal slab in the morgue. Would this be the hour that she would join him?

Suddenly, a sharp knock interrupted the interrogation. When the door opened, Tamara recognized the two men standing on the other side. They belonged to Sergei and Tamara's church in Dushanbe, the one that had sent the Bessarabs to Isfara. They had already heard what happened to Sergei. Tamara breathed a deep sigh of relief. The men were from a church officially registered with the government, and this status carried with it a measure of clout. When these brothers arrived, the police released her. Tamara was not alone, the authorities had realized. There were others who loved and supported her.

As Tamara left the interrogation room, she glanced at the interrogators. Their faces betrayed their frustration.

Tamara returned to her home where, just hours earlier, her husband had still been alive.

⁓ello⁓

Sergei's funeral felt like a dream, as if Tamara's eyes were shrouded, obscuring everything in view, while Sergei's mother sobbed next to her son's coffin.

Missionaries, former prisoners, mosque leaders, and representatives from the Tajik government all attended Sergei's funeral. Many people spoke passionately during the service, testifying one after another about the God whom Sergei had served. Each of the speakers prayed for Sergei's killers, that the Lord would touch their hearts.

The funeral was a farewell to a faithful man the Christians knew they would see again one day in heaven. Mosque leaders and Tajik officials offered their condolences to Tamara and the community as they heard the gospel and the powerful testimonies about this man who had been murdered.

Tamara was in a daze with only a coffin, a body, and an understanding that something terrible had happened. *I am in such a fog,* she lamented. Even so, Tamara prayed for God to help her continue her husband's work in Isfara. She knew the only way she could move forward was with His help.

Standing beside her was Tamara's teenage son, Seryozha. As his stepfather's coffin was lowered into the ground, the young man cried out to God in repentance and gave his life to the Lord. In his death, Sergei was able to lead his son to Jesus Christ.

Sergei was buried in a grave on a rocky stretch of ground just outside his hometown of Konsoy.

For twenty days after her husband's murder, Tamara couldn't even bear to hold a Bible in her hands. "Why, God, why?" she cried, tears streaming down her face. *Perhaps Sergei's death, even this horrible loss, was part of God's plan.* Wanting to continue as a small group leader, she reluctantly opened her Bible. Inwardly, though, she struggled. Tamara resented God for taking Sergei away. The healing in her heart would take time, but God's Word and His love would eventually break through to Tamara. The Holy Spirit would speak to her through Romans 8:28, and Tamara would cling to those precious words: "And we know that for those who love God all things work together for good, for those who are called according to his purpose."

Letters of sympathy poured in from around the world. "This man had a big heart," one family wrote, and "he left the best impressions about himself. When he led the church gatherings and talked about God, it was accessible, I think, for every soul. With his thoughtfulness in communication, he managed to instill hope in any person." The church in Isfara, they said, "has suffered a great loss" in Sergei's death.

Many of the letters were from former prisoners who had come to Christ through Sergei's ministry in prison. "Our Lord Jesus was killed for preaching God's Word . . . Sergei [is] now with Christ. His tragic demise shook me a lot," wrote one man who'd been imprisoned with Sergei both as a teenager and again as an adult. He relayed that a constant refrain among the prisoners who'd learned of Sergei's death was, "It's a big shame that such a genuine person, who always pointed at God's path, died from the godless people's hands."

"Sister Tamara," he assured, "don't be distressed. Know we are always with you and we love you."

For several weeks after Sergei's murder, most of the church members stayed away from their regular worship gatherings out of fear the killers would come back. After some time, though, church members returned, and Tamara stepped in to lead the flock.

One day, as Tamara discipled new Christians and distributed Christian literature around the city, she realized she no longer wanted to leave Isfara. *We have church members, and we baptize new believers. People are coming to God.* After Sergei's death, people still came, and she knew she couldn't abandon them. She would stay, if only to strengthen the Christians who also stayed. In time, Tamara came to understand that when God has His own plan, and we move in it, it will always be a blessing.

Tamara moved into a nearby apartment, and a different family moved into the church. She couldn't go back to her home. She was afraid, and it was beyond her strength to spend the night where her husband had been shot. *Everything reminds me of him.*

Late one night, she was awakened by banging on her door. Two men, dressed in clothing that suggested they were mullahs,[2] stood across the threshold from Tamara.

"Why were you distributing literature?" the men demanded. "Why were you there?"

Tamara stood silently.

"We don't want to kill you," one of the men warned, "but if you don't stop this activity and get out of here . . ." He glared at Tamara as his threat lingered in the air. Finally, the men turned and walked away.

Tamara's heart was racing as she locked the deadbolt and leaned against the door. *It wouldn't cost them anything to kill me.* Immediately, her fear turned to anger. *God, I will never live according to these Islamic laws. Strengthen me and make me even bolder!*

---

2. Mullahs are educated in Islamic religion and law. They are often leaders in the mosque.

Over time, word of Sergei's murder spread. *We prayed a long time that God would pay attention to Isfara,* Tamara realized, *and now He has turned the attention of many people around the world to Isfara. God is preparing a special blessing for Isfara because we are praying and staying on our knees.*

Tamara still wanted justice for her husband's killers. When one of them was arrested and brought in for questioning, Tamara went to the station, stood behind a large plate-glass window, and stared menacingly at him as the interrogation began. But Tamara wasn't content just to watch. She grabbed a piece of paper from a desk and scribbled, in large black letters bold enough for the man to read, the word *scum*. She slapped her handmade sign against the glass and glared at the man who had killed her beloved husband.

"When you get to prison," she called, "you're going to be given such a reception that you will regret what you have done."

Tamara despised Sergei's murderer, but she also wondered if one day she would be able to forgive him. In the midst of it all, Tamara asked God for one thing: to continue her ministry — Sergei's ministry — in the place where her husband was killed.

ele

Tamara walked through the prison gate and made her way to the prayer room, just as she had countless times before. As she arrived, she found Viktor, a fellow prisoner who Sergei had led to the Lord while he was still incarcerated. Now, Viktor led the prison worship services.

Tamara stopped abruptly just inside the prayer room. Dressed in a prison robe like all the other convicts, with a Bible splayed open in his lap, was the man who had murdered her husband. Tamara saw exhaustion in the man's eyes. He lowered his gaze and Tamara quickly looked away, a storm raging inside her.

She turned to Viktor. "What is this piece of scum doing here?" she spewed.

"This 'scum,'" he said gently, "is looking for God. He's here all the time and has a lot of questions about Christ. We work with him."

"Is this for real?" Tamara asked, her eyes fixed on the man who killed Sergei.

"It is."

As she stared at the young man, Tamara knew the Lord was speaking to her. *"Don't interfere,"* she heard Him say. *"I understand your pain, but this man is looking for God."* In an instant, the boiling rage she had carried for so long was gone. In its place, a warm wave of forgiveness flooded her heart and mind.

Tamara walked out of the prison freed from the pain of unforgiveness.

After a year of faithful witnessing, of talking late into the night on side-by-side cots, and inviting him to worship services, Viktor led his young cellmate to the Lord.

Tamara marveled at this turn of events. Long before he was killed, Sergei had led Viktor to Christ. Years later, in the very prison where he himself had become a Christian, Sergei's spiritual son now led Sergei's killer to Christ.

Sergei had become the spiritual grandfather of his own murderer.

ele

Tamara continues to faithfully minister in Tajikistan. She mentors widows who are struggling through the tragic loss of their husbands, helps in children's ministry, and disciples women in an impoverished neighborhood. She continues to reach out to Muslim women. She has also befriended and mentored women whose husbands were imprisoned for their Christian faith.

One in particular was a pastor's wife whose husband had converted from Islam to Christianity and was later arrested and imprisoned when he refused to renounce his faith during a violent surprise raid of his church. With no support from their Muslim families, this pastor's wife was left in the difficult position of providing for her three teenage children alone. When her husband was transferred to a prison eight hours away from their home, and the woman's health prevented her from visiting often, the situation felt unbearable, and she was spiraling into despair.

Tamara befriended the pastor's wife and brought with her a word of challenge that would help her to persevere. With a compassionate but firm perspective, one that had helped Tamara survive countless situations that seemed impossible, she reminded her new friend of one simple truth: "At least your husband is still alive. He will come back. Mine is gone."

༶༶

Tamara sees how God worked through the darkness and evil of Sergei's murder. When asked if following Christ has been worth the persecution she has experienced, she said, "For Christ's sake, I can safely say now that it was worth it! If I had been offered another life, I would have said 'no.' I understand, by the end result, that when you are filled with God's strength and continue on not with your own strength, but with God's power, that it's all worth it.

"No longer do you say, 'Oh I can't, oh this is scary, oh it's dangerous.' He's the One who gives you strength. Yes, it will be scary. I know what is going to happen next because it is in the Scripture: 'I was persecuted, and you will be persecuted.' Who wants that? But I know there is One who will give strength to endure."

In Her Words:
Vee

Vee, a widow in her late 70s who lives in Laos, trusted Christ when Christians prayed for her and she was healed from a long-term illness. Soon, a village leader confronted her about her newfound faith.

I was in my own home minding my own business when a village leader came to see me. He said, "Mrs. Vee! Why do you go out to that certain village often?"

"I go to that village for Christian fellowship," I told him.

"What fellowship or gathering? Your daily life and routine are in this village, no? Do not go to that village anymore," he replied. "Stop going! You are old and it is not worth going! You will die if you keep bowing to that Western belief. Why are you so ignorant? Stop doing what you are doing and listen to what we say!"

I thought in my heart . . . *Sheesh, why must you act and say harsh things to me? What did I do wrong?* I did not understand why he said that or what they were planning to do.

"Not go? I will go," I answered.

"Who told you to go?" he asked.

"No one told me to go!" I replied. "No one came to share with me about Jesus. I went to find it myself. I never knew there were Christians near me until I was ill and heard that their prayers to Jesus could help me. I looked for Christians to pray for me. I was ill and poor, yet they did not disregard me in any way. They prayed for me, and I was healed. Once I was healed, I wanted to believe and go fellowship with the Christians. I wanted to believe this Jesus so much! I was so happy. I never thought of not wanting to join them. My heart was with them."

The village leaders tried to evict me the next morning. I was about to have breakfast. One of the villagers came and yelled at me, "Vee, go to the village office right away! They are looking for you."

When I got to the village office, I was questioned again.

"Where are you going and what do you do with this religion?" they asked, pointing their fingers at me. "Who are those people? They are not good people. Who told you to go believe this religion? Who told you to go to that village? Why do you not respect the spirits of our ancestors?"

"I do not care about the spirits of my ancestors," I replied. "Why do you keep bothering me about this? Do you not have eyes? I was very ill. Yet I prayed, and Christians came to pray for me and I was healed. Of course, I will go worship the One who healed me and fellowship with the Christians. No one told me to or forced me. I go of my own free will. Whoever says anything negative to me about this religion, I will not listen. I will keep going to fellowship with them."

"Do not live here. Leave!" they demanded. "If you are not dead, then leave. If you die in this village, you will not be buried in the village with us. Your body will be buried in the jungle, far away from this village! Your farm that we gave, we will take it and split it among ourselves."

But I did not leave. I stayed at my home. Then the village leaders came almost every day to tell my son to kick me out of the house, to stop giving me food or even hide the food.

My son started to beat me. I felt I was going to die. He beat me three times. I kept thinking, *How can my child do this to me? I raised that child since he was a baby with my own two hands. Why would he do this to the person who raised him?*

But even though he beat me, I have no hate for him. And when the villagers persecuted me, I was not scared. I said that whatever they want to do, then do it. I will believe no matter what they do. They kept telling me to stop. I did not and will not stop. The thought of renouncing my faith never crossed my mind. I will continue to keep believing. I will not listen to them.

Those people want me to die. Yet I pray, and the Lord is giving me strength daily. I feel stronger by the day. Many things have been done to me—from not giving me food, to my clothes being taken away, to even being forced out of my house. Yet God helped me during the difficult times. This is a blessing.

I will not be discouraged by any persecution. I will keep fighting until I pass away.

Boupha

A Teenager No Longer Afraid

LAOS
FEBRUARY 2020

Sunday was Boupha's favorite day of the week, and she woke up eager to teach the Bible study lesson to the children at her church. Inside the stilted, bamboo home she shared with her parents and five siblings, eighteen-year-old Boupha began her usual Sunday preparations and assembled her family's breakfast of vegetables, hard-boiled eggs, and chili sauce.

As the rice steamed, she opened her booklet of Bible study lessons and carefully selected the music, games, snacks, and activities for her Sunday school class. She enjoyed teaching the children about the love of God and prayed they would experience the same joy and happiness she felt when she first placed her trust in Christ.

Boupha's parents first heard the gospel when she was a young child. A man named Nuud, who lived in their village, had gone to the nearby city of Vientiane for Bible training. When he returned, he immediately began evangelizing his Khmu village. The Khmu are one of the largest minority ethnic groups in Laos. Many Khmu trusted Christ, including Boupha's parents.

Each week, Boupha, her parents, and siblings would gather with other Khmu followers of Christ to worship in house churches scattered among the country's villages and cities. Christians gather in house churches to avoid detection by the Laotian government, which views Christianity as a foreign religion used by the West to undermine the Communist regime. In an attempt to control and oppress the Christian activity in the country, Laotian authorities sometimes arrest Christians and detain them for up to a week. And in some villages, new Christians are driven from their homes by family members and fellow villagers who are afraid their newfound faith will offend the spirits.

Even as a child, Boupha knew following Jesus Christ meant risking persecution. She remembers being scared when her parents first became Christians. Police officers were assigned to monitor the residents in her village, threatening to handcuff and imprison anyone who continued to attend church. Instead, Nuud gathered the Christians together to worship at night, making it harder for the officers to discover them.

Boupha vividly recalls one Thursday night when she and her parents were attending a worship service. Villagers stood outside their house church and hurled heavy items onto the corrugated metal roof. The loud clanging terrified the young girl.

Why would people do this? Boupha wondered. *If my parents continue to go to church, they could get arrested. And if they get arrested, how could I live without them?*

Her parents' faith also attracted opposition from the parents of Boupha's non-Christian friends. Their conversations would include unflattering comments about Christians whenever Boupha was present. "Sure, Christians didn't lie or cheat," they said, "and they don't get drunk on alcohol. But they are certainly bad people. Christians are drug addicts who go to church every Thursday night to sing nonsense songs. And then they turn off all the lights. What are they doing during that time?" they mused, exchanging knowing glances with each other. "Whose wife is whose?" Boupha didn't miss the negative and false insinuation of her church's worship services.

"Don't listen to what others say about Christians," her parents assured her. "Whatever they say about our faith, listen only to us and let them be." As Boupha talked with her parents and became more immersed in church life, she realized that all the negative rumors she'd heard about Christians were just that—rumors. Boupha saw for herself that Christians were the most virtuous, joyful people she'd ever met.

Years later, through the influence of a Sunday school teacher, her pastor, and a longtime friend, Boupha became serious about her faith. After observing her take responsibility with the smaller tasks she was assigned at church, Pastor Kim asked her to teach the youth Sunday school class. When Boupha agreed to step into the new role, she did so knowing she must fully commit herself to following Christ. It would be impossible to teach others without growing in her own faith. Soon after, she and other Christians from various villages were trained to teach children. That was how Boupha came to be teaching Sunday school that fateful morning.

Once Boupha finished eating breakfast and preparing her Sunday school lesson, she slipped on a beautiful white dress. Sunday was a sacred day to Boupha, one worthy of the best clothes she owned.

On her way out the door, Boupha grabbed her hymnal, lesson booklet, and a notebook full of games. Her parents would join her later when the service began, but Boupha left early since the children would arrive soon for Sunday school class. Besides, she was eager to ask Pastor Kim for advice on ways to get the children to listen and pay attention.

During the five-minute walk to the house church, Boupha was unaware that within the hour, her journey would take a decidedly different path—a road that would test her faith and help her overcome fear.

"*Sabaidee!*" Boupha sang out in greeting as she was warmly welcomed at the village hut where her church met. As was the custom, she pressed her palms together and bowed slightly to Pastor Kim, then proceeded to ask him questions.

After their brief conversation, Boupha gathered the dozen students—ranging in age from two to thirteen—and ushered them into the Sunday school room, an extension on the back of the hut covered by a corrugated metal roof and supported by wooden poles.

Ready to put into practice some of Pastor Kim's advice, Boupha took a piece of chalk and drew a line on the ground. "Heaven!" she suddenly yelled, pointing to one side of the line. The children scurried across the line to one side of the Sunday school room. "Hell!" she called out, the children laughing as they sprang back to the other side. The game gave her young pupils a chance to work off some of their energy.

After a few minutes, Boupha settled her students and began to teach her lesson, which came from Genesis. The children listened attentively, their minds focused on Adam and Eve and what happens when humans don't listen to God.

Suddenly, the light that spilled through the doorway into the Sunday school room vanished. Sensing something was wrong, Boupha turned to see what was blocking the entryway.

Three men walked into the room and surrounded the children. Dressed in casual clothing, two of them looked to be in their

mid-thirties while the third man appeared to be about twenty-five. Fear gripped Boupha as her eyes rested on the pistol holstered on the youngest man's hip.

Police! Boupha panicked and struggled to concentrate. *Did they hear what I was teaching?* Since she was speaking in Khmu, she hoped they didn't understand.

"What are you doing in here?" one of the officers asked.

Boupha felt her heart thumping in her chest. "I'm teaching these children in our Sunday school class," she said.

The man shot her a doubtful glance. "Why is this class so loud?"

"We've been playing a game," she responded. "And now we're having a lesson. We're having fun with one another."

"Why? Why are you doing this?"

Boupha tried to conceal her nerves, but her entire body was shaking. "I have to," she replied. "It's my responsibility . . . I'm their teacher."

"You should stop," another officer said.

"Why is that?" Boupha asked, hoping her voice sounded confident. The officer did not respond.

The third officer held up a camera and took photographs. "For evidence," he said.

Evidence? Evidence of what?

Boupha had never experienced anything like this before. The officer called the children to line up. They obeyed, staring in worried silence as the camera shutter clicked.

"Now you," the man said, gesturing at Boupha. Reluctantly, she joined the children for a second photograph without making eye contact with the officer.

When they finished taking the photos, the officers moved back toward the doorway. One turned back to Boupha and sneered.

"Did you know that teaching these children here is against the law?"

Lord, please help me. Give me wisdom in this situation. Give me wisdom in answering whatever questions they have. Mustering every ounce of boldness, Boupha looked directly at the officer and responded, "How is what I'm doing against the law when our religion teaches us to instruct children?"

Noticing other Christians were now arriving for the church service, the three police officers left the room. Boupha looked down at the children, their eyes wide and their mouths gaped open. She knew they were shocked by what they'd just experienced.

They inundated Boupha with questions. "Who were they? Why did they ask those questions? Are they police officers? Why did they come here? Are they going to arrest us?"

"Don't worry," Boupha said, scrambling for an explanation that would calm their fears. "They might just want to worship with us!"

As she watched the concerned expressions evaporate from the children's faces, her own fears began to fade. She wiped her sweaty palms on the skirt of her dress and continued with the lesson.

Her relief was abruptly shattered when one of the officers reappeared in the doorway.

"We need you to come with us to the police station," he said.

The situation, Boupha realized, was more serious than she'd thought.

He instructed her to go home and get her border checkpoint passbook before proceeding to the police station. Police issue an identity document on behalf of the Ministry of Home Affairs. It is the required form of identification that all Laotians are expected to present. When moving from village to village, citizens often pass through police checkpoints where they must show their identity cards.

As the policeman escorted Boupha out of the Sunday school room, she turned to catch one last glimpse of the children. She looked into their wide and fearful eyes and smiled, trying to alleviate their worry as she instructed them to continue working on the coloring assignment for the day.

When Boupha saw her parents, she quickly pulled them aside to tell them she was being summoned to the police station.

"If you have to go, then you should go," her father said, as he eyed the policeman standing near his daughter. "If anything happens, call us and call Pastor Kim."

As Boupha rode on a police motorbike to her home, her thoughts returned to the children. She wanted them to know that everything was going to be okay and hoped the coloring assignment would overshadow the intrusive encounter with the police. *Perhaps it will keep their spirits up . . . at least until I see them next Sunday.*

Boupha hoped that she would, in fact, be back with the children the following week.

ele

After retrieving her documents and her own red motorbike, Boupha's thoughts began to race as she tightened her grip on the handlebars and throttled the bike onto the dusty, unpaved road. One police motorbike drove in front of her; the other followed closely behind.

Boupha knew the police had a reputation for getting violent with those they took in for questioning. She was just over five feet tall and didn't know how she could defend herself if they got abusive. Her thoughts were tormented by the terrible things that could happen to her—like arrest, prison, or worse.

As her motorbike sped along the countryside, she passed a Hmong village. Like the Khmu, the Hmong are another people group in Laos. Tribal groups like the Hmong and the Khmu are especially targeted for persecution by the government and local villagers. Boupha remembered the time she and her friends had tried to visit some Hmong Christians their age, and how the local authorities had set up a checkpoint on the road and stopped them.

The police had asked Boupha and her friends where they were going, and they replied they were going to worship with some of the Hmong youth. The police seized their Bibles and scolded them. Their Bibles were never returned. Meeting with Christians in another district, Boupha learned, was not allowed.

Boupha kept her eyes locked on the road ahead, focused on dodging potholes, while trying to calm her anxious mind. Her heart was beating so rapidly that she felt like it was no longer in her chest. *Why would the police bother with someone like me? I'm just a Sunday school teacher for children.* Boupha's motorbike kicked up dust as she bumped along the dirt road. *Will I be arrested?*

Thirty minutes later, Boupha and the officers arrived at the police station—a structure that looked more like a normal village hut, one that might be used for social gatherings.

After an officer instructed her where to park her motorbike, she walked inside the station, glancing around nervously as she had never been inside one before. Piles of scattered documents sat atop small tables; beds were set up in several adjoining rooms.

"Please, have a seat," the officer said, motioning toward an empty table in what Boupha assumed must be the interrogation room. She sat down and placed her Bible study booklet, hymnal, and notebook on the table in front of her. From where she sat, Boupha could see a half dozen police officers milling around the station, along with a frowning man who appeared to be in charge. Boupha's eyes darted around the room, and she suddenly felt surrounded by men with guns.

The man in charge walked toward her and sat down. He, too, was wearing a gun on his hip. Four other officers walked into the small room. Carrying a notebook and pen, the fourth man sat down at the table, waiting for his superior to speak.

"Who made you teach these things?" the boss asked abruptly, as he leaned menacingly toward Boupha. "Don't you know that believing in this religion is against the law?" Boupha knew that in Laos, it isn't actually illegal to be a Christian, but officials often operate as if it is.

Boupha's frazzled nerves threatened to steal her voice. She prayed for wisdom and courage, asking the Lord that her answers would not betray her fears.

"Where in the law does it say I cannot believe in this religion?" she replied confidently.

"Why do you teach those children at your church?" he replied, ignoring her question. "Other children are good children without needing to be taught this Bible stuff."

"What I am instructing these children is how to grow as Christians," she said. "The other children who do not learn what I teach do not go the right way in life."

Seeing the policeman's curious look, Boupha continued.

"For instance, I know ten-year-olds who smoke. I can teach the children not to smoke because it's bad for their health."

Boupha took a deep breath and explained her desire to see the children mature in Christ, following in the Lord's ways and loving their parents and neighbors.

"You must stop teaching these children," the man said. "Your church does not have a building, and without a building we cannot allow you to teach your beliefs. If you want to teach, you must build a church."

"Why do I need a church building?"

"You must meet all the requirements before you can instruct the children. There must be a church. It is *wrong!*" The man paused and glared at Boupha. "You know, we can take you to jail right now if we want to."

Boupha panicked. "And what crime will you charge me with? What did I do wrong?" She felt tears welling up, but she refused to let herself cry.

"Who gave you this role to teach the children?" the officer demanded, again ignoring her questions. "Who is paying you to teach?"

"Who gave me this role is not important," Boupha replied. "What is important is that I fulfill my responsibilities to the best of my ability, just like you in your role as a police officer."

The man slammed his palms down on the table. "Who is paying you to teach?" he screamed.

"I am a volunteer," Boupha insisted firmly. "A Christian trainer in Vientiane taught me and gave me this booklet, but no one is paying me."

The conversation continued for nearly an hour as the man bombarded Boupha with questions. Her fear was reaching a breaking point, and she wondered if the interrogation would ever end.

Perhaps this officer had heard her lesson from Genesis because his line of questioning unexpectedly shifted.

"How do you know the God you believe in is the one who created everything?"

Sensing the Lord replacing her fear with courage, Boupha sat up straighter in her chair. "I passionately believe God created everything because He made me," she declared. "In the Bible, God says it clearly that He created the heavens and the earth and everything within it. What the eye can see and not see, He created it all."

"You people believe in Jesus," the officer said. "What do you get out of it?"

Boupha thought for a moment. "Even if we do not get money or material things from being a Christian," she replied, "we get everlasting life."

The officer smirked as he mentioned the name of a local Christian leader who had died several years earlier. "If you get everlasting life, then why isn't he back from the dead?"

Boupha wasn't sure how to respond.

The officer repeated the question, only louder.

Boupha was dumbfounded, not knowing how to answer his question. Feeling the weight of the officer's intimidation, she began to tremble uncontrollably, her nerves clouding any chance of rational thought. She felt detached from her body, like her soul was watching the situation from above.

Lord, please help me.

As she prayed, a comforting thought struck her—a thought that could have come only from the Lord: *What I am facing right now will not be a problem. This is the Lord's will for my life. The Lord has a plan in this.*

Looking down at her hands, Boupha noticed they were no longer shaking. She had an idea. "May I make a phone call?"

When the officer gave the okay, she quickly walked outside and called Pastor Kim.

As soon as he answered, she asked, "What should I do? The police are threatening me to stop teaching Sunday school."

He told her she could put the classes on hold for now or as long as she wanted. "If you want to continue to teach the children, then you will have to do it secretly."

When Boupha returned to the interrogation room, the officer pointed at her stack of documents on the table and told her to give him her book. Sliding the Bible lessons across the table, she watched as he flipped through the colorful pages and then told her he was confiscating it.

"Why would you want this teaching booklet?" Boupha asked. "Do you know the written language in it?"

She doubted the officer knew how to speak more than the official Lao language; the booklet was in Khmu. But if he could read it, perhaps the content in the teaching materials might lead him to Christ.

"It doesn't matter!" he snapped. "We will do a thorough examination of this booklet."

The man darted his eyes back to Boupha. "You must promise that you will not teach from these materials anymore," he said. "If you do, we'll bring you back in." The officer paused and arranged a stack of papers in front of him. "And the next time, we will put you in jail for two weeks."

Hearing their threat, Boupha was still unwilling to make such a promise. The children needed to know about Jesus, and God had called Boupha to teach them. But she wondered if there was a way to satisfy the officer.

"You took the materials already," she said, gesturing toward her Bible lesson booklet, "so there's no need to promise you that I will never teach again."

Pleased with her response, the officer told her she could go home. Boupha promptly gathered her things and scrambled out of the interrogation room. Even though she had been at the station for only an hour, she felt like the experience had lasted much longer.

Feeling the warm afternoon sun on her face once again, Boupha hopped on her motorbike and drove straight home, relieved that the officers hadn't arrested her or even worse. And she was able to share the gospel with the police.

Thank You, Lord, for loving me and for having mercy on me.

When Boupha arrived home, she parked her motorbike under the house, walked inside, and began preparing the evening meal for her family. Then she started getting ready to return to school the following day. She knew she hadn't done anything wrong. She hadn't broken any law. Surely these were empty threats from the police. While she was still worried and scared, wondering if her answers to the police would eventually cause trouble, her desire to be faithful to God had grown larger than her fear of arrest and imprisonment.

If you want to arrest me, Boupha thought, *then go ahead. Say what you want. I won't waver. I will not back away from the Lord or from other Christians.*

Although the interrogation with the police had been short, more persecution was to follow.

‿ℓℓ‿

It didn't take long before Boupha's worst fears became a reality.

Her first couple of weeks at school went smoothly; but then one day a teacher called her out of class to meet with him. As Boupha rose from her seat, the classroom buzzed with a flurry of gossip.

"Hey, Boupha," the students said, "what did you do wrong? Something bad must have happened."

"No, I didn't do anything wrong," Boupha assured her peers. "It must be a normal meeting to discuss my academics or something like that."

As soon as she arrived in the teacher's office, she realized that it was not a meeting but a confrontation.

"Why do you have to believe in Jesus?" he asked repeatedly. "Why do you do these things as a Christian?" He continued to ask Boupha one question after another.

After the teacher's interrogation, high school never returned to normal. The questioning continued for the next three months with school officials creating more difficulties for her. While she excelled academically, her teachers refused to acknowledge her accomplishments. Her classmates excluded her from school activities and continued to make fun of her, saying, "You Jesus person! You are not a good person." Though Boupha was certain the school had been informed about her arrest and questioning, she was determined to persevere.

ele

Boupha knows that persecution will likely happen again. But despite threats of arrest, ridicule from schoolmates, and harassment from school officials, she chooses hope over discouragement. She shares her story as a reminder that nothing is too hard for the Lord. He promises in His Word to help us, and she draws strength remembering God did not abandon her during her interrogation by the police—and He will continue to be with her to the end. If the police come again, her heart is at peace, and she is confident about answering their questions.

With a smile on her face, Boupha continues to rise each Sunday—still her favorite day of the week—to prepare the morning meal and nourish not only her family, but also the children in her Sunday school class. She is eager to continue serving the Lord and sharing the gospel.

"During this time of trouble, I know who loved me the most— the Lord. The Lord would not leave me nor forsake me in any situation."

In Her Words:
Surita

Worshiping Hindu idols, requesting prayer from a Buddhist priest, and visiting witch doctors did not bring Surita of Nepal relief for her illness or her four-year-old son's stomach issues. Then she met Christians in her village who shared the gospel with her and prayed for her family.

When I first went to church, I was searching for healing; but within two months, I realized that healing was not the most important thing. I realized that I was lost. I was just running around in the darkness, and I needed forgiveness for my sins. Healing was a secondary thing. The primary thing I needed was a relationship with Jesus Christ.

Now I have come into the light, and this miracle of forgiveness has come only from the true God. I felt joy and happiness, and I accepted Jesus Christ as my personal Lord and Savior.

My husband and I lived in the same home as my father- and mother-in-law. Even though my husband permitted me to go to church, I endured torture from my Buddhist in-laws from the very first week I attended. When my father-in-law would get drunk, my mother-in-law would tell him, "Go and beat her because she is going to church." She also encouraged my husband to attack me.

One day, I saw my father-in-law—who was drunk at the time—go into my room. A few minutes later, he came out with my Bible. He grabbed me by the hair and beat me over the head with my Bible. For nearly ten minutes, he beat me with all the effort he had.

At the time, I remembered the pain of Christ on the cross. I thought if Christ suffered for me and gave His life for me, then this was a privilege for me to suffer for Him. Even if I died here, it didn't matter because eternal life was secured for me. I felt privileged to suffer for Christ.

After my father-in-law finished, I started thinking that even Christ my Lord was attacked by many people. They spat on Him and despised Him. If Christ suffered that much for me, this is nothing compared to His suffering. I immediately thanked God that I had suffered for Him. Then, I prayed for my father-in-law because he didn't understand what he had done. But one day he will have to stand before God for judgment—and God will judge him.

Since then, my father-in-law has tried to attack me again. He is very weak from drinking, and he gets sick often. I go to him with boldness and tell him, "Stop drinking. If you can, join me in the church. I wish that you would come to church."

My desire and prayer is one day I will see my father-in-law kneeling before Christ, praying and asking for forgiveness. I know he can be forgiven, be saved, and have eternal life. That is my honest prayer that I am praying.

Surita's husband, Kamal, attended church with Surita until his father began threatening them. Kamal was away for work during Surita's attack, but when Kamal returned home, his parents told him that he and Surita had to leave because of her Christian faith. Kamal told them unapologetically that his wife could follow Christ if she wanted, and he and his family moved out the next morning. Though he has not professed faith in Christ, Kamal's bold rebuke of his parents in defense of Surita's Christian faith cost him his inheritance.

Huldah

A Life Hidden Under Christ

INDIA
MAY 1, 2018

Huldah watched anxiously from her front step as her seventeen-year-old son, Aman, hopped onto his father's black motorbike and revved the engine. It was nine o'clock at night, and the moon above the village was nearly full, as bright and wide as Huldah's eyes.

For the past three hours, Huldah had been waiting for her husband, Abraham, to return home; she grew more worried by the hour. Huldah thought about the powerful businessmen in their community, men who were associated with radical Hindus and who had become unhappy with Abraham. "These people hate Christian activities," a neighbor had recently warned. "Especially your work evangelizing villagers."

"Take your father's motorbike and go look for him," Huldah instructed her son. "Look around and see if his vehicle is broken down somewhere. Ask the neighbors if they know anything."

The moon illuminated the dust kicked up as Aman sped away. Wringing her hands, Huldah walked back into her home thinking over different scenarios for why Abraham would be late. *Has one of these men done something to my husband?*

Aman raced toward the nearby bridge, just over a mile ahead. Monsoon season was still a month away, and the roads had not yet turned to mud. The dense jungle trees whizzed by as he twisted the throttle and picked up speed.

Within minutes, Aman saw a glow in the distance. Panic shot through his body. A column of black smoke rose into the night sky. He rushed toward it until the scene unfolded clearly before him.

A vehicle sat engulfed in flames.

Aman screeched the motorbike to a stop as he stared in disbelief. A crowd had gathered to watch as flames spilled from the broken windows of the blazing Jeep.

A *white Jeep*. The same vehicle his father had departed in that morning.

ele

Huldah was born in a small Indian village in the middle of the jungle, thirty miles from the state's capital. In those days, reaching her village was strenuous; the roads weren't paved, and the family had to hike through mountainous jungle to reach their home.

While Huldah's father devoted most of his days to tending the small plot of land he owned, her mother cared for the children at home. To make ends meet, her father also farmed other people's land as a daily wage worker. Every morning he awoke at three o'clock to sing hymns, pray, and study his Bible by the light of a small candle. By five o'clock, he began his household and agriculture work. Every Sunday, he took his family to church.

Huldah liked being a part of the festivities at church. Every Christmas, she looked forward to decorating the village church.

She and her young friends cleaned the building and adorned its hallways and exterior with paper crafts. And Huldah loved celebrating Easter, when her family would gather with other church members to sing resurrection hymns as the sun rose. Her church had also tasked her with collecting rice from each church family—handfuls of grain that had been set aside as an offering for the poor of the community.

Huldah attended a mission school near her village. Following her graduation, her father managed to scrape together enough tuition money to send her to a government boarding school in a neighboring district, a three-hour mountain hike followed by an hour train ride.

The classroom and dorm room were mud structures with mud-tiled roofs. Because Huldah shared her small space with a roommate, there wasn't much privacy. The surrounding bush and shrubs served as their bathroom—typical for a rural school.

Sulami, Huldah's classmate, also came from a devoted Christian family. Huldah took notice of her personality and countenance—her face always seemed to shine so brightly. Sulami cared for the girls who were sick and shared the sweets she'd received from her parents. No matter what she was doing, Sulami was always smiling and cheerful, even when tackling the more unpleasant chores at the school hostel.

Huldah had never before witnessed a life that radiated such joy. *How could I be like her?* she wondered. She also realized that at fourteen years old, though she'd been active in church life, she didn't really know Jesus as her Lord and Savior.

During a visit to Huldah's cousins, who lived just a few miles away from her family, she experienced the Lord's protection in a personal way, causing her to seek a relationship with Him.

Around eleven o'clock one night, hours after Huldah and her cousins had drifted off to sleep, a noise outside the room startled

Huldah. She opened her eyes to see a tall man standing on the veranda, no more than ten feet away. He wasn't alone.

Huldah muffled her gasp with a blanket as four men quietly opened the bamboo door and crept inside the bedroom. She couldn't make out their faces in the dark or tell if they were armed. But she knew these men could hurt her and her cousins, even without weapons.

"*Help!*" Huldah shrieked at the top of her lungs. Her cousins bolted upright. The men, startled by the sound, turned and fled out the door.

That night, as Huldah struggled to fall back to sleep, one thing became clear in her mind: God was with her. He had protected her.

When Huldah returned to school, Sulami gave her a copy of the New Testament. Huldah pored over its words, seeking God in prayer, and soon placed her trust in the God who protected her—the Lord Jesus Christ. But not everyone was pleased with Huldah's decision.

One of Huldah's sisters-in-law opposed her reignited faith. To keep Huldah from spending time praying and reading Scripture, she gave Huldah a burdensome number of household chores.

On a day Huldah had chosen to devote to fasting and prayer, her sister-in-law asked her to take the cattle to the forest to graze. When Huldah explained her plan to focus on spiritual commitments that day, her sister-in-law accused her of shirking family responsibilities and neglecting household work.

But Huldah's faith would eventually influence her sister-in-law. When the woman became gravely ill and felt discouraged by her inability to get well, she sent word to Huldah. "Please, pray for me," she begged. Huldah returned home and prayed fervently for her sister-in-law. Soon, her health was restored. Persuaded by this miracle they had witnessed, Huldah's brother and sister-in-law became dedicated Christians.

Huldah discovered immense joy in telling others about Christ, and she soon led a group of students who gathered for prayer and Bible study. Even after one of the school wardens scolded her for her evangelism, Huldah continued to share her faith.

This desire to spread the love of God did not end after she finished her schooling; it was just beginning. Huldah returned to her village, using the hours she worked in the rice paddy as opportunities to share the gospel with other villagers who labored beside her. At times she was well received, other times she wasn't.

One day, as she and other women planted rice, Huldah began sharing her story. Suddenly, three of the women stopped planting and began arguing with Huldah. Before the conversation became even more heated, Huldah knew she needed to diffuse it. Calmly, Huldah asked the women to turn their attention back to the work at hand. They would all be able to talk more later, she assured them.

That night after work, one of the women asked Huldah to accompany her back to the house where the three women lived so she could pray for a problem plaguing the family. Huldah arrived at the house, gathered the family, and began to pray. When she finished, the women felt more at peace. "We are thankful for your visit," they told her, "and for praying for our family."

When she wasn't working in the fields, Huldah traveled throughout the area to share the gospel. Twice, she was chased from a village by angry residents who wanted nothing to do with her message or her God. Huldah would soon learn that persecution was a normal part of the Christian life.

Everyone saw how different Huldah's life had become, even her father. And because of his daughter's steadfast witness for Christ, he recommitted his life to God. His reinvigorated faith, however, came at a cost. Because of his faith, Huldah's father felt convicted about some of his behaviors. When those convictions compelled him to stop participating in the village social activities, where alcohol and tobacco were often abused, he was ostracized from the community. "No one is allowed to go to this family's home," the village leaders warned. "And whoever helps them in any way will be fined."

All of these experiences shaped Huldah into a woman of fierce faith, a woman who had experienced ridicule, slander, and marginalization because of her relationship with Jesus Christ. The experiences also helped shape her into a woman who would one day meet a godly man named Abraham and prepare her for the ministry they would share together.

ele

Huldah first met Abraham when she attended a Christian event with her family and friends.

Abraham was considerate and friendly, and because he spoke the same language as Huldah, he was able to help her and her friends secure meals and find places to sit during the event. His personality impressed her, as did his kindness. Abraham smiled from his heart—a contagious smile that brightened the moods of everyone around him.

Huldah was attracted to him, but she didn't mention her feelings to anyone. She had once decided not to marry long ago, but she later changed her mind. As she shared the gospel, she now prayed for a husband who would join her in her ministry work. Now, Huldah wondered if Abraham was the answer to her prayers.

Abraham's pastor knew of Huldah's reputation as an evangelist. "She is the one who will climb all the mountains to share the gospel," he told Abraham. "Why don't you pray and consider marrying her?"

Having had no success finding a bride, Abraham kept thinking about Huldah. *Has God kept her for me?* he wondered.

On May 20, 1998, in a joyous ceremony, Huldah and Abraham were married.

ـعلے

Abraham brought his new bride to live with him in the small hut where he ministered to his church. It was a lively church, quite different from the church of Huldah's youth. Her new husband was an effective preacher, a man who spoke simply and directly to the heart. Before each sermon, he spent hours in prayer, carefully selecting illustrations and real-life stories he knew would resonate with his listeners. He was a good reader, too. In addition to the Bible, Abraham studied two books that helped him prepare his messages: a Bible commentary and a sermon preparation resource used by many evangelists throughout India.

With Abraham's small salary as a pastor, life was hard for the newlyweds who struggled to pay rent. Their possessions amounted to little more than three tin boxes to store their clothes, a few cooking utensils, and one wooden bed. It would be a long time before they could afford a table and a few chairs.

For extra income, Abraham raised pigs and farmed the land surrounding their hut. Huldah sold rice in their village market. The jungle provided the villagers with firewood, fruit, and food for their cattle. But life in the jungle presented all kinds of dangers, especially because of the bears, elephants, and monkeys they often encountered. In the evenings, Abraham and Huldah would carry a tin bucket filled with burning brush to light their path and keep the hungry animals away.

But there were other dangers, too. Each day, as Abraham and Huldah ministered to the poor and marginalized, they trekked over a dozen miles to visit new Christians in hard-to-reach rural areas. On the sunniest of days, the tropical landscape could be unforgiving. But in the monsoon season, when the sky unleashed its relentless torrents of rain, the jungle transformed, making it too muddy for travel and swarming with disease-carrying insects.

Eventually, Abraham and Huldah saved enough money to purchase a black motorbike, the family's only means of transportation. The journeys were still arduous, though, and the motorbike could only take them so far. They'd often ride for an hour before having to hike another hour on foot. Nevertheless, Abraham and Huldah traveled throughout the district to preach the gospel, lead Bible studies and prayer sessions, and worship with like-minded Christians in their homes.

To them, the ministry was worth the difficulties.

On one occasion, the couple traveled to a distant village and planned to spend the night to avoid risking the midnight venture home. That evening, after holding a prayer service for the sick, they were getting ready for bed when they heard shouting outside their hut.

"Call the priest who came to pray for the sick!" a man demanded.

Abraham and Huldah hurried to the front door. Behind the man stood an angry mob of about twenty men, some of them armed with guns and thick bamboo sticks.

"You've come to defile our village god!" a Hindu villager shouted. "You've come to try and change our religion!"

Surveying the mob, Abraham and Huldah knew they had to escape. Before the men could grab them, they dashed back to the bedroom, stuffed their Bible and hymnal into their small travel bag, and snuck out the back door. They fled through the darkness, fearing for their lives. After traveling all night, they finally arrived home at two o'clock the next morning.

Exhausted and shaken, Abraham and Huldah spent the next day in prayer. "We need to pray for those believers to stay strong in their faith," Abraham said. "And we need to continue to pray for the villagers who attacked us."

Huldah agreed. "God has given this ministry to us," she said, affirming that the Lord would continue to provide opportunities for them.

ele

Three years into their marriage, Abraham and Huldah purchased a plot of land and constructed a two-room mud house. They covered the roof with mud tiles and spackled the exterior of their home with a mixture of mud, cow dung, and burnt hay. They placed additional hay in the front yard for villagers to sit on when they gathered for worship every week. The couple funded their ministry by raising pigs and growing rice, onions, garlic, and corn to sell.

Abraham and Huldah tried unsuccessfully to have children. After a doctor's examination revealed a medical issue that would require expensive treatment, they turned to adoption. However, their weak financial situation and lack of a higher education disqualified them from fulfilling the necessary government criteria. Still, they continued praying for a miracle. Amid all obstacles, they prayed that God would give them a child.

Their prayers were answered when a relative was unable to care for his young son. Huldah burst into tears when she and Abraham first saw little Aman smile at them. He was a miracle. And with arms outstretched, the couple welcomed him into their family.

ele

Morning of May 1, 2018

"Abraham," Huldah murmured, "I just had the most disturbing dream."

Abraham rolled over in bed to look at his wife, who was visibly upset.

"People were chasing me," she said. "I fell down. Someone poured something from a bottle, and then all of the people ran away."

"Don't worry about the dream, Huldah," he reassured her, smiling. "Just focus on today's work."

After their morning prayers, Abraham and Huldah got ready for the day. It was Tuesday, their busiest day of the week, and the village market would soon open. Huldah wrapped herself in a yellow and green cotton sari and gathered the goods she planned to sell that day.

The market was located only a few yards from their home, and it had become a strategic connection point for their ministry. Not only did the market allow Huldah to sell rice so she could contribute extra income to the family, but it also provided Abraham with opportunities to connect with villagers.

Every Tuesday, one of Abraham's relatives loaned him a vehicle, and Abraham enlisted a man from a nearby village to drive him. For the past two months, the man had taken Abraham throughout the mountainous jungle, canvassing the roads for villagers to shuttle from their houses to the market. It was a ministry on wheels, and Abraham always engaged passengers in conversation and shared the gospel with them.

On this particular morning, Abraham was in such a hurry to meet his driver that he left home without even eating breakfast. Hours later, just after lunchtime, Huldah walked to the market to buy a few groceries. She saw Abraham standing in the parking area.

"Do you have some money for me to buy some vegetables?" she asked, noticing his face, which had just received a fresh shave from the market barber.

Abraham knew she was concerned about saving money, especially because they were expanding their home to make it more conducive for worship services. "Don't worry about the small things," he said, and handed her some rupees. "I'm going to visit some believers in a nearby village, but I'll see you tonight."

Huldah took the money and watched her husband walk to meet his driver by their vehicle. Abraham turned and gave her a smile, then disappeared behind the door of the white Jeep.

Huldah went back to her house to plan the evening meal. She knew Abraham would be hungry when he returned home after squeezing in only a few bites for lunch in the market. She pulled her dark hair into a tight bun and prepped his favorite meal. She thought about him as she gathered the spices, washed and chopped the vegetables, then placed them in a simmering pot on the stove.

After a few hours, Huldah glanced at the clock. The afternoon had turned into evening, and she expected Abraham to return any minute. Another hour passed. Seven o'clock. Then another hour passed. She walked into her son's bedroom.

"Aman," she said, "your dad hasn't returned yet. What should we do?"

Aman flipped over in his bed, equally concerned. "Have you tried calling him?"

Abraham carried a simple mobile phone, one that didn't have a voicemail service. Huldah punched in the number and waited for the ring tone, but the call immediately disconnected. She tried again, feeling panic rise in her chest, but the call wouldn't go through.

Maybe it's out of batteries, she thought. After one more failed attempt to reach her husband, Huldah went outside and sat down on the step.

God, please protect my husband, she prayed. *Keep him safe. Bring him home.*

ele

Aman stared in horror at the flames lapping around the white Jeep. He tried to catch his breath as his heartbeat pounded in his ears. Inching the motorbike around, he worked to steady his shaking arms. He revved the engine and wobbled back down the bumpy path as he began the return trip home to his mother.

In the distance, Huldah heard the faint rumble of Aman's motorbike growing louder. It had only been ten minutes since he'd left to go find his father. The engine died, and Aman burst through the front door.

"Mom, I got to the bridge and saw a burning vehicle." Huldah waited as her son paused and struggled to control his trembling voice. "It was Dad's Jeep."

Huldah collapsed to the floor, tears streaming down her cheeks. *I just know Abraham was in that Jeep,* she thought.

Aman helped his mother up and sat her on her bed. "A crowd had started to gather, so I hurried back," he said. They both knew that such a crowd could quickly turn into a mob.

The next two hours were agonizing. Aman and his mother waited and prayed, crying out to God for help, hoping for the best but fearing the worst. Huldah knew her husband was a target. She knew there were men in the village who saw him as a problem and wouldn't mind seeing his work stopped.

At 11:00 p.m., the phone rang.

"Huldah?"

She recognized the voice on the other end of the line. It was Abraham's relative, the owner of the white Jeep.

"Huldah, I've just learned from the police that my vehicle has been stolen by unidentified men with guns."

Is Abraham alive?

Just before dawn, Huldah received the answer to her question when relatives came to deliver the news.

Abraham's beheaded body had been found next to the burning Jeep.

୬ℓℓ

The next morning, the police arrived at her front door.

"Are you Abraham's wife?" one of the officers asked.

Huldah nodded.

"Last night, masked gunmen abducted your husband and his driver on their way home. They released the driver but murdered your husband." The police officer hesitated, then he continued. "We need your help for the investigation. Could you come with us to identify the body?"

Still in shock, Huldah shook her head. The request was too painful, so her brother volunteered to go in her place. He and Aman climbed onto Abraham's motorcycle and traveled the short distance to the bridge, the site of the murder.

In the bright morning sun, Aman saw what had remained hidden in darkness the night before. At the water's edge, beside the smoldering remains of the charred white Jeep, Aman saw his father's beheaded body.

Aman and his uncle held each other and wept.

Over the next few days, the investigation unfolded. The driver of Abraham's Jeep provided information to the police, as did several villagers who had witnessed the crime.

Abraham had been kidnapped, beaten, stabbed, and shot before his murderers slit his throat and beheaded him. His killers were twenty-five armed and masked Naxalites, members of a Communist group that generally opposes the government and claims to represent the poorest among India's society. Hindu radicals have often paid or incited Naxalites, or "Maoists," to persecute Christians.

The handwritten note found beside Abraham's body stated in bright red letters: "Death to police spy. Long live PLGA" (People's Liberation Guerrilla Army). It was signed "Your Maoists."

After the arrest and interrogation of one of the Naxalite gunmen, the police learned that the group responsible for Abraham's death was intentionally misguided by local Hindu businessmen who wanted the Christian pastor dead. Radical Hindus circulated the rumor that Abraham was a police informant, angering the Naxalites and manipulating them into killing the pastor.

Abraham was murdered just nineteen days before he and Huldah would have celebrated their twentieth wedding anniversary. Huldah buried her husband in a small plot of land behind their home. A large crowd of Christians, including many pastors from the surrounding churches, gathered for the funeral service.

Tears streamed down Huldah's face as she stood beside her husband's grave, staring at the fresh hole dug in the ground. But, for a moment during the funeral, Huldah was comforted by one particular hymn the congregation sang: *"We will go across the blue sky where our Jesus lives. We will meet in the cloud and after that we will also see our loved ones . . ."* Though Huldah was devastated, she knew Abraham was with Jesus—and that one day she, too, would join him in heaven.

A large, white stone marker would later be placed above Abraham's gravesite, with the words "Martyred for Christ" engraved at the top. At the bottom of the stone, written in Hindi, was Abraham's favorite Scripture verse: "I have fought the good fight, I have finished the race, I have kept the faith" (2 Timothy 4:7).

For the next two weeks, Huldah felt restless and unbearably lonely. She couldn't eat, cook, or visit the village market. The only activity she could manage was walking to Abraham's gravesite, standing for hours, and thinking about her husband's smiling face. Without him, she didn't know what would happen to their ministry.

On the couple's anniversary date, Huldah spent the day in prayer. Even though her life had been torn apart, she thanked God for comforting her in her grief.

You have kept me alive for some specific purpose, she prayed. *You have already planned this purpose for me, and I need to discover what it is.*

Some of the pastors encouraged Huldah to hand over Abraham's ministry to someone else, to go to the city and live in the housing available on their church premises. As the weeks passed, Huldah's relatives also began to worry about her safety, fearing the Naxalites might murder her as well.

"Why do you want to continue living in this village?" one of her relatives asked. "Come to our house. It's safer for you here."

Each time, Huldah responded with the same conviction. "God has called me to this place for ministry," she said. "My husband did his part faithfully, and now it's my turn to do my part. I will not leave this place. I will continue the ministry that Abraham has left."

Villagers informed Huldah about those responsible for killing her husband once they learned the men's identities. One day, as she was walking through the village market, she saw one of the men. A wave of anger swept through her.

Why did you kill my husband? she wanted to shout. *Abraham never harmed anyone and was always available to help people who were in need!*

But instead of confronting her husband's killer, Huldah decided to surrender her anger to God. *Please, God,* she prayed, *change him, and change the others who were involved in killing my husband, so that someday they might accept Jesus and become evangelists and do the work Abraham has left.*

Two years later, Huldah would discover that God was answering her prayer. The leader of the men who murdered Abraham, the most wanted Naxalite in the entire community, fell gravely ill and surrendered to the police.

In his confession, the man admitted something that Huldah had known all along—something known by everyone who knew Pastor Abraham.

"I killed an innocent man," he said.

ele

Along with her son, Huldah eventually resumed the ministry she and her husband used to fulfill together, driving to remote house churches, following the same paths she and Abraham had once traveled through the mountainous jungles.

Everywhere she goes, Huldah encounters people who knew about Abraham's life, death, and love for Jesus Christ. She knows her ministry is different without him, but she stays with the rural villagers, ministering to those her husband died to serve.

Huldah also planted three more house churches with the help of Christian women active in the congregation's fasting and prayer services. She joins the small groups outside their homes, sitting on palm leaf mats, singing praise songs, and studying God's Word.

When reflecting on her ministry, Huldah has often wondered why God called her to serve the community without a life partner. She had prayed for so long to have a husband, only for him to be taken away.

Those feelings of loneliness, however, have reminded her that God always has a purpose. She has been able to use her own horrible experience to minister to other widows who lost their husbands while serving the Lord in India. "God has provided for me," she said. "God has provided much more than I ever could have imagined."

And so, Huldah's work continues—in the same village where her husband was murdered, among the same people who were responsible for his death.

"It's worth following Christ," she said, "in spite of all the persecution and hardship in life. In the future, if more persecution comes, I am ready to face it because I know my Redeemer lives and my life is hidden under Christ."

In Her Words:
Karen

In 2014, Karen Short's husband, John, was detained and interrogated inside North Korea. He was forced to write a confession for his "crimes," including the offense of wanting more North Koreans to follow Jesus. During his fifteen-day detention, Karen had no contact with him.

When I first heard John had been detained, I thought, *Ah, the Lord is in this.* I knew the Lord was in control. I never thought about brutality or how he would be treated. I didn't go to the "what if" situation in my imagination. "What if" is not in my dictionary. I simply trusted the Lord in it, that it was God's will. My only request for John was that he be able to keep his Bible. I thought, *If he has the Word of God with him, he will be fine.* Thankfully, God answered that prayer.

John and I shared a habit where we would read a certain chapter of certain books [of the Bible] every day. So I thought if he had Scriptures, we would be on the same page. I knew what he would be reading each day he was detained. It was so practical and so encouraging that we would be united in prayer at the throne of grace, totally confident in the Lord. I knew that John was a light in a dark place.

During that time, the Lord's people were supporting me in prayer, and I received many words of encouragement. Whether it was text messages, emails, or phone calls, they were tremendously uplifting. The letters from children were precious because there is truly not a moment of doubt in the prayers of sweet little children. I know the Lord hears their prayers.

While John was detained, several people asked me, "What are your demands? What do you want from the North Korean government?" I said, "Nothing." I don't expect anything from any government. We are Australian. I thank God for our Australian privileges. But I didn't expect the government to do anything because it was beyond government; it was in God's hands, not the hands of men.

I went to the Australian Consulate in Hong Kong, and they interviewed me at length after John had been detained for about ten days. I gave gospel tracts to every one of the officials. They would ask me, "Aren't you upset? Don't you miss him? Don't you love your husband?" I replied, "That's a given, but God is first in our lives, and he is there for God's purpose."

Different people asked me, "What about this? What about that? And what if he doesn't come back?" I told them, "Please don't talk like that. I don't think like that. We are in today, and we are praying for the men who are guarding him, whatever his situation is for now, for today, and we are very thankful."

John and I often fast together, so I didn't eat for fifteen days. I think that gave me a clear focus on the Lord. Everything that was not of necessity fell away. I was totally focused on praying for John to be spiritually calm and quiet to deal with all the demands that may come at him. I just knew I needed to be quiet before the Lord, that I couldn't be scattered.

When I married John, my father's advice was, "Stay near the Lord, read the Word of God for your life, and you will overcome in whatever situation you are in." I believed that. You have to have an anchor and a foundation that is God first. Trust God with all your heart; do what He wants you to do. It is not a mystery. Where you are today is where God wants you to be unless He puts it in your heart to go elsewhere. The Lord knows; but if you are willing to be willing, you will know what to do because His will is perfect.

Listen to both Karen and John share about his ordeal in North Korea by visiting vomradio.net/short.

Marziyeh & Maryam

Two Ordinary Girls

TEHRAN, IRAN
2006

Maryam Rostampour and Marziyeh Amirizadeh stood in the living room of their urban apartment surrounded by piles of small New Testaments. Each young woman held a backpack and crammed the Bibles one by one into the bags. Tonight would be the first time implementing their new ministry plan, one that filled them both with equal parts excitement and trepidation.

By the time they finished, their backpacks were bulging with 114 copies of the New Testament. Just before they stepped out into the chilly evening air, they walked over to the large map taped to their living room wall. Before them stretched the sprawling city of Tehran. At the bottom of the map were these words in English: "God is Love. He loves us. We love Him." A tiny blue cross punctuated the handwritten reminder.

As they scanned the map, their eyes landed on the neighborhood where they'd be distributing Bibles that evening. They each prayed aloud over the area and its residents. They prayed for protection and for each New Testament the men and women would receive. When they finished, the two women looked at each other nervously and walked out into the night, knowing that if they were caught with so many Bibles, they would surely be arrested.

Traveling north in Marziyeh's car, they soon arrived at their destination. At each home, they slipped a copy of the New Testament into the mailbox. If a home had no mailbox, the women crouched down and slid the copy under the door. A few times, when neighbors noticed the two women, they ducked their heads and ran, thankful for the cover of night. Adrenaline coursed through their bodies as their bags became lighter and lighter.

When their backpacks were finally empty, they made their way back to their apartment—exhausted, thrilled, and grateful that the first night of distributing Bibles had been a success. Using a green ballpoint pen, the two marked the completed neighborhood on their wall map with a small circle and a cross. They smiled at each other and exhaled sighs of relief. Together, they prayed again for the area they'd visited, asking God to grow hundreds of faithful Christians from the small seeds they had planted.

Now, they wondered, studying their large map once more, *where should we go tomorrow night?*

ﻌﻠﻌ

MARZIYEH

Marziyeh was born in Iran, just a few months before the 1979 revolution that replaced Iran's government with an Islamic republic under the rule of Ayatollah Ruhollah Khomeini. Consequently, she grew up in a radical Islamic country with one of the most oppressive regimes in the world. Leaving Islam is illegal, and Christians face constant threats of imprisonment and false charges of acting against national security for owning Bibles or even talking about Christ.

As a child, Marziyeh wrestled with many questions about Allah, the god of Islam. She found Islam's description of him as a cruel ruler eagerly waiting to punish people for the slightest sin entirely unsatisfying. Growing up, she had a close relationship with her father, and she wanted Islam's Allah to be like him.

Marziyeh's questions about Allah grew more pressing in her teenage years. "Why do I have to talk to Allah in Arabic instead of Farsi, my native language?" she asked her teachers. She wondered why the one who created her was not able to understand her heart language.

Not only did she question Islam, she also questioned the Islamic government, especially the stringent rules placed on women. "Why should I cover myself when I talk to Allah?" she asked. "And why do I have to bow down in front of Allah at specific times during the day? Can he not hear me if I pray to him at other times in the day?"

"You shouldn't ask questions," the teachers cautioned. "Just obey the rules of Islam. If you want to be closer to Allah, and if you want him to be satisfied with you, then you should practice the Islamic rules."

Marziyeh was thirsty for truth, but without another way to know Allah and develop a close relationship with him, she obeyed her teachers and embraced Islamic rituals. For two years, she devoutly read the Quran, practiced Islamic rules, and prayed Islamic prayers. However, all of that changed one night when, while Marziyeh slept, the One True God spoke to her in a dream.

In the dream, Marziyeh stood praying toward the sky when, suddenly, it opened, and a white horse came down. "Sit on my back," it said. Marziyeh climbed onto its back and held on as it galloped into a city. There, Marziyeh saw a mosque. Scores of Muslims stood outside the building, waiting for the start of evening prayers.

At first, Marziyeh sat proudly atop the horse, observing the Muslims from a safe distance. But then, as she watched, she noticed their faces distorting into the savage features of wild animals. At the same time, the Muslims also noticed Marziyeh. They rushed toward her and began attacking her, violently pulling at her legs.

Immediately, the horse ran, carrying a terrified Marziyeh away from the crowd to safety. Grasping the horse's mane, she felt an unmistakable love emanating from the animal beneath her, a pure and powerful love she had never before experienced.

The week after her dream, all Marziyeh could think about was the deep love she had felt in the dream. She had never known a love like that in the world. "God, why did You let me wake up?" she asked. "I wanted to be in this dream forever!"

Soon she came to the conclusion that what God cares about most is her heart, and she decided to set aside her religion. Instead of following the Islamic guidelines for prayer, Marziyeh decided to simply talk to God as her precious Father.

One day a friend who had converted to Christianity approached her. This friend knew Marziyeh was thirsty for the truth; she told her that in Christianity, Jesus Christ is the Son of God and the Savior of all humankind.

Marziyeh was shocked. She had only ever been taught that Jesus was a prophet. *But He's actually the Son of God?* She began reading the Bible, determined to study other religions and to know if Christianity told the truth about Jesus. But soon she felt overwhelmed. *There might be some faith in the world that I would never be able to know in full.*

One day, finally fed up with her confusion, she knelt and prayed a simple prayer to God: "If You created me, if You are my Father, You should find me. You should show me the truth about Jesus. If Jesus is the truth, show me and prove it to me, because I don't want to be misguided in this world."

Not long after, a friend invited Marziyeh to church where she experienced Christians worshiping God joyfully and praying to Him in their own language, Farsi. At the time, Marziyeh was battling a painful disorder in her back, one that had plagued her for a while. During the worship service, however, she heard a voice say in her heart, "You are healed." Over and over again, Marziyeh heard the voice repeat the message: "You are healed." Wanting to ignore the voice, she told her friend. "The voice belongs to Jesus," her friend explained, "and He can heal you."

Marziyeh left her friend and went to her doctor's appointment, as she needed to refill her prescription that helped manage her symptoms. But when her doctor started to write the prescription, he suddenly paused and put down his pen.

"Miss Amirizadeh, I don't know why, but I can't write anything for you right now," he told her. "Would you please come back another time?"

What's wrong with him? Marziyeh wondered. *Why doesn't he want to write my prescription?* And then God reminded her: "Marziyeh, trust Me, I healed you."

Finally, Marziyeh decided not to resist and left the doctor's office. When she later realized she no longer had symptoms, she thanked God for that miracle.

In her heart, Marziyeh had begun to believe in Jesus. But still, she had some doubts. As she read the Bible, she didn't understand certain things about the Holy Spirit, like how the apostles spoke in other tongues after receiving the Holy Spirit. *God, please show me the truth,* she prayed. *I don't want to have any doubts.*

Then one day, while praying in her room, Marziyeh began to pray in a different tongue. Though it wasn't a language she had ever heard before, somehow Marziyeh understood the words she spoke to God. She knew it was from the Holy Spirit. And as she worshiped God and prayed to Him, she had a vision of Jesus in front of her, standing next to a large throne. Immediately all her doubts disappeared; she felt that God had removed a curtain from her eyes, and she could see the truth clearly. She just kept worshiping Him. From that day forward, she dedicated her life to Jesus Christ.

Being a Christian isn't illegal in Iran; however, converting from Islam to another faith like Christianity, and evangelizing Muslims on behalf of that faith, are both crimes punishable by death. But this didn't stop Marziyeh from sharing her new faith. She was a manager of a cosmetology school in Tehran, a job she had worked hard to secure over many years. Through this position, she shared the gospel of salvation with the women who crossed her path.

Eventually, Jesus gave Marziyeh another message: "Leave your job and follow Me." Marziyeh wrestled with the decision. She had built her business from nothing, working tirelessly for years until she achieved a level of success that afforded her a significant salary. But ultimately, she knew what her response must be.

"Marziyeh, are you crazy?" her friends asked. "For years, you've worked so hard, and now you can enjoy the success of your career! What happened to you?"

"I am in love with Jesus," she said, "and all I want to do is follow Him."

In 2005, Marziyeh heeded the advice of her pastor and traveled to Turkey to attend a Christian conference. It would change the course of her life.

ele

MARYAM

Maryam was born into a family of nominal Muslims in Iran. They didn't practice the Islamic rules and rituals and were Muslim in name only, like most Muslim families in Iran.

From a young age, Maryam desired a close relationship with God. She wanted to talk to Him, to have two-way communication with Him. She wanted to know Him and the truth about Him. She would ask her family members questions, and she tried Islamic practices, like reciting *namaz*[1] and reading the Quran in Farsi. And as she grew older, she researched other religions and discovered another branch of Islam that promised a more intimate relationship.[2] No matter what she tried, however, Maryam never felt close to God. She never felt He could hear her voice, and she couldn't hear His.

At sixteen, her mounting frustration culminated in the decision to abandon her religious rituals. Maryam stopped praying. She also stopped researching about God and trying to understand other religions. Instead, she stood on her balcony for hours gazing up at the night sky. There, on the balcony, she talked to God.

She didn't know who God was, but she knew He existed and could hear her voice. In the quiet of the evening, Maryam spent hours talking to Him. She enjoyed these moments, but she also felt like there was some sort of barrier between her and God.

One afternoon, her older sister returned home from her college classes with a small booklet. Maryam glanced at the title: *His Name Is Wonderful*. A man at the church across the street from her sister's university had given her the book.

"I know that you want to know the truth about God," her sister said, handing the book to Maryam. "Just don't read the last page,"

---

1. *Namaz* is the Persian word for prayer. The daily *namaz* is one of the five pillars of Islam.

2. Sufism is a mystical form of Islamic belief dating back to the seventh century. In Sufism, a follower seeks to experience divine love and knowledge through the transmission of divine light from the heart of the teacher to the student.

she warned. "It is a confession prayer for anyone who wants to become a Christian."

Maryam took the booklet and hurried upstairs to her room to read it. As she began to learn who God was, she felt a powerful presence enter her room. Every word she read spoke directly to her heart, and she wasn't reading the words alone. Maryam knew she was in the presence of someone else.

In the booklet, Maryam discovered that Jesus Christ is the Son of God—a claim blasphemous to Muslims. But she knew in her heart it was true. About this, Maryam had no doubt. She felt Christ drawing her to Himself, preparing her heart to accept the truth.

The presence of God in her room was so powerful, so palpable that she sat and cried for nearly three hours, voraciously reading every word of the thirty-page booklet. On the last page, she saw the printed prayer and read it without any doubt or hesitation. And it was at that moment Maryam repented and gave her heart to Jesus Christ.

After Maryam shared her experience with her sister, they began attending church. Soon, her sister also gave her life to Jesus.

At age nineteen, Maryam was secretly baptized at midnight in the basement of a small church.

All the while, Maryam felt the heavy, oppressive atmosphere of Islam. But in the midst of that darkness, she experienced the living, breathing truth—the love of God—and she couldn't help but share it with her family members. Some of them began following Jesus. However, other members of Maryam's family weren't as receptive to the sudden change of faith. "You know your house is dirty now," one of them told Maryam's father. "Your children are dirty because they've become Christians."

Nevertheless, nothing could stop Maryam from telling people about God's love and inviting them to church. When Maryam's pastor saw how passionate she was to share the gospel, he recommended she attend a Christian conference in Turkey to learn more about Christianity.

It was there she met her new best friend, Marziyeh, a woman who would soon become closer than a sister. The two had a unique passion for Jesus. As they shared their stories, a fierce connection was forged, one that was noticed by others at the conference.

"How many years have you known each other?" people asked.

"We've just met today!"

༄

When Marziyeh and Maryam returned home to Iran, they both struggled to figure out how best to serve the Lord. Evangelizing Iranians was dangerous for anyone; but as women, they knew they needed to be especially cautious. Strict Islamic rules governed how they must dress in public and limited the interactions they could have with men.

The two friends leased an apartment perched on a hill in a residential and commercial district of Tehran. The windows in the two bedrooms looked out onto the beautiful Darkeh Mountains in the distance, but the view from their kitchen balcony was far more ominous.

From there, the new roommates could see the high walls of the notorious Evin Prison, a compound holding 15,000 political prisoners, including Iranian converts to Christianity. The two women had heard stories of solitary confinement, rape, and torture within the prison walls. A year and a half earlier, at dawn on July 27, 2008, the Iranian government had executed twenty-nine inmates by hanging in the prison yard. Evin Prison stood as a constant reminder of the perils often awaiting Christians in Iran—but Marziyeh and Maryam longed for a way to share the love of God with the people of Tehran.

As Marziyeh was reading her Bible one day, God spoke to her once more. "First, you need to plant some seeds, and I will grow those seeds with the power of the Holy Spirit." Maryam had a dream with a similar message. As the friends shared their individual callings, they were now certain of their new assignment: to give Bibles to the people of Iran.

Marziyeh's first phone call was to a pastor whom she knew during her training in Turkey.

She requested to have thousands of Bibles sent to her in Iran. "Marziyeh, are you serious?" he asked. "You need thousands of Bibles?"

"We believe this is something from God—a vision He gave us—and we can do it."

It wasn't a simple request. The Bibles would need to be printed and smuggled illegally into the country. Marziyeh and Maryam prayed fervently, and within a few months, the first of their New Testaments arrived. The women bought a large map of Tehran, hung it on their apartment wall, and planned their first mass distribution of Bibles. They would begin in the northern part of the city and then move southward. In order to avoid attention, they would work at night.

ele

The pair quickly learned that distributing Bibles in the southern, more conservative part of the city was far more dangerous. There, the residents supported the Islamic government and advocated strict adherence to Islamic law. To blend in, the two friends donned Islamic coverings and tried to slip, unnoticed, into the neighborhoods. But almost immediately, locals spotted the women and offered a suspicious, "Hello, stranger."

They've identified us! Marziyeh thought as fear gripped her heart. She and Maryam understood just how vulnerable they were. As women walking alone at night, they were vulnerable to men harassing or even attacking them on the street. But evening after evening, as the two friends canvassed neighborhoods across Tehran, God protected them and their Bibles.

They hid the stacks of New Testaments in their apartment and in the basement of the building, then loaded the copies into their bags each day to distribute across the city. In the winter, they even trudged through snow three feet deep. Their map became covered in small crosses as they checked off each area.

During the day, the women shared the gospel. Once, Maryam walked into a bookstore in search of several texts. She didn't plan to evangelize that particular morning, but when a young man approached the manager looking for a Bible, Maryam couldn't help but overhear. Once their conversation concluded, Maryam walked over, pulled a New Testament from her backpack, and handed it to the young man. "May I ask why you were looking for a Bible?"

"Last night, I had a dream about Jesus. He asked me in my dream to go to a bookstore and find a Bible, and then go to the mountain." The man slipped the New Testament into his own backpack and left.

Over the next three years, the two women passed out more than 20,000 New Testaments, placing copies in every part of Tehran. They left copies in taxis and cafes, and even once in a mosque. They also started two house churches. One was among prostitutes, widowed women who entered into temporary "marriages" with men in order to earn a living. The Quran permitted the practice, so Marziyeh and Maryam faced tremendous difficulty convincing the women that God had something better for them than sexual encounters with scores of men.

Marziyeh and Maryam invited curious people they met during their daytime evangelism back to their home. Oftentimes, God had already prepared their hearts to hear His message of salvation through dreams or visions, and they were thirsty for the truth. But the house churches were also risky since the two women could never be sure who was entering their apartment.

By the end of 2008, the young teammates began facing resistance to their ministry. Areas typically brimming with Muslims eager to hear about Jesus and receive a Bible were now sparse with few interested people. Instead of returning home with empty backpacks, the women now struggled to hand out a single New Testament. They had always felt passionate to evangelize, but now, their ministry just felt like work.

Is God changing our mission? Maryam wondered. *Maybe we need to do something different.* Something was different, and both women knew it. Marziyeh thought back to a dream she'd had five years earlier, one in which God told her she would one day go to prison.

"This is going to happen," she told Maryam. Both women could feel that something was about to change.

ele

MARCH 5, 2009

Maryam unlocked the door to her apartment and walked into the kitchen to pour herself a glass of water. Her jaw throbbed from her morning trip to the dentist, and she desperately needed a dose of pain medication. Since Marziyeh wasn't home yet, Maryam hoped to stretch out on the living room couch and take a nap.

Just then, the phone rang. Maryam's sister, Shirin, was on the other line. She sounded anxious.

"I'm so glad I caught you at home," Shirin said. "I had a terrible dream about you last night. I dreamed you had disappeared, and a voice told me you would be in a dark and dreadful place where you would be afraid." Shirin hurried through the rest of the narrative. "Suddenly, the sky opened above your head, and you were pulled upward by your hair into a beautiful green landscape. Then the voice said, 'This is what is happening to your sister.'"

"Forget about it," Maryam said lightly, not wanting to worry Shirin. "You're getting yourself all worked up over nothing. Everything's fine." Maryam walked into the living room, her prescription bottle in hand. "Marziyeh and I are going on vacation for two weeks during the New Year's holiday. We can talk more about it while we're on the road."

Maryam swallowed her medicine with a gulp of water and lay down on the couch. Shirin's dream bothered her more than she cared to admit. She and Marziyeh did, in fact, have a trip planned—but it wasn't the vacation she'd described to her sister. That was the story they told their friends and family for their own safety. In reality, the two women planned to travel throughout other Iranian cities to hand out copies of the New Testament.

But Maryam had experienced a disturbing dream of her own. She and Marziyeh were standing on a hill accompanied by a group of boys and girls. An old man was there, glowing brightly in a shroud of light, and he was prophesying over each of the children. When he finally came to Marziyeh and Maryam, he offered the women a chilling prophecy.

"You two will be taken."

ele

Maryam blinked rapidly as she woke from her nap. *Did someone ring the doorbell?* She heard Marziyeh's muffled voice in the hallway, along with several others she did not recognize.

That's odd. Why doesn't she just come in? Maybe she forgot her key. Maryam peered through the peephole and saw her friend standing with another young woman in Islamic dress and two young men.

"Open the door," the young woman ordered. Maryam's mouth ached and her brain felt fuzzy from her pain medication. She needed a moment to think.

"You'll have to wait until I change my clothes," she said through the door. Islamic law required her to observe the Quran's strict dress code if an unrelated man were to enter the apartment. But the woman pushed her way into the apartment anyway and escorted Maryam to her bedroom to change.

When they returned to the living room, Marziyeh was sitting on the couch as the two young men ransacked the apartment. The two friends watched in horror as the men methodically rummaged through every corner of every room, emptying cabinets and closets and pawing through their books.

The officers had no search warrant. They were *basiji*, part of the Revolutionary Guard.[3] The status of the basiji fell somewhere between government militiamen and common thugs. They wore no uniforms, and they needed no permission to do anything.

The home was not only the girls' personal refuge but also the meeting place of their illegal house church. Stacks of plastic chairs and a stash of New Testaments were in their bedrooms, along with other Christian literature.

While the men searched, Marziyeh and Maryam quietly slid their cell phones into the couch cushions. If confiscated, their contact lists, text messages, and photos would certainly put their friends in danger.

---

3. The Islamic Revolutionary Guard Corps, or the "Revolutionary Guard," was established following the 1979 Islamic Revolution in Iran and exercises significant power in defending the Islamic Republic against perceived threats from outside or within the country.

Before long, the men discovered the New Testaments in the bedrooms. "Have you become a Christian?" one man asked Maryam.

"Yes," she said, her voice strong and confident. "I've been a Christian for eleven years."

The man turned to Marziyeh. "Why did you become a Christian? What has our imam ever done to you?" he said, referring to one of the Islamic religious leaders.

"I became a Christian because I met Jesus," she said. "I turned toward Jesus because He came into my heart and called me to Himself."

The man scoffed and continued his systematic destruction of the apartment. "The Lord seems to be everywhere in this house," he said.

They don't even know about the thousands of Bibles in our basement, Maryam thought.

Marziyeh and Maryam knew it was only a matter of time before they were brought in for questioning. As the men began to pack up their evidence—New Testaments, CDs, private journals, personal belongings, and identification documents—Marziyeh helped them.

The female basiji handcuffed Marziyeh and Maryam and escorted them out of the apartment and into a small white car. By now, it was evening, and the wind was cold. The men followed, carrying boxes of belongings. The two friends weren't allowed to bring any extra clothes or supplies, and they had no idea where the basiji were taking them or when they would be allowed to return home.

As the car sped through the neighborhood, the roommates looked out at the holiday shoppers preparing for the Iranian New Year, called *Nowruz*.

They soon drove past the towering brick walls of Evin Prison. The women had passed the walls nearly every day as they headed into the city to share the gospel. They often wondered what it would be like to be imprisoned there.

Were they about to find out?

ele

Several days earlier, Marziyeh had renewed her passport. One of the forms asked her to indicate her religion, and she had checked the box for "Christian." The clerk was indignant. "How is this possible?" he demanded. "You have an Islamic name. How can you be a Christian?"

"With the Lord," Marziyeh told him, "anything is possible."

On the morning of Maryam's dentist appointment, Marziyeh had been called to the police station under the guise of a problem with her car registration. But when she arrived, the officials questioned her about her religion and her Christian activities. She quickly realized the problem with her car registration had been a ruse. They knew about the New Testaments stored in her apartment. Eventually, they handcuffed her and hustled her into a police car to accompany three officers back to her apartment to search the home. Marziyeh felt frightened for a moment, then she remembered a promise she had made to the Lord. *I will never deny You. I trust You to be with me always and overcome my fear.* She then leaned over to the female officer.

"I am a Christian. You have shackled me for my faith and for no other reason. I am honored to serve Christ this way, and I want you to know I'm not upset with you for what you did."

ele

When the car carrying the two friends and the basiji finally came to a stop, they were in front of the neighborhood police station, a three-story brick building that typically handled motor vehicle registrations. The main entrance was busy, but instead of taking the women through the front door, the basiji escorted them to a quiet back alley, out of public view. Marziyeh and Maryam would soon learn this was Base Two, the facility for the secret police who deal with crimes against the state.

Maryam began to doubt. *Will we truly go anywhere to follow Jesus and do His work?* The commitment seemed easy enough when they were talking about it alone in their apartment, or when they were distributing Bibles each night without being caught. But now they were both in police custody, and the prospect was a far more serious matter. From the look on Marziyeh's face, she could tell her friend felt the same way.

Fighting her rising panic, Maryam felt weak, not brave. *Will we deny Christ to save ourselves?* She prayed for the Lord to keep them strong. She knew they could be brave and resist only in His strength, not their own.

The officers led the women up a flight of stairs to a small office with bare walls and a large desk. Confiscated property belonging to previous detainees was piled on the desk and all over the floor.

Maryam's painkillers had long worn off, and her jaw throbbed. Dizzy and weak, both women realized they had not eaten since morning.

In front of them sat an officer named Mr. Rasti, one of the men who had questioned Marziyeh earlier that day. "You will tell me the truth from now on," he snapped.

"I have always told the truth," Marziyeh answered sharply. "But you have not! You lied to me about the car this morning to bring me here. I told you I've been a Christian for eleven years. I've handed out New Testaments. I could have denied everything, but I answered honestly." She could feel her voice rising.

The female officer spoke up. "They have become Christians!" she accused. "We discovered a bunch of Bibles and other Christian propaganda in their apartment." She turned to the two women. "Don't you know that makes you *kafar*?" she asked, using the Farsi word for "infidel."

Exhausted and in pain, Maryam explained the Christian belief that Jesus is the Savior of humanity. "He wasn't just a prophet, as the Quran claims." She continued to explain that He was God in the flesh, the One who had taken on the sins of the world.

For hours, the officers and the two women went back and forth, arguing about Christianity and Jesus. They were questioned together and separately about the people they had given Bibles to, along with other specific details of their house church and friends. A significant part of the interrogation involved whether the women had, indeed, converted to Christianity. The case against them seemed to hinge on this point.

When Mr. Rasti finally slid a stack of papers in front of Marziyeh, it was nearly 11:00 p.m. The women had been interrogated for more than two hours. "Sign," he demanded. She didn't have a chance to read them and was too tired to argue, so she acquiesced. When Mr. Rasti presented Maryam with a similar stack, she did the same.

⟞⟞

It was nearly midnight when another guard entered. "You will remain in custody," he informed them. "I will take you to the detention center."

Marziyeh and Maryam climbed into another car and soon arrived at the Vozara Detention Center. There, guards ushered them into a room to be processed. "What is the charge against you?" a sleepy soldier asked from behind the counter.

"Christianity," the pair said in unison.

Marziyeh raised their handcuffed hands and said, "We are proud of these handcuffs because we're wearing them on account of our faith in Jesus Christ!"

"I have faith in Jesus too," the soldier said, "but I would never try to convert someone else to my beliefs. You're not in custody for believing in Jesus; you're in custody for promoting Him to others."

A guard soon led the women down a long flight of stairs into a basement, through a series of steel doors, and into a room where two female guards waited. The women removed their clothes for the guards to do a body cavity search. Then, the guard guided them through another metal door to a hallway with open rooms on either side. The two friends took crusty, damp blankets from a dirty stack as the guard clanged the door shut behind them.

In the dim light, Marziyeh and Maryam saw blanketed figures on the floor of the other rooms. They found an open spot in a room with an overwhelming stench of sweat, vomit, and clogged toilets. There, the two friends huddled together on the freezing floor and held hands, the smell of dried urine wafting up from their blankets.

The rush of emotions was unlike anything either had ever experienced: bone-tired confusion, hunger, thirst, and repulsion. *How will our family or Christian friends find out what has happened? How long will we be here? Are our lives in danger?*

The women were too tired to be afraid. Everything was too raw. All they could do was turn their situation over to the Lord. After trading stories of their separate interrogations and praying for protection, Marziyeh and Maryam fell into a fitful sleep.

It would be the first of more than 250 nights behind bars.

ele

Shouts of frustrated prisoners looking for cigarettes woke the two women the next morning. In their haze, they finally remembered where they were. The guards passed out single pieces of bread for breakfast, but they couldn't eat.

Neither Marziyeh nor Maryam had ever been imprisoned before, and the first few days were tremendously difficult with little to eat, dirty water to drink, and the stress of the unknown. Soon, they had a realization: many of their fellow prisoners were the same prostitutes they had struggled to evangelize in the streets of Tehran. Every day, more women arrived, some as young as sixteen.

For two weeks in the Vozara Detention Center, Marziyeh and Maryam sat and listened to the women tell their heartbreaking stories of abuse and desperation. On the cold, filthy, concrete floor, they also prayed with them and shared the message of salvation through Jesus Christ. Late one night, a young girl arrived. Her body was emaciated, and she appeared to be addicted to drugs. When the girl cried out in terrible pain, Marziyeh hurried to her cell and sat next to her.

"Why are you here?" the girl asked. "Why aren't you asleep?"

"Because I want to sit here with you," Marziyeh told her with a smile. She laid the girl's head in her lap and stroked her hair. *She's younger than my little sister, Elena.* Marziyeh prayed silently, and soon the girl fell asleep.

Early the next morning, the girl came and found Marziyeh. "What kind of prayer did you pray for me last night?" she asked.

"I prayed for Jesus to heal you."

"I became so calm, and my pain is much less." Together, Maryam and Marziyeh explained the gospel to the young girl.

We are in the best place we've ever been for witnessing to people hungry for the gospel of Jesus, Maryam thought.

The two women had prayed diligently for more opportunities to share their faith, and now, the Lord was answering that prayer. In the darkness of prison, their only light was Jesus.

Several days later, Marziyeh and Maryam's first court appearance arrived. They, along with the other inmates, would be transported from the detention center to the courthouse. As they waited, prisoners were called one by one from the cell block until only the two friends remained. Finally, the guards came for them. As they stepped outside the detention center, they breathed deeply, grateful to inhale fresh air for the first time in weeks. The bright sun nearly blinded them as their eyes acclimated to being outdoors once again. *What a blessing to be out in the world again, if only for a moment!* Marziyeh thought.

Suddenly, they heard their names and turned to see their own two sisters, Elena and Shirin, running toward them. They were shocked their sisters had found out about their case.

"Ignore them!" one of the guards barked. "Keep moving!" But Marziyeh and Maryam couldn't. The joy of seeing their sisters was too immense, and they threw themselves into their sisters' arms, handcuffs restricting their movements. In an urgent whisper, the pair hurriedly told their siblings about the supply of New Testaments still hidden in their apartment building. "Will you hide them for us?"

Elena and Shirin hastily shoved a supply of chocolate and juice to their sisters, who hid the contraband under their clothing. The two inmates also learned that people around the world had heard about their arrest and were trying to help free them. In the days to come, Elena and Shirin would be their lifeline to the outside world.

"Into the car!" the guard ordered. The two women hugged their sisters one last time and maneuvered into the backseat of the waiting car. They learned they were headed to the Revolutionary Court, a special court system established after the 1979 Islamic

Revolution and tasked with trying defendants charged with crimes like blasphemy or attempting to overthrow the Islamic government. In the Revolutionary Court judicial system, a single judge presides over each trial, and the trials are not public.

Marziyeh and Maryam eventually arrived at the office of Mr. Sobhani, who had received their case from Mr. Rasti. Mr. Sobhani was a stern-faced judge with a dark beard who preferred his prisoners flatter him and beg him for mercy.

Glancing around the office, Marziyeh noticed evidence of Mr. Sobhani's dedication to Iran's regime: framed photos commemorated the Islamic Revolution and the Islamic martyrs who had been killed, and there were photos of the Ayatollah Khomeini. She also noticed his huge ring inscribed with verses from the Quran and the red mark on his forehead that devout Muslims get when they pray for long periods of time with a prayer stone pressed against their brow. *He heated the stone before using it,* Marziyeh thought to herself, knowing Muslims do this to show their "dedication" without investing all the time in actual prayer.

The judge wrote out a list of questions for the two women to answer. They weren't allowed to confer with each other as they wrote their answers. But since the questions were ones they'd answered countless times already, their answers were nearly identical.

Do you accept the charge of advertising activities against the regime and insulting religious authorities?

No.

Do you accept the charge of distributing Bibles and evangelizing in a restaurant in Tehran?

No. We gave New Testaments as gifts only to people who asked for them. We did not initiate conversations about Jesus with anyone in a restaurant.

They continued through the questions then signed and finger-printed their answers. Instead of returning to the detention center, the guard drove the two women back to the police station. There, they met again with Mr. Rasti.

"I hope you've been thinking carefully," he said, nibbling on a piece of bread.

"What should we have been thinking about?" Maryam asked.

"About telling us what we want to know about you and your activities, about people you have worked with." He paused and stared at the two women. "We have other ways of getting prisoners to communicate. Tell us what we want, or we will beat you. You might as well tell us now and save yourselves."

If we are tortured, the women prayed, *give us the strength to stand fast.*

ele

Prisoners were only to be kept for three days in the Vozara Detention Center, but Marziyeh and Maryam had already been there for fourteen. They had no bed, no sufficient meals, and not even a hint of justice — but they had survived, and the Lord was with them. During this time, they had witnessed to dozens of women they never would have met if the authorities had followed their policy.

Two weeks into their detainment, they found themselves alone in the cell block. The other prisoners had all attended their court hearings, and all but one — a woman who was sentenced to prison — had been released on bail. The once-bustling basement cell block was now quiet.

As Marziyeh and Maryam moved from cell to cell, they prayed for all the women who had been locked up there, that they would continue to listen to the Holy Spirit moving in their hearts.

But what about the women who will be locked up here after we're gone? Marziyeh thought. *How can we reach out to them?*

On the walls were damp places where little chunks of plaster had fallen off. Using the pieces of plaster as chalk, Marziyeh and Maryam wrote Bible verses and Christian messages of encouragement all over the walls and on the ceilings where prisoners could read them as they fell asleep. All alone in an underground prison cell, the two friends prayed aloud and sang songs until late in the night. They still shared a joyous celebration of faith.

"What a miracle it was that we've been able to meet and encourage so many women," Marziyeh said as she and Maryam walked through each cell praying. "What man meant for evil, God used for His good and His glory."

The next morning, the two women returned to the Revolutionary Court. If they could each come up with 200 million *tomans* ($100,000 USD) by five o'clock that afternoon, the judge said they would be released. If not, they would be transferred immediately to the notorious Evin Prison.

There was no way Maryam and Marziyeh could come up with so much money so quickly. Besides, it was a holiday, and the banks were closed.

Instead, they became the newest inmates of Evin Prison, one of the most brutal prisons in the world.

⁓

Marziyeh and Maryam entered Ward 2, the section reserved for women accused of murder, prostitution, fraud, or crimes against the state. Mrs. Mahjoob, the prisoner in charge of keeping order in that ward, led them to a room already so crowded there was scarcely room to sit. Eight triple bunk beds were crammed into the fifteen-by-twenty-foot space.

For the first time in two weeks, under ice-cold streams of water, Marziyeh and Maryam finally showered.

Cellmates inundated the newcomers with questions. "You have become apostates," one woman said harshly after learning of their charges. "This is very dangerous."

"Don't worry," another woman said. "We're all political prisoners in this room."

Slowly, they got to know the other women in their cell. The first night, they heard Mrs. Mahjoob crying quietly on her bunk. "Could we pray for you?" Maryam asked.

As Mrs. Mahjoob cried, the two women prayed—not loudly, but not silently either. Gradually, the other women around them stopped their conversations to listen. By the time Marziyeh and Maryam finished, nearly the entire room was silent.

"Your heart is pure," someone called out, "and God will listen to your voice. Will you pray for me, too?"

Evin Prison, the dreaded hellhole of Tehran and a symbol of radical Islamic oppression, had become Maryam and Marziyeh's church.

༒

Within a few days of their arrival, Marziyeh became sick from showering in the icy cold water. What began as a sore throat quickly became a serious infection, and she struggled to keep her balance.

Maryam told Mrs. Mahjoob that Marziyeh needed to see a doctor, but he was evidently on vacation and wouldn't be back until after the holidays. Instead, the woman secured some expired antibiotics. It was the best she could do.

For nearly a week, Marziyeh stayed in bed, miserable, shivering, and exhausted. Other prisoners brought her tea and fruit juice, and once in a while a few bootleg painkillers. All they could do was pray.

The food in the prison did nothing to help Marziyeh heal. The prisoners received one meal a day, often a stew consisting mostly of dirty water and fat with a few unpeeled carrots and potatoes. Once a week they had sausage, a horrible concoction that gave the women diarrhea.

In addition to their physical challenges, Maryam and Marziyeh also experienced relational challenges with some of the women in their cell. For weeks, the Muslim inmates called them "dirty infidels." Initially hesitant to talk with strangers during their breaks outside, the two women didn't know who might be spying for the regime or who might try to hurt them. But gradually, they began mingling and looking for opportunities to engage in conversations. These conversations soon fostered friendships with other inmates.

When they were first arrested, all Marziyeh and Maryam could think about was their release from prison. But now, they had come to embrace the place God had sent them, and the friends settled into a routine. In the mornings, they knitted, exercised, and talked. In the afternoons, they invited other prisoners into their room for tea and snacks and spent the whole afternoon in conversation. They prayed with fellow believers and shared their faith with the others.

Marziyeh and Maryam were extremely grateful their sisters had set up an account for them at the prison commissary so they could buy snacks and a few other luxuries. They always tried to keep a supply of chocolate and the best snacks on hand to give away to the poorest prisoners who couldn't purchase anything. These acts of kindness did not go unnoticed by the other inmates.

Usually, prisoners were excited to hear their names called over the prison loudspeakers. This often meant they were being released, or at least their case was moving forward.

Six weeks after they arrived in Evin, the two women heard their own names called. They were apprehensive, as were their two new friends: Shirin, a political prisoner; and Silva, a Christian in prison under scrutiny for her work with an American charity. "Do you know why you are being ordered to report to the prison office?" they asked, rushing into Marziyeh and Maryam's room, but they had no idea.

The pair reported to the prison office. There, a woman behind the desk offered a terrifying explanation: "You are being transferred to Ward 209," she said. "Go downstairs and wait for a guard to escort you."

Ward 209? With no warning or explanation, Marziyeh and Maryam were being sent to the dreaded ward where Silva had been kept in solitary confinement for eight months, and Shirin was beaten unconscious and had her teeth knocked out.

Marziyeh and Maryam went back to their ward to say a quick goodbye to Silva, Shirin, and the others they had come to love so much. Then, they waited. After half an hour, a rotund, bearded guard appeared, barking an order to follow him.

They followed him for several hundred yards until they came to a small white door in a red brick building. He handed blindfolds to each woman and ordered them to put them on. Marziyeh and Maryam stumbled inside and heard the door lock behind them.

In Ward 209, the two friends were subjected to more interrogations—manipulative attempts to force them to renounce their faith. The interrogations were conducted separately, each lasting as long as four hours. Each time, the young women remained faithful and shared the gospel with their questioners.

Before long, the full horror of Ward 209 became painfully clear. One of their cellmates, a young woman named Zeynab who was imprisoned on murder charges for defending herself against an abusive husband, was hanged in the prison yard. There were no words to describe the pain and sorrow Marziyeh and Maryam felt as they mourned the evil act of injustice.

ele

In the months that followed, periods of relative peace were interrupted by periods of intense questioning. "If you continue your Christian activities here," one interrogator warned Marziyeh, "it will be very hard for you."

"Do what you wish," she said, defiantly. "Unless you cut out my tongue, I will keep feeding the people's hunger for the truth about Jesus. And if you do cut out my tongue, I will share His gospel with sign language!"

Marziyeh and Maryam were housed in separate cells and isolated from one another, then shuffled occasionally from the prison to the Revolutionary Court in a black, unmarked car. The Holy Spirit was their constant companion. But despite the assurance that the Lord loved them and would never forsake them, a fierce loneliness crept into Maryam's heart. She struggled to eat, and she felt an emptiness she'd never known. She prayed for the Lord to comfort her, and she sang hymns. It wasn't long before one of the guards asked Maryam to pray for him. As she prayed, she felt the presence of the Lord wash over her and dispel her fears and loneliness. She knew there was purpose in their imprisonment, and she felt more blessed than she had ever felt before.

While Marziyeh and Maryam had little contact with the world outside, interest in their case was growing. Their story was gaining attention on satellite TV and the internet. Christians around the world were praying for them; they were being lifted up as part of a spiritual family that circled the globe.

One day, a guard came to Maryam's cell with shocking news. "You have a room full of letters," he said. "People from all around the world are sending you letters."

Each day, approximately fifty letters were delivered to the prison. Some were from adults, the guard said, and many were from children who drew pictures and wrote Bible verses for the two imprisoned women. The letters sent to them surpassed even the quantity of official mail arriving at the prison, and the prison staff was angry. "We have to open your letters and read them," the guard said, "because the Iranian government forces us to check all incoming prisoner mail." He paused, a bewildered expression on his face. "What does it mean that 'Jesus is our Shepherd?'"

Praise the Lord! Maryam thought. *Even though we can't read our letters, God is using them to send His message to the guards and prison staff!*

When their sisters were finally allowed to visit several weeks later, the women learned more details about the growing interest in their case. Their global spiritual family was supporting them through prayer and through writing letters to them. They no longer felt alone.

The prison staff, along with the government, now also knew the women were not alone. Countless people worldwide were following the women's situation closely and, even from far away, were holding the prison staff and the Iranian government accountable for their treatment of Marziyeh and Maryam.

⚬⚬⚬

Eventually, the two friends were thrilled to learn that their time in Ward 209 had come to an end. They would be transferred back to Ward 2, to their friends Shirin, Silva, and the others.

Six months after their initial arrest, Marziyeh and Maryam still had not met with a lawyer who could represent them in court, and they had not seen the charges against them in writing. Following a turbulent presidential election, the whole country was in chaos. The pair had come to terms with the fact there was nothing more they could do to gain their freedom.

Serious health problems plagued both women, and they felt sick or in pain every day of their imprisonment. One night, Maryam suffered from an unbearable stomachache, and the prison refused to give her medication. The whole night, Marziyeh sat by her side and prayed.

The encounter had a powerful impact on their cellmates. "Your friendship is amazing," one woman remarked. "We can't believe the way you love each other and care for each other."

One morning, the two were called to the prison office and transferred, again, to the court. There, they finally met their attorney. "I'm sorry we haven't met yet," he said. "I'm still trying to get the judge's permission to visit you in prison." The lawyer began working on their defense, and with this new turn of events, Marziyeh and Maryam felt hope that they might, one day, be released.

Before their next court hearing, their lawyer encouraged his two clients to soften their stance on Christianity in exchange for more favorable treatment in court.

"Your court date is coming up soon," he said, "and you'll finally have a chance to defend yourselves. Would you be willing to think about changing your position on your Christian beliefs?" During their last hearing at the Revolutionary Court, the judge warned that if Marziyeh and Maryam didn't change their story, their case would be transferred to the infamous Bureau 15 for a final verdict. There, the judge was known for sentencing prisoners either to death or to life in prison.

But the women refused. "There is nothing to think about," Marziyeh said. "We will never turn from Christ, never water down our story, never deny our Savior." She knew their faith and their lives were hanging in the balance, but that God's hand would guide whatever happened next.

ele

Within a week, Maryam and Marziyeh heard their names called once again over the prison loudspeakers. Tomorrow would be their trial, they learned in the prison office.

The next morning, they met their attorney at the court. International pressure had continued to mount, and Marziyeh and Maryam learned they had been assigned a new judge. Officials at the United Nations had telephoned and asked the judiciary to sort out the case as soon as possible.

What great news! Marziyeh thought. *Will today be a day of resolution?*

"Do you realize," the judge asked, "that due to your perseverance, our enemies have taken advantage of the situation and have run several negative campaigns against us?" The two women knew about vigils in front of the Iranian Embassy in London and others around the world. They hoped the judge's frustration wouldn't boil over into a harsh punishment. Both women felt their stomachs flutter as they stood silently. Nothing in their lawyer's countenance revealed his thoughts.

"The charges of propaganda against the regime and insulting our sacred values are baseless," the judge continued. "There is no substantial evidence to support them."

Marziyeh and Maryam were shocked. *Is this really happening?* The judge leaned forward and continued.

"I don't suppose you've insulted any other religions or religious beliefs, have you?"

"No," the women replied.

The judge sat up straight behind his bench. "Therefore, I hereby acknowledge your acquittal from the charges of instigating propaganda against the system and insulting our sacred values."

Just like that, without a word of testimony, Maryam and Marziyeh were cleared of the charges. But the judge wasn't finished. The charge of apostasy still remained.

"Are you a Christian?" the judge asked. "Are you called to follow Jesus?"

As the questions hung in the air, Marziyeh felt chills. They were the same questions asked four years earlier at her baptism. Slowly, she explained her faith in Christ and her personal relationship with Him. "I consider Jesus to be the Son of God and my Savior."

The judge was visibly startled by such a bold statement from a prisoner whose freedom was so close at hand. He pressed Marziyeh, but she became more insistent. Her lawyer jumped in to try to explain, but Marziyeh's statements seemed to undermine his planned defense. The judge left the room for a brief recess, and the women's lawyer angrily asked why they refused to simply sign a statement renouncing their evangelism efforts.

"There would not have been a problem if you had simply agreed to sign the statement I prepared," he ranted. "It would have set you free!"

"We would not sign because we didn't agree with it," Maryam interjected.

Without any resolution, Marziyeh and Maryam were returned to Evin once more. Their friends were eager to learn what had happened in court, and some told the two Christians they were crazy for not accepting the government's offers.

"We believe in our God," Marziyeh assured the other prisoners. "We're sure God can show His victory. We can't do it, but God can show His power."

᠊ᡇᠯᡄ᠊

Over the coming days, the women received confusing, mixed messages about their status from the prison staff. Some days, it seemed like promises of freedom had been a lie; other days, their release felt imminent. Every night, they wondered whether it would be their last in Evin Prison. *Will this be our last night to do God's work behind bars?*

Finally, the day arrived. Marziyeh and Maryam learned they would be released the very next day. The women were thrilled, but they also felt conflicted about leaving the place that had been their home and their family for nine months. Evin Prison was no longer strange to them. It was their university, teaching them things they never could have learned anywhere else. It was their church, a place of sincere, deep faith and trust in Jesus Christ. It had become a part of their very existence, representing the worst days of their lives as well as some of the best.

Shirin asked to pray for them, and their friends threw Marziyeh and Maryam a going-away party, singing songs and giving the two women poems, notes, and small gifts to remember them by. That night, no one slept. Finally, God was finished with the work He had for them in Evin Prison, and the next evening, they would find themselves in a different world.

At two o'clock the next afternoon, November 18, 2009, the two friends finally heard the words they had longed for: "Your freedom papers have arrived!" They heard their names over the loudspeaker, then picked up their few belongings. Friends from all over the ward swarmed into their room to hug the women and wish them well. Now, there was nothing left to do but walk through the corridor, out of the ward, and into the sun. They waved to the sea of faces until the guard closed the door behind them.

"Are you the two Christians?" the guard asked. "I've heard a lot about you. I'm very happy that you are finally released."

A sentry led the two women to the main gate of the prison, opened it, and ushered them through.

Marziyeh and Maryam were finally free.

Just outside the prison gate were their two sisters. Through tears and laughter, the four women embraced until a soldier told them to leave. For months, Marziyeh and Maryam had dreamed of this moment, but as they drove away to their apartment, Marziyeh felt strange. *My body is free, but my soul and spirit are still with our precious friends suffering terrible injustice inside.*

Their sisters had cleaned their apartment, and Marziyeh and Maryam took in the sight that had once been so familiar. They looked at their furniture, their photos, their stacks of music CDs. The belongings that had once seemed so necessary now seemed frivolous. From their kitchen balcony, they could still see the walls of Evin Prison.

∽

For two years before their arrest, Maryam and Marziyeh had hosted two churches in their home and given away New Testaments. For nine months in prison, they had spent every day praising Jesus and proclaiming His gospel. But now, their evangelism work was stopped dead in its tracks. Iranians wanting to know more about Christianity dared not contact them. People who once attended their home churches wouldn't come near them.

Soon, the two women heard indirectly that news of their faithfulness to Christ had led others to Him. When people learned they were willing to die rather than deny their faith, they wanted to know what it was that was worth such a sacrifice. People whom they'd spoken to in the past—ones who hadn't been interested in Christianity—now read the Bible eagerly and asked probing questions about Marziyeh and Maryam's faith.

Months passed, and the two friends eventually learned their court appearance on apostasy was scheduled for April 13, 2010. Depending on the outcome, there was a chance they would be sent back to prison. They packed suitcases to take with them to court, just in case, and passed word to their friends in Evin that they might be rejoining them soon.

On the day of their hearing, they arrived at the courthouse and waited an hour for their names to be called. Finally, they walked inside the courtroom to stand before a panel of judges. For ten minutes, no one spoke.

Eventually, the chief judge recited a prayer to Allah and then ordered the charges against Marziyeh and Maryam to be read.

"Miss Rostampour," he said, "do you accept these accusations against you?"

"No."

"Miss Amirizadeh, do you accept these accusations?"

"No."

The women watched as their lawyer wrote down his clients' defense, the words that would determine Marziyeh and Maryam's future. When he finished, the chief judge called them to the bench and leaned over to speak. "Sign this statement that you were in court, and you are free to go home."

"But don't think it will always be so simple," another judge barked. "We've let you off the hook this time, but if you ever step into this courtroom again, you will surely be sentenced to death."

Outside the courtroom, their lawyer could barely contain his joy. Finally, it was over. And for the first time since their arrest, Marziyeh and Maryam felt free.

ـelـ

Their feeling of freedom didn't last long. Although they had been physically released from Evin Prison, they still felt as if they were being held captive by a regime that was monitoring their every move and could arrest them again at any time. Iran was their home, their motherland, but if they had to decide between their faith and their country, they would choose Christ.

On May 22, 2010, Maryam and Marziyeh left Iran, unsure if they'd ever return. As their plane rose through the early morning sky, they looked out the window at the lights of Tehran below. They were heading to an uncertain future, forced from the land of their birth. Behind them, they were leaving a lifetime of memories. Most of the country was still asleep—their suffering friends in the crowded cells of Evin Prison and their Christian brothers and sisters in their homes.

However, they knew their future was in the Lord and in His mercy for the suffering and persecuted people in Iran. "This unjust and cruel regime cannot last forever," Maryam said. "The day will come when God will cause this country to rise from the ashes and give them 'the oil of gladness instead of mourning, the garment of praise instead of a faint spirit'" (Isaiah 61:3). Maryam and Marziyeh prayed that the Lord would continue to use the two of them as part of His plan to allow the freedom of the gospel to flourish in Iran.

The friends eventually settled in the United States, where they began their new lives. They knew very little English but began working on a book about their experiences in prison.

Reflecting on her time in prison, Maryam said: "When people experience living in Evin Prison, they will never be the same again. The stress is too much. We can't be the same people. We can't be as happy as before. We don't enjoy activities like normal people because all the time we think of those who are still there."

"I believe God had a purpose from the beginning to change me and prepare me for the worst experiences that I had in prison," Marziyeh said. "I am very grateful that God gave me the opportunity to taste a little of His sufferings. Compared to what He did for us, it was nothing. It was an honor for me to suffer because of His name."

In the years following their release from prison, Marziyeh and Maryam have had opportunities to travel the world and share about their imprisonment in Iran. They gratefully share with people about their ministry of distributing Bibles, the time they spent imprisoned for following Jesus Christ, and the ways God continues to use them.

As they stood at a podium and spoke in Australia, Marziyeh and Maryam noticed an Iranian couple sobbing in the audience. *Why do they keep crying?* the friends wondered. Afterward, the couple approached the two women and shared that years earlier, their family had opened their mailbox to find a New Testament inside. As a result of that one Bible, the whole family placed their trust in Christ—first the daughter, then her fiancé, and soon the rest of the family. They eventually immigrated to Australia but always prayed for the mysterious person who put that Bible in their mailbox. When the couple's friend told them about hearing Maryam and Marziyeh's story in a radio interview, the husband and wife knew they had to meet the women whose faithfulness changed their lives.

"It was God's plan really from the beginning to bring us together," Maryam later said. "If we were alone, we couldn't do all we have done. I think there is power in unity. We have the presence of the Holy Spirit with us, but there's also a reason that

God put people around us in our life. We can encourage each other, and we can strengthen each other."

The friends take great comfort in the mighty ways God used them for His purposes in Iran. Sometime after they began handing out New Testaments in Tehran, a Christian friend told them their ministry had been announced in the Iranian Parliament as a security threat. With so many Bibles scattered throughout the city, the government assumed a large Christian organization must be behind such a massive distribution. Marziyeh smiled as she thought back to that day. "They did not know that it's just by the faith and work of two ordinary girls," she said.

In Her Words:
Gao

In the 1940s, Gao Shao Xiu placed her trust in Christ after being healed from a chronic illness. Well into her 80s, she served as a house church leader and continued to faithfully disciple Christians under the Chinese Communist government's increasing restrictions.

When I was little, I was diagnosed with inflammation of the brain. I was in constant pain. The doctors told my parents not to invest too much money in me and my education because I would not live long. These were the 1930s.

Fortunately, I was born into a relatively wealthy family with parents who loved me very much. I was moved from hospital to hospital in hopes of finding a cure. These futile treatments lasted for over ten years. When I was fifteen years old, a quack convinced my parents he could heal me within three months. They invited the so-called healer to move into our home. How much money they gave him, I do not know; but one night he simply disappeared—and with him my hope to be free from pain. At the age of sixteen, my parents were openly speaking of my funeral. I was to wait patiently to die.

Then two Christians visited us. They had heard of my situation. They simply said, "We have good news. There may be hope." My parents were obviously desperate for good news. My father invited them to stay with us so he could hear more.

They told him God does exist and He is powerful and capable of saving my life if we ask Him. Of course, my father was skeptical after the grave disappointment with the quack doctor, but he allowed them to stay anyway.

The guests did not charge any money. They remained for three days, and all they did was pray. I began to feel pain free for the first time in my life. It was then my father chose to believe in the Lord and he publicly dedicated me to God. Shortly after, I also believed and chose to follow the Lord.

As a young adult, I had not yet seen an entire copy of a Bible. Our fellowship had some chapters that were hand copied. During my school years, I had been too ill to attend school, but I wanted to enhance my education, and I thought, *What better way to do this than to hand copy the portions of the Bible we have available!*

So, I started to copy the Bible portions. The more I copied the Scripture, the healthier I became both physically and emotionally.

During the Cultural Revolution,[1] I experienced trauma like many other Christians. Angry people tied me up, put a pointed hat on my head to humiliate me, and forced me to march in the streets with a sign on my chest saying "anti-government." I was forced to walk in public like this for many days.

Even then, I did not renounce my God. I knew He was real. He was powerful, and because of Him, I was not dead already. By then I had a knowledge of God's Word. In it, I found the means of truth, life itself, and clear guidance to the path I should be on.

Today, this same Book is the vital resource of my life.

I still maintain the habit and discipline of hand copying God's Word. Though I have committed many verses to memory, my favorite verse is still John 3:16.

---

1. The Cultural Revolution (1966–1976) was a failed attempt to revive the spirit of China's Communist revolution, led by Mao Zedong, when the Communists took power of the country in 1949. Anything associated with China's pre-Communist past was destroyed, including artwork and cultural monuments. Given Christianity's ties to Western missionaries, Christians were specifically targeted.

Anita

Nothing Greater than
Living for Jesus

AUSTIN, TEXAS
DECEMBER 19, 2013

Anita Smith swept her long, sandy brown hair to one shoulder as the production assistant clipped a small microphone to the lapel of her gray cardigan. She adjusted her earpiece, squinted into the blinding studio lights, and took a deep breath. In minutes, she'd be speaking with the veteran anchor of a well-known global media newscast.

Attending her husband's memorial service earlier that day had left Anita emotionally drained, but she was determined to do this interview. She stared into the camera lens, waiting for the camera operator to give her the cue she was patched through to the journalist who was broadcasting from a skyscraper in New York City.

Suddenly, Anita heard his clear voice coming through her earpiece. She kept her eyes focused on the camera as the host offered his condolences for her loss.

Anita was prepared and ready. While she didn't have anything especially lofty or winsome to say on television that night—she wasn't concerned with impressing viewers with her speaking ability—the thirty-one-year-old widow did have a specific message she wanted to share with the world, and this interviewer was about to give her the opportunity.

Nodding to the camera to offer a quick "thank you so much," she listened for the journalist's first question. Not surprising, it was about Anita's husband, Ronnie, asking about the comments his students had been making about him. They were remarks Anita had seen as well, descriptions of Ronnie as a "light" and a "silver lining in a tumultuous city."

Anita drew a breath and took a brief moment to gather her thoughts: *What do I want people to know about my husband?*

ele

BENGHAZI, LIBYA
TWO WEEKS EARLIER

Ronnie Smith unraveled the knot of his necktie and tossed his dress shirt onto the bed. With his dark, closely cropped hair, he blended easily into the ethnic diversity of Libya. Even though he was American, a native of Detroit, people on the streets often assumed he was Turkish.

It was an unusual day for the high school chemistry teacher. Typically, Ronnie's responsibilities kept him at the International School of Benghazi until at least three in the afternoon. However, with his students taking their midterm exams, he'd been able to leave work early and go for a midday jog.

Ronnie laced up his tennis shoes and opened the door to his apartment. The Mediterranean air felt cool against his skin as he ran down the stairs of the building where he and his family had lived for less than a year. He couldn't wait to join his wife, Anita, and their two-year-old son, Hosea, who had flown back to the States for the holidays. Just one more week, and Ronnie would be on his way.

elle

Ronnie and Anita first met during freshman orientation at Wayne State University in Detroit when Ronnie, a chemistry major, was grouped with Anita, a future pharmacist. A fast friendship developed. They spent hours together in the lab and in difficult classes studying high-level math and science. Anita loved Ronnie's sense of humor and sarcasm, his athleticism and quick smile.

Anita's church background differed from that of her future husband. Raised by Assyrian Catholic parents who immigrated to the United States from Iraq, Anita grew up attending mass on significant holidays with her family. Though Anita observed her mother participating in the traditional sacraments and could recite religious doctrines, Anita had not understood the importance of developing a personal relationship with Jesus Christ. But through Ronnie's influence, Anita became aware of her need for a Savior, and of her Heavenly Father who desired to know her personally.

Ronnie grew up in a Christian home. His parents served in leadership within their Pentecostal church community, and Ronnie frequently participated in the youth group. In college, Ronnie remained active in his church. He picked up Anita in his white Saturn one Sunday and took her to his church. For the first time, Anita learned that Jesus wanted a relationship with her, and that true repentance leads to a shift in lifestyle and desires.

Over their shared interests and her growing faith, Ronnie and Anita fell deeply in love. They were married after graduation in a joyful summer wedding and then moved to Austin, Texas, where

Ronnie worked on his master's degree in chemistry and Anita started her career as a pharmacist.

In Texas, they discovered a year-old, Bible-based congregation that gathered in a downtown high school. The church taught and lived out being the hands and feet of Jesus and sharing God's love with those in desperate need of it. Anita joined their refugee ministry and devoted countless hours to loving and serving the Middle Eastern refugees who had arrived in Austin.

"Why do you want to come and help us?" they asked Anita, over and over again.

"God gave us love," she said, "and we're trying to show that to you."

At the church, Ronnie developed such a passion for understanding and articulating the Word of God that—though he was pursuing a PhD in chemistry—he instead decided to go to seminary.

Ronnie and Anita's son, Hosea, whose name means "salvation," came into their lives several years after they married and just as Ronnie completed his seminary training. The couple began thinking about what they would do next with their lives. Should they stay in Austin and continue serving at their church, or should they move to share God's love in another place?

As Ronnie and Anita prayed for guidance, Anita became more involved in their church's outreach work. They enrolled in a small group Bible study where they discovered the need for Christians to share the love of God in their neighborhoods, communities, and to the ends of the earth, even if it meant discomfort, danger, or sacrifice.

The intensive Bible study covered different topics, but it was the one on suffering for Christ that resonated with Anita. During that class, the couple read a chapter from *Foxe's Book of Martyrs* and began praying for persecuted Christians around the world.

They prayed for the Christians ministering in difficult places, suffering for their faith, and that all believers would have strength to be unashamed of Jesus Christ. Anita began to reflect deeply on what it meant to suffer for her beliefs. *Persecution is not an "if" thing, it's a "when" thing. Christ's followers can't escape suffering. It's part of the Christian life.*

This thought was new to Anita, who was still relatively young in her faith. She had been a Christian only five years, and yet she felt compelled to pray that the Holy Spirit would give her a spirit willing to embrace suffering for the sake of Christ. Not in a foolish or unwise way—she didn't want to suffer for the sake of suffering or put herself in unnecessary danger. Rather, she prayed for a humble willingness, a reverence and calm assurance that would enable her to follow Christ wherever He took her family.

When Anita returned home from her Bible study one day, she said, "Ronnie, I want you to know I am praying that we will undergo suffering."

He looked at her, a bit confused. "You're praying for us to undergo suffering?"

"Well, yes," she said. "Through suffering, we're going to learn how to persevere and have stronger faith."

Ronnie wrestled with that idea too. What would this mean for their future? Was God calling them to share the love of Christ in a place where it would be dangerous to do so?

It was during this time the couple heard a sermon by Pastor John Piper that had a profound influence on them. "[T]he volatility in the world today against the church is not decreasing," Piper said. "It is increasing . . ." Referring to Colossians 1:24[1], Piper said,

---

1. "Now I rejoice in my sufferings for your sake, and in my flesh I am filling up what is lacking in Christ's afflictions for the sake of his body, that is, the church" (Colossians 1:24).

"Paul's self-understanding of his mission is that there is one thing lacking in the sufferings of Jesus: *the love offering of Christ is to be presented in person . . . to the peoples for whom He died.* And Paul says he does this in his sufferings."[2]

"Golgotha is not a suburb of Jerusalem," Piper shared. "Let us go with him outside the gate and suffer with him and bear reproach."[3]

Those words, echoing in their hearts, confirmed Anita's prayer and influenced not only their theological passion for showing Christ's love, but also the geographical trajectory of their lives.

Ronnie and Anita sensed God calling them to do something other than church planting in the US.

They prayed for God to show them an area of the world where they could share His love. And after going on a trip to Tunisia, the couple decided to move to North Africa.

Anita's family, however, stood completely against the idea. "You're throwing yourself in the fire," her mother warned, drawing on a familiar Assyrian quote. "You don't have the ability to do this. You're young Americans; you don't know the culture we lived in. You can't do it. You don't even know the language!"

"Then we'll learn it," Anita gently assured her.

Anita knew it was going to be a painful transition. The cost of being obedient to Christ would tear her family apart, impacting her relationship with her mother most of all. The decision to follow Jesus meant leaving the comforts of America, the comforts of home; but it also meant leaving behind a family that didn't understand or embrace her decision. Hosea was her mother's only grandchild. To move him across the world and separate the two of them was a huge disappointment for her mother. At every

---

2. John Piper. "Doing Missions When Dying Is Gain." October 27, 1996.

3. Hebrews 13:13

juncture, Anita's desire to move was met with opposition from her family.

Eventually, Ronnie and Anita decided to move to the North African country of Libya, a land fraught with internal warfare and crisis since the nation's leader, Muammar Gaddafi, had been removed from power only a year earlier.

Living in Libya would be dangerous, undoubtedly. But Ronnie and Anita felt ready to leave behind their family and American lifestyle to show the people of Libya that the love of Christ was more important than physical comfort. Believing that all things work together for the good of God's people and that to die is gain, they decided to serve God in a land that desperately needed His love.

It wouldn't be long, though, before the couple's commitment to demonstrate the love of Christ—knowing it could cost them— was put to the test.

⁓

Four months before Ronnie and Anita moved to Libya, Islamic militants attacked the US diplomatic compound in Benghazi. In the nighttime ambush, four Americans were killed, including the US ambassador to Libya.

Ronnie and Anita were living in Alexandria, Egypt, at the time, preparing for life in Libya, learning Arabic and other skills they would need to form deep relationships with people in their new culture. Not long after they had arrived, Ronnie learned of a position teaching chemistry at a school in Libya. Since Ronnie had not used his chemistry degree in about eight years, he and Anita believed God was showing them an opportunity to share His peace with war-torn Libya, and their time in Egypt was cut short.

While the attack on the diplomatic compound rattled the entire world, it did not discourage Ronnie and Anita from moving

to an apartment in Benghazi. When they arrived in the city in January 2013, political tensions were at an all-time high. The sound of explosives detonating at night became so commonplace that Ronnie and Anita's neighbors even joked about them. "Have you gotten used to the bombs yet?" their Libyan friends asked. The US State Department had also warned all US citizens against traveling to the city.

For Ronnie, who lived an extremely disciplined life and settled quickly into the daily routine of teaching at the International School, the transition to Benghazi had been a fairly easy one. He loved his students and enjoyed joking around with them. They loved him, too, and in rudimentary, heavily accented Arabic, Ronnie spent hours talking to them about life, delving into deep and meaningful conversations that challenged and inspired them. On his Twitter profile, which his students regularly visited, Ronnie described himself as "Libya's best friend," an affectionate moniker bestowed upon him by his students.

Anita's life in Benghazi was far more cloistered than her husband's. It was unusual for a woman to be outside alone, so she stayed in the apartment most of the time, taking care of Hosea, who was now a toddler. For a while, she didn't know any of her neighbors and didn't have a car. When the weather warmed to the mid-eighties, she and her young son absconded to the flat rooftop of the apartment building. There, she could wear a T-shirt and shorts, and Hosea could splash and play in his blue bucket. When he outgrew the bucket, Ronnie and Anita bought their son a kiddie pool.

Soon, Anita began forming relationships with her neighbors. When she visited her friend's house in a nearby apartment building, she walked quickly in her beige hijab, trying her best to appear as Libyan as possible.

She befriended the family who lived in the apartment below her own, and on Thursday or Friday evenings, the women sat on the floor eating and drinking tea while their children played. When she and Ronnie bought a car, Anita loaded her neighbors and their children into the small vehicle and drove them all to the beach.

Anita found it easy to talk to the women about God. "What do you believe about Jesus?" her new friends asked. "What do you believe about Muhammad?"

For Anita, showing God's love to her new neighbors was a relational activity. Like Ronnie, she wanted to forge friendships with the people of Libya, and they were easy to love—friendly and hospitable, and always looking out for their American neighbors.

Libya was experiencing enormous civil and social unrest. After the execution of Gaddafi, rogue militias took over different sections of Benghazi. The city became a hotbed for terrorist attacks, and Christians were encouraged to stay indoors for their safety. When one of these militias caused strife in a nearby outdoor recreation area, Ronnie's friends quickly informed him and urged him to shelter in place. "Please don't go out there to go jogging," they said. "If you're going to do anything, just run in our neighborhood."

The area was quiet, and Ronnie usually felt safe enough to enjoy his runs. But as the city became increasingly tumultuous, a close friend advised Ronnie to reconsider even those neighborhood jogs.

On October 5, 2013, US Army Delta Force operators seized al-Qaida operative Abu Anas al-Libi in a pre-dawn raid in Tripoli, Libya, just 600 miles up the coast from Benghazi. The resulting political unrest threatened the safety of the Americans living in the city, so Anita's neighbors took extra effort to protect her as well. "Stay indoors," they warned her. "We'll pick up your groceries for you."

ele

The stress of living in Libya had taken its toll on Anita. Though she knew God had called her family to Benghazi, she often battled the fear that one of them might be kidnapped—a fate even worse than death. She sometimes wondered how she could ever bear not knowing what had happened to Hosea or Ronnie.

In November, she and little Hosea boarded their flight to the United States to be with family for the holidays. As the plane lifted off, Anita looked out the window at the Libyan soil below and felt an immense sense of relief. She and Hosea had made it out safely. They'd be back after the new year, but for the moment, Anita felt like she had escaped. *Now,* she thought, *Ronnie just has to get out.*

On December 1—while Anita and Hosea were still in the United States, and Ronnie was administering mid-term exams in Benghazi—al-Qaida decided to respond to the US military's October raid. Adam Gadahn, a US-born convert to Islam who once served as Osama bin Laden's spokesman, denounced Abu Anas al-Libi's capture and urged his Libyan followers to "teach the Crusaders[4] a lesson they will not forget." He urged them to "rise up and take vengeance against America, the enemy of Islam and the Muslims."

Gadahn's goading was well received in Libya, and in Benghazi it became even more dangerous to be identified as an American citizen.

---

4. "Crusaders" is a term of derision used by Islamists today. It hearkens back to the medieval Crusades from the 11th to the 13th centuries when Christian powers fought militarily to retake the Holy Land from the Muslims and recapture formerly Christian territories, among other aims.

ele

BENGHAZI
DECEMBER 5, 2013
11:30 A.M.

Inside a car parked on the street, a man who lived in Anita and Ronnie's neighborhood waited patiently for his elderly mother to exit her home. He looked up as Ronnie jogged past his vehicle. Moments later, he noticed four men in a black Jeep following Ronnie.

"Are you an American?" he heard one of the men ask Ronnie. From inside the car, the man could hear the brief conversation, and he was relieved when the Jeep drove away. He watched as Ronnie continued his jog, keeping close to the curb as he ran.

Moments later, the man in the car noticed the black Jeep once more. It had circled the block and was again following Ronnie. The Jeep turned the corner, and suddenly rapid-fire gunshots pierced the air. Ronnie's body crumpled on the side of the road, his torso riddled with bullet holes and blood pouring from his body.

Neighbors heard the gunshots and called for an ambulance. The medics arrived quickly and loaded Ronnie's body onto a gurney. They rushed him to the hospital, but it was too late. Ronnie was already dead.

ele

DETROIT, MICHIGAN
8:30 A.M.

Anita wiped the oatmeal from her toddler son's cheeks, smiling to herself as she cleaned his chubby, sticky fingers. The warm breakfast felt especially comforting on such a cold December morning.

Christmas was three short weeks away, and Anita was excited to celebrate the season in Texas with Ronnie and his family. In the weeks since they'd been apart, Anita had spoken to Ronnie on a video call, but she longed to have him by her side. It would be wonderful to be together again, spending the holidays with their friends and family. Anita couldn't wait to be back with Ronnie in the familiar places where they had first sensed God's unique calling on their lives. So much had changed since their early days in Texas.

As Anita finished cleaning up the breakfast remains while chatting with her mother and older sister, her cell phone rang. She glanced at the clock.

Eight thirty. It's a little early for a call.

Anita wiped her hands and glanced down at the screen. It was an incoming video call from her friends in Benghazi, an American couple she and Ronnie knew well. She answered the call and found herself face to face with both her friend and the young woman's husband.

"Anita?" he asked. His serious tone matched the strained look on his face. "Are you with Hosea? Can you find somewhere private to sit down?"

Slipping out of the kitchen, Anita walked down the short hallway to her mother's bedroom. She closed the door and sat on the bed.

Anita's friend took a deep breath as tears filled her eyes. Her husband stared gravely at the phone. Finally, he spoke.

"Anita," he said, "I'm so sorry, but Ronnie is dead."

The shock of his words rendered Anita speechless, and seconds passed as she struggled to make sense of what she'd just heard.

"What?" she finally managed to say. "No. No, that's not possible." Anita felt her stomach turn over, and she fell to her knees.

"I'm so sorry, Anita," her friend said, choking back sobs. "Ronnie's gone."

~ele~

In the aftermath of Ronnie's death, Anita's mother, sister, other family members, and friends surrounded her with support. Keeping with the traditions of her parents' culture, loved ones flooded the home. Anita appreciated their care but at times felt overwhelmed by the sheer number of people in the house. She needed to get somewhere quiet and process what had happened. Close friends from Texas arrived that night and took Anita to a coffee shop to get away from the numerous family members coming in and out of her mother's home.

Ronnie's young students hashtagged their condolences on Twitter with #ThankYouSmith. "#ThankYouSmith for being a great teacher and an amazing friend," one student wrote. "#ThankYouSmith for risking your life every single day to help us reach our full potential in life," said another. "I am sorry you had to go this way."

Still in shock, Anita couldn't believe Ronnie was really gone. *How will Hosea grow up without his father? How will I go on without my best friend? What will happen to our life in Libya?*

Ronnie's students also sent messages directly to Anita, expressing their shock, sadness, and embarrassment that Libyans were responsible for their teacher's death.

As she processed her grief, Anita knew what she needed to do—what Ronnie would want her to do. She needed to speak directly to the people of Libya.

On December 12, just one week after Ronnie's murder, Anita wrote a public letter in English and Arabic, titled "An Open Letter from the Widow of Ronnie Smith to the Libyan People."

My husband and best friend, Ronnie Smith, loved the Libyan people. For more than a year, Ronnie served as a chemistry teacher in a school in Benghazi, and he would gladly have given more years to Libya if unknown gunmen had not cut his life short on December 5, 2013.

Ronnie and I came to Libya because we saw the suffering of the Libyan people, but we also saw your hope, and we wanted to partner with you to build a better future. Libya was very different from what we had experienced before, but we were excited to learn about Libyan culture. Ronnie grew to love you and your way of life, as did I. Ronnie really was "Libya's best friend."

Friends and family from home were concerned about our safety, as were some of you. We talked about this more times than I can count. But we stayed because we believed the Libyan people were worth the risk. Even knowing what I know now, I have no doubt that we would both make the same decision all over again.

Ronnie loved you all so much, especially his students. He loved to joke with you, tell stories about you, help you with your lives, and challenge you to be all that you could be. He did his best to live out his faith humbly and respectfully within a community of people with a different faith.

To his attackers: *I love you and I forgive you. How could I not? For Jesus taught us to "Love our enemies"—not to kill* them or seek revenge. Jesus sacrificed His life out of love for the very people who killed Him, as well as for us today. His death and resurrection opened the door for us to walk on the straight path to God in peace and forgiveness. Because of what Jesus did, Ronnie is with Jesus in paradise now. Jesus did not come only to take us to paradise when we die, but also to bring peace and healing on this earth. Ronnie loved you because God loves you. Ronnie loved you because God loved him—not because Ronnie was so great, but because God is so great.

To the Libyan people: I always expected that God would give us a heart to love you, but I never expected you to love us so much. We came to bless you, but you have blessed us much more. Thank you. Thank you for your support and love for Ronnie and our son, Hosea, and me. Since Ronnie's death, my love for you has increased in ways that I never imagined. I feel closer to you now than ever before.

I hear people speaking with hate, anger, and blame over Ronnie's death, but that's not what Ronnie would want. Ronnie would want his death to be an opportunity for us to show one another love and forgiveness, because that's what God has shown us.

I want all of you—all of the people of Libya—to know I am praying for the peace and prosperity of Libya. May Ronnie's blood, shed on Libyan soil, encourage peace and reconciliation between the Libyan people and God.

Austin, Texas
December 19, 2013

What do I want people to know about my husband?

"Ronnie wanted to shine the light and the love of Jesus to the Libyan people that he knew," Anita said, speaking calmly and clearly, looking directly into the camera. "He really did. He didn't want any attention on himself—of being a good guy or a good teacher or the fun teacher—it was just about the love and the forgiveness that we know from God. That's what he wants to leave behind."

The host moved to his next question. He'd heard about the letter Anita had written to the people of Libya and to the men who killed Ronnie. He couldn't believe Anita was able to tell her husband's murderers that she loved and forgave them. As he shifted under the bright lights of his studio in New York, the host expressed, with a significant measure of incredulity, how extraordinary he thought Anita's action had been.

"I honestly do not have any anger toward them," Anita explained, "and I want them to know this. I don't want any revenge. I just really want them to know that I do love them, and I forgive them, and Ronnie would want this. I pray and hope that our son, Hosea, will believe this, and I pray with all of my heart that the attackers—that maybe this incident will call them to know the love and forgiveness that's found in Jesus. I really do."

The next question didn't surprise Anita. Did she feel love and forgiveness toward her husband's killers right away? For the benefit of the viewers at home, the anchor explained that it had been only a few weeks since Ronnie's death. He'd known of others who were able to arrive at a point of forgiveness months or even years after a loved one's death, but he was astounded that Anita had been able to feel those emotions so quickly. The host was a seasoned journalist, one who had covered tragedies all over the world, and he knew Anita's claims were going to surprise many of his viewers.

"The first day of the incident," Anita said, "I wasn't even thinking in regards to any emotions to the attackers, but it came really soon. It came within that evening or the second day. It's got to be God's Spirit pouring into me, replacing that anger with His love. Yeah, they took away my husband. I love my husband. But it's got to be God's Spirit that's pushing me to show them that, look, this is what God wants them to see. He wants them to see that love and forgiveness is real, even if they've done this to my husband, and I want them to see this and to know this."

She didn't feel angry? She didn't feel hatred toward the men who killed her husband? The host was visibly perplexed. He apologized for staying on the same line of questions, but he still couldn't quite understand how Anita was able to express such extraordinary mercy.

Tears welled up in Anita's eyes, and for a brief moment, she struggled to continue.

"I just envision the black Jeep driving up to him. And I don't know their faces, I just want them to know that God loves them and can forgive them for this. And I don't know them, but I just, yeah, that's how I honestly feel. It may sound crazy, but, it's God's Spirit that's putting this inside of me. And I believe it."

The host softened, and his next words were full of tenderness. He assured his grieving guest that no, he didn't think she sounded crazy. Rather, to him, he thought she sounded like a remarkable person.

Then, the interviewer shifted his attention toward the subject of Anita's young son, Hosea. What did Anita plan to tell her child when he grows up? What would she tell him about why his father was in Benghazi, what he was doing there?

Anita sensed in his tone that the interview was coming to a close; the segment was edging toward a commercial.

"We want Hosea, our son, to know that we love him so much," she concluded. "And Ronnie loved him so much. And what Ronnie and I would want as parents for Hosea is that God loves him more. And God wants him to know, just as Ronnie and I want him to know, that there's no greater thing to live your life for than to live for Jesus."

EPILOGUE
Anita would conduct other interviews with the media, in English and in Arabic, sharing the same message: forgiving her husband's killers and wanting them to know the love and forgiveness that is found in Christ.

In Her Words:
Vanda

For more than a decade, Vanda Jašek's husband Petr, a Czech citizen, led the work of The Voice of the Martyrs in Africa, requiring him to travel to dangerous places where Christians endure persecution. On December 10, 2015, when Vanda did not receive a text from her husband before his flight departed from Khartoum, Sudan, she began to worry. Soon she learned that he was arrested. Vanda shares how God used the Scriptures and the faithful prayers of the global body of Christ to sustain her during Petr's 445 days in prison.

I was aware of the danger related to Petr's work for our persecuted brothers and sisters. I had even accompanied him on several dangerous missions. But it was a big shock when he did not return home from his routine trip to Khartoum. At first we contacted our pastor who immediately initiated a prayer chain. Then our daughter contacted the Czech Embassy in Cairo and the Czech Ministry of Foreign Affairs.

Many brothers and sisters and friends encouraged us through visits, phone calls, text messages, and emails. The Lord reminded me of many encouraging Scriptures, and I was making note of them. In the early days of his imprisonment, one of the most encouraging verses that helped me to remain calm was 2 Timothy 1:7, "For God has not given us a spirit of fear, but of power and of love and of a sound mind" (NKJV).

After those first stormy days, the words from Psalm 37:5 spoke to my heart. It says, "Commit your way to the Lord; trust in him, and he will act." It is easy to say that but may be difficult to stay focused on it. It was not about my strength or determined mind.

There was an occasion when I felt like Petr would not be coming home. One day I was at a gas station, and a newspaper stand caught my attention. A big headline on the front page of the daily newspaper said: "Czech citizen arrested in Sudan facing the death penalty." This was definitely a big shock to me, and all my thoughts were like: *Is this really going to happen?*

All the while, I was mainly praying for Petr's release, and this prayer was eventually answered in due time. However, later on when we were able to communicate with Petr through letters, I found out how the Lord was using him to share the gospel with fellow prisoners. This changed my perspective and even my prayers: *How could I ask the Lord for Petr's immediate release when He wanted to use Petr to bring people to Him?* So, I prayed rather for God's will to be done in everything.

There were many answered prayers: Petr's good health despite many diseases around him, and he was able to experience the peace of the Lord in his mind and heart. One big answer to prayer was when Petr received a Bible from the Czech Consular Officer. I learned about other answered prayers after Petr's return home. We flipped through our daily devotional book and found out when the Lord had explicitly answered our fervent prayers when Petr needed them most.

I believe the reason I was able to remain calm and experience the peace of the Lord was that so many people were praying and interceding for me. The many prayers of other believers helped me to overcome my doubts and fears.

Hannelie

The One Who Was Spared

KABUL, AFGHANISTAN
NOVEMBER 29, 2014

Hannelie Groenewald walked down the stairs of her family's apartment building into the crisp autumn air. She saw Hassan was on duty at the gate surrounding the compound, and she paused to exchange a few friendly words as he opened the gate for her to leave. Hannelie's driver, Sayed, was waiting on the other side. Traffic on their morning drive would be especially chaotic; the city was on high alert for a possible attack that day and had blocked certain roads.

Hannelie's first stop was a medical conference in a lavish meeting room of the Kabul Star Hotel. The agenda failed to hold her attention, so she slipped her cell phone from her bag and texted her children—seventeen-year-old Jean-Pierre and fifteen-year-old Rodé—but neither responded. She assumed the two teenagers were still asleep, so she spent her time responding to emails on her phone. Finally, the meeting adjourned after lunch, and Hannelie was on her way.

Sayed drove Hannelie to the medical clinic where she worked as a doctor. Though she didn't typically work on Saturdays, the United Nations had received credible intelligence that a Taliban attack in Kabul was likely. They asked Hannelie and her coworkers to be on standby to care for the expected casualties. Hannelie wasn't particularly bothered. There were attack alerts often, and she suspected this would be just another ordinary day.

The afternoon was fairly quiet. Several of Hannelie's patients failed to keep their scheduled appointments, and the predicted attack hadn't transpired. When Sayed texted her around four o'clock that he was waiting outside, Hannelie was glad to leave. She climbed in the backseat of the car, and as they drove, Sayed did his best to navigate the frenzied afternoon traffic.

Ten minutes later, Sayed's cell phone rang. By the tone of his voice and the expression on his face, Hannelie could tell something was terribly wrong. Concerned, she leaned forward. "What happened?"

Sayed glanced back at his anxious passenger. There had been an attack after all, he said. Softly, he explained what had happened.

The attack had been on Hannelie's home.

Hannelie leaned back against the seat, her mind attempting to process the information. She reached for her cell phone to call her husband, Werner, but his phone only rang.

Not wasting a second, she tried calling Jean-Pierre and Rodé, but no one answered. Paralyzing fear mounted. *Maybe they tried to find shelter in the basement of the building, and they left their phones behind in the rush. Or maybe their phones were set to silent because they were too afraid of the noise drawing attention.*

For the next few minutes, Hannelie continued to frantically phone her children and her husband.

When she couldn't reach her family by phone, Hannelie focused on the congested traffic to avoid feeding the fear growing in her heart. It seemed to take forever to reach Street 5 in Karte Se. Multitudes of Afghan police officers and large armored vehicles cordoned off the streets.

As soon as Sayed parked the car near the intersection on a side street, Hannelie bolted from the vehicle, rushing toward the street where her family lived and worked. Pushing through the crowd gathered in the street, she tried desperately to move through the barricade, but the police wouldn't let her pass. She begged for information, but no one would tell her what had happened. Hannelie craned her neck for a view of the top-floor apartment where she and her family lived.

A terrible, deafening silence hung in the air. The crowd was disturbingly quiet, and even the usual cacophony of traffic, car horns, and barking dogs was absent. News of the attack had circulated throughout the city, and journalists approached Hannelie for an interview. Waving them off, she tried to withdraw from the crowd, but their cameras flashed as she walked away. Tears burned her eyes, ready to burst like water over a fracturing dam.

Hannelie cried out to God for help.

ell

2002

The tragedy of the terror attacks on September 11, 2001, introduced Hannelie and Werner Groenewald to a new chapter in their lives. At the time, they enjoyed a happy, fulfilling, and relatively easy life in an affluent suburb of Pretoria, South Africa. Hannelie worked long hours as a physician, rotating among several emergency units across the city. She earned a good salary, and at the end of each shift, she looked forward to returning home and relaxing with her family.

Her husband, Werner, was a pastor at a large church where he spent most of his days working before rushing to the nursery to pick up their two children. At night, Werner visited inactive church members and served in other ministries wherever there was an opportunity to reach out.

Werner and Hannelie were content. For them, their life was idyllic.

Neither Werner nor Hannelie was especially missions oriented. The mission field, they thought, was for "super Christians." For the adventurous. For those who held a "special key to God's throne." The Groenewalds, in contrast, thought of themselves as simple people who served in simple ways.

Not long after Islamic terrorists attacked the World Trade Center in New York City, Werner came home from work and approached his wife with a surprising idea. "I am considering going on a short-term outreach trip to Pakistan," he said softly. "There is an organized group at church that is scheduled to leave soon, and I would like to join them. Would it be okay? Of course, I would love for you to go along." Werner explained that he felt a gnawing urge to visit the country in order to pray for its people with more insight. He revealed that the idea had been on his heart for some time.

Hannelie was speechless. It was one thing for Werner to want to go on this kind of trip, but she definitely didn't want to join him. For a while, she put it at the back of her mind; she didn't want to think too much about it. And she certainly never anticipated how his desire to go on this trip would soon change their family's lives.

When the day of Werner's departure arrived, Hannelie accompanied him and the team to the airport with a heavy heart. She wished he were back already, and the trip was a pleasant memory they could look back on as they returned to their everyday lives.

At the airport chapel, Hannelie was asked to pray for the team. The request made sense as she was the minister's wife, but Hannelie sat frozen in her seat, unable to utter a word. She'd never felt comfortable praying in front of other people, and now she suddenly felt overwhelmed by the uncertainty of the journey to this dangerous country. In that moment, she realized she didn't want to let Werner go. *What if he doesn't return?*

With a trembling voice, she uttered a few words of prayer. Unable to make it past the second sentence, she fought back tears and sat in silence. After a long, uncomfortable interlude, someone else spoke up and prayed for the team's journey, for God's hand of blessing, and protection to rest upon them.

Gathering their coats and bags, the team excitedly chatted about the new adventure that awaited, but Hannelie's heart still felt heavy. She realized deep inside that her relationship with God was not what it was supposed to be. She didn't want to minister with Werner in Pakistan, and she felt ashamed that she couldn't even pray for the team. *Why can't I hear God's voice like everybody else?*

Ten days later, Werner returned from Pakistan. To celebrate his return, Hannelie booked a table at an expensive restaurant. Once they'd placed their orders, Werner looked intently at his wife. Hannelie was surprised to see his eyes filled with tears. Stories of his time in Pakistan poured from his lips, describing the difficulties the team had experienced. Nothing had worked out well, and chaos surrounded them the entire time. He told Hannelie about eerie black crows he saw everywhere he went. Their endless caws filled his soul with an unceasing sense of darkness and evil. Werner couldn't shake the feeling that the crows were a reflection of the spiritual climate of the country.

Then he told her about the day the group drove to the Khyber Pass, the mountain gorge separating Pakistan and Afghanistan where tribal warlords—not police or military—ruled. The road over the pass, known as "The Silk Road," had long been the key trade route between Central Asia and South Asia.

By this time, tears were running down Werner's cheeks. Hannelie glanced uncomfortably at the other guests in the restaurant, but her husband cried unashamedly. He had clearly experienced the Lord calling him to Afghanistan. He saw thousands of Afghans who would be eternally lost if nobody told them about the love of Jesus Christ.

It was at that moment, Werner said, while standing with both feet on the "no-man's-land" border between the two countries, that he dared to challenge God. "Lord," he said, "You know Hannelie. She will never agree to leave our comfortable life in South Africa and exchange it for a life of sorrow and difficulties in Afghanistan. You will have to call her Yourself. I can't do this."

Waiters brought their main course, and for a few moments, the couple ate in silence. Then, Werner lifted his eyes to Hannelie's once more and hesitantly asked, "Will you consider going on a short-term medical trip to Afghanistan in a few months? I'll arrange everything, but I want you to go with me."

Lost in the pool of her husband's gray-green eyes, Hannelie couldn't muster the courage to tell him no. She had no desire to go to Afghanistan, but she nodded. Silently, though, she hoped he'd forget about it all. *Surely this is just a phase he's going through, some kind of post-outreach enthusiasm or culture shock,* she thought.

But it wasn't. Just a few weeks later, Werner had enlisted enough medical professionals to form a team, and Hannelie agreed to go along. *It would be good to do something adventurous, something outside my comfort zone,* she told herself. In preparation for their trip, Hannelie and the other team members received cultural training, learning a few words in the *Dari* Persian dialect spoken in Afghanistan. Then the day arrived for their departure.

The team landed in Peshawar, Pakistan, on a Wednesday and then planned to cross the border into Afghanistan. But when they discovered a glitch with the visa process, they realized they wouldn't arrive in Kabul in time for their first scheduled medical clinic that Monday. Instead, they spent the weekend at a guest house in Peshawar and planned to worship with a local house church. As Hannelie walked to the home, she was stunned by the open sewage system. A sickening stench hung in the air as the contents of the ditches had turned green in the intense heat.

At the house church, expatriate Christians welcomed the team as they squeezed into metal folding chairs in the living room. When a group of toddlers stood up to worship the Lord with a song of praise, something strange came over Hannelie—something she'd never experienced before. The Holy Spirit touched her in a way she never thought possible. She tried to swallow her tears, but they escaped down her cheeks. Hannelie felt at peace here. In her heart, she knew God was showing her something new. This place could be her home.

She looked up at Werner and was surprised to see tears streaming down his cheeks as well. *Is this how God calls people?* she wondered. *Is this why our departure to Kabul was delayed?*

Early Monday morning, the team members received their visas, and they began the thirteen-hour journey from Peshawar to Kabul in a minibus taxi. They hired an armed soldier to accompany them on the trip as they traveled through the notorious Khyber Pass and into the Hindu Kush mountain range, an especially dangerous tribal area where terrorist groups like al-Qaida, the Taliban, and ISIS trained. These same mountains sheltered Osama bin Laden for months.

The arduous, uncomfortable journey took a total of thirteen hours. At the border checkpoint, Hannelie used the lone squat toilet. To flush, she used a bucket of water from the corner of the filthy room, while trying to keep her layers of clothing out of the way in the process. Later in the journey, she and the other ladies would use their head scarves as makeshift partitions when they needed to use the restroom; public toilets for women were nonexistent.

Dust easily found its way into the sweltering taxi once the group was back on the road. The passengers opened their windows wide and wiped the sweat from their faces with dusty hands. For hours, the unconcerned driver bounced through an endless succession of potholes and swerved around rocks. Without any extra water in the vehicle, Hannelie wondered what would happen if they broke down.

Finally, the exhausted team arrived in Afghanistan's capital city. Over the next several days, they set up mobile medical clinics in villages on the outskirts of Kabul and provided medical care for Afghan women. In the evenings, they returned to their guesthouse tired but fulfilled.

ஓ

When the Groenewalds returned home to South Africa, they felt they needed God to confirm their new calling. For Hannelie, this happened early one morning during her quiet time with the Lord. She suddenly felt the urge to turn to Luke 5:31–32, where Jesus said, "Those who are well have no need of a physician, but those who are sick. I have not come to call the righteous but sinners to repentance." Hannelie's stomach fluttered. *God has called me as a doctor to serve the sick in Afghanistan.*

Hannelie spent more time in God's Word, searching the pages for His truth. She prayed and earnestly sought His face for guidance and answers. Werner did the same. Soon, Hannelie realized her relationship with the Lord had deepened, and for the first time in her life, she experienced the Lord speaking to her through His Word. In order to be as useful as possible to the women of Afghanistan, Hannelie tried to enroll in the obstetrics and gynecology program of the University of Pretoria. After her interview with the dean of the faculty, she was put on a waiting list and told that when a vacancy for a clinical assistant became available, she would be called. For months she waited, without any response to her application.

One evening during her quiet time with the Lord, Hannelie read 1 Corinthians 7:20: "Each person should remain in the situation they were in when God called them" (NIV). She read the context of the verse and saw where the Apostle Paul repeated the same admonition three times. In that moment, Hannelie realized she didn't need to leave her expertise as an emergency room doctor and specialize in gynecology to serve effectively in Afghanistan.

Seven months later, in April 2003, Hannelie and Werner returned to Kabul to find a nonprofit organization to join, secure suitable housing, and investigate schooling options for their children, who were six and almost four. They needed to formulate a plan for fundraising and decide on a date for their family's move to Afghanistan.

That was when Hannelie and Werner encountered more challenges. When they visited the small international school, one operating out of a private home, they learned there was no available space for their children. Hannelie left the meeting wiping away tears, knowing she would have to prepare herself mentally to homeschool Jean-Pierre and Rodé.

Once again, Hannelie experienced an intense need for God to confirm their calling. That night, she and Werner, along with another South African Christian worker, made plans to visit an older Afghan woman who had been run over by a motorcycle several weeks earlier. When her clothes became entangled in the bike, she was dragged for several meters, breaking both bones in her forearm. Doctors had performed surgery—but without anesthesia.

By the time Hannelie visited the fragile woman at her home, the lady was in shock from the trauma of her procedure, along with excruciating pain and fever from the infection in her open wound. Hannelie wrote her a prescription for painkillers and antibiotics but was frustrated how the language barrier prevented her from communicating effectively. Her group prayed for the woman, for her family, and left. Deep inside, Hannelie knew the people of Afghanistan desperately needed her love and knowledge. Once again, she had an unmistakable impression that she and Werner were supposed to move to Kabul.

When it was time to share their calling with their family and friends, most were supportive and encouraged them to go where the Lord was leading. However, Hannelie's family resisted. Her parents firmly believed the Lord would never call a family with young children to go and serve in a dangerous country like Afghanistan. They strongly opposed Werner and Hannelie's plans, and the conflict drained the couple of much-needed energy during their time of preparation. Werner and Hannelie didn't want to take her parents' only grandchildren away from them, but they knew they had to obey the Lord.

Many times, the worsening relationship between Hannelie and her parents left her sitting in despair and immense discouragement. She couldn't understand why the Lord would give her such a clear calling and repeated confirmation, and yet allow these difficult circumstances to continue. Only years later did she realize God used the trials she was experiencing to grow her roots deeper in Him and strengthen her faith.

Within two months, Werner had successfully secured nearly all of the financial support the family needed to relocate to

Afghanistan. However, during this time, they also learned they would have to cancel their life insurance policies. No life insurance company would pay any death claims since Afghanistan was a war zone. The discovery deeply troubled Hannelie, and her worries kept her up at night. *What would happen to the children and to me if Werner were to die?*

Hannelie also struggled with professional questions. *If I practice medicine in Afghanistan, how will I ever be able to re-enter the medical world again in South Africa?* The old proverb, "If you don't use it, you lost it," consumed her thoughts, filling her with anxiety.

After worrying about these issues for some time, she eventually understood that God wanted her to place her worries in His hands and trust Him totally. *Jehovah Jireh*, Hannelie thought. *That is His name—the Lord, our Provider.* God wanted her to realize that He is ultimately in control, and He wanted Hannelie to trust Him for her family's financial security and the future of her medical career. She learned to trust Him to be her Helper, her Guide, and her Rock. Hannelie's job was to live each day to the fullest and give herself to Him and His purposes.

ele

2003

On the day of the Groenewalds' departure, their families gathered at the airport to say goodbye. Tears flowed freely, as if their families expected Hannelie, Werner, and their children never to return. The farewell was so emotionally draining that Hannelie made a mental note that when they returned for a visit, they would say their goodbyes at home—not at the airport.

The family of four flew from South Africa to Dubai. From there, they would continue on to Afghanistan. During their layover, sleep evaded Hannelie, and she experienced the most intense fear she had ever felt in her life. It was as if an unseen demon was striking her flesh with his fangs to suck the life out of her.

As she lay on the hard airport floor and listened to the endless drone of passenger announcements, Hannelie looked at Werner, Jean-Pierre, and little Rodé, and felt totally paralyzed. *Lord, what on earth are we doing?* In those moments, uncertainty grabbed her by the throat and threatened to choke her; she cried out to God for help. When the time arrived to move to their departure terminal, she swallowed hard at the lump in her throat, gathered her carry-on luggage, and boarded the plane.

⁓

Adjusting to life in Kabul proved to be quite an undertaking for Hannelie and her family. The turbulent, war-torn country was 99 percent Muslim, and travel within all areas of Afghanistan was unsafe due to the ongoing risks of kidnapping, landmines, suicide bombings, and insurgent attacks. Only recently had the Taliban government been overthrown, but militants still plagued the country. The Afghan police were largely uneducated and underpaid, and they often supplemented their meager salaries with bribery.

The arid climate and extreme pollution in Kabul caused a fine layer of dust to sift continuously over the city like a fine powder. Hannelie quickly learned that dusting furniture was a waste of time.

The director of the non-profit organization Hannelie and Werner would be working with helped their family get oriented to their new surroundings. But after a couple of weeks, when he traveled back to Switzerland for the birth of his first child, Hannelie and Werner were left on their own. Life was so difficult that Hannelie was ready to pack her bags and return to South Africa.

Communication was a primary hindrance, and the Groenewalds worked to learn Dari as quickly as possible. When they struggled to find enough time for formal language training, they canceled their lessons and tried to master it themselves. Hannelie soon learned that the Dari language borrowed words from many other languages, and learning it was a slow process requiring willpower, endurance, and never-ending repetition. She focused on learning the vocabulary she would most often use — household and medical phrases that would help her manage her home and treat patients.

As a South African woman, Hannelie found Afghan cultural practices to be an even greater challenge. Afghanistan is one of the most dangerous countries for females. Young girls are commonly engaged to be married by the age of twelve, often to men decades older than themselves. Islamic extremists insist that women and girls stay home and leave only when fully covered and accompanied by a male relative.

It took Hannelie four months to muster the courage to venture onto the streets on her own to buy bread. She learned that customers in Afghanistan didn't line up orderly while they awaited service, but instead forced themselves to the front in a chaotic mass. In the crowded bakery, Hannelie knew men would likely grope her bottom or rub their arms against her breasts.

While Werner and Jean-Pierre were free to wear Western clothing anywhere, Hannelie was expected to cover her body from her neck to her feet. Afghan women are expected to be fully covered in a burqa,[1] but as a foreign woman, Hannelie had to only wear a head scarf. She struggled most with the head scarf since it got in

---

1. A burqa (also spelled burka) is a conservative Muslim garment worn over a woman's clothes that envelops her entire body and face. A mesh screen covers the woman's eyes and allows her to see.

her way as she examined patients and worked among body fluids and blood.

Tall and blonde, Hannelie stood out among the Afghan people, and it was not uncommon for men and young people to harass foreign women in the streets. Hannelie soon discovered that when a woman makes a noise in the street, everyone knows she has been touched indecently; if she doesn't make a scene, the offender will assume she is a prostitute and repeat the behavior. When Hannelie broached the subject with Afghan women on visits to their homes, she was surprised to hear the women deny what she'd witnessed. *I know they are victims as well. Are they defending the men?*

Hannelie didn't share her fears with her husband. Werner was already shouldering a heavy burden at work, and she didn't want to add to his stress. Instead, when she had to leave their home, she buttoned up her loose black overcoat, pulled a large scarf over her head, walked quickly to wherever she needed to go, and worked hard to suppress her fearful thoughts.

Hannelie also discovered that young girls were often subject to unwelcome attention from men on the street, too. Whenever Hannelie had Rodé with her on the streets, she would cover her daughter's back with one hand clenched in a fist and her handbag ready to punch or slap the offender, which would accomplish the dual purposes of publicly shaming a man while protecting a woman's honor.

The streets of Kabul felt like a busy, dusty ant's nest. Only a few traffic lights functioned, and no one followed traffic rules. Whenever there was a gap, vehicles rushed in, bumping and knocking against each other in a power struggle that certainly didn't help the congestion.

In addition to the chaos outside her home, Hannelie felt uncomfortable when she visited Afghans in their homes. While she always tried to show Christ's love, she felt as if she didn't belong there. Many times, neighbors invited her to visit, but then they'd hand her booklets about Islam and explain what she needed to do to become a Muslim. At first, Rodé reluctantly accompanied her mother on these visits, but she, too, felt uncomfortable and soon refused to go.

Sometimes at night, Hannelie stood on the roof of their home and watched the neighboring houses. She wanted to understand more about the Afghan people and their daily lives. During the day, their curtains were usually tightly drawn, keeping sunshine and fresh air outside the musty homes. But when their curtains were open, Hannelie could catch a glimpse of the Afghan households. She saw extended families living together, and when the homes were small, this living arrangement led to quarreling among the multiple wives and among in-laws. Women rarely left the home; men often sat outside on their empty verandas, squatting motionless and staring at nothing for long periods of time.

To Hannelie, the Afghan lifestyle seemed empty, as if the men hadn't yet discovered how different it would be to feast with their wives and children in the cool shade of the trees. Instead, the women—the heartbeat of every home—were left at home without any voice and without any rights. They were locked inside, bound to bear children, raise them, and look after the household chores.

In time, the Groenewalds settled into a familiar routine. They gathered each morning at seven o'clock and enjoyed coffee, cereal, and family devotions. Werner was in his office by 8:00 a.m., and Hannelie prepared to homeschool six-year-old Jean-Pierre and four-year-old Rodé. Eventually, Rodé was accepted into a preschool program while her older brother stayed home and raced through both first and second grades in a single year. Ultimately, both children gained admittance at the local international school.

Werner spent each day training Afghans in community development, agricultural skills, and English. All the training material had to be translated into Pashtu and Dari. Their eight staff members—from the cleaner to the gate guard—were Afghan and joined Hannelie, Werner, and their children for lunch each day. Hannelie and Werner talked with them like one big family, something unheard of in Afghan culture because of class prejudice and the separation of sexes. Several months would pass before their cleaning lady felt comfortable enough to sit and eat with all of them at the table.

Hannelie worked several days each week as a physician in a local medical clinic, and on the days she was home, she helped the children with their schoolwork and treated patients in the basement of their home. She, along with Werner, also visited South African prisoners in the Pul-e-Charkhi prison east of Kabul, a notoriously harsh penitentiary known for torture and executions. In order to win the favor of prison guards, she would dole out medical advice and prescriptions to them when needed.

As she served the people of Afghanistan, Hannelie soon experienced a change of heart. In the first difficult months of adjustment, she felt the Lord helping her and revealing His character to her. The promises of the Bible gained new meaning to Hannelie and pulled her from the dark well she was in. God showed her that He really is love, and that He cares for those who sincerely seek Him.

Hannelie had always loved music, and she longed to play an instrument again. She slowly learned to play the guitar and started to experience a wonderful satisfaction when worshiping the Lord. While she'd previously lived only for herself and her family, Hannelie now opened a loving hand to some of the poorest people on earth. The feeling of joy and satisfaction she felt in her new work lifted her up amid arduous circumstances. She felt like she could embrace this new life.

Nine years after moving to Kabul, the Groenewalds' pastor from South Africa made a short visit to Kabul to convey some bad news: the large church Werner and Hannelie belonged to would be cutting their financial support by almost half. The South African economy had experienced a downturn, and the church was struggling financially. Shortly afterward, Werner and Hannelie learned that several of their other supporters could no longer afford to continue their financial support either.

It would be nine long months before the Groenewalds could return to South Africa to raise more funding, so they took a close look at their situation and realized they'd have to drastically cut expenses. They removed Jean-Pierre from the private school he'd been attending; their son was devastated. He thrived on the social interaction of school and had wonderful relationships with his classmates. He served proudly on the student council, appeared on the academic honor roll, and spent hours playing sports. Jean-Pierre experienced isolation and depression after the difficult transition to return to homeschooling.

By the following year, the family's financial situation had deteriorated even more, and Werner pitched the idea of moving the family into the apartment above his office, just a few blocks away. The proposed change upset Hannelie. Their spacious home was surrounded by fruit trees, a grapevine, and a beautiful rose garden.

She made jam and candy from the abundance of prunes and apricots and enjoyed giving them as gifts to neighbors and coworkers. Their front yard held a plastic swimming pool where the family could cool down in the summers, the backyard had a wide veranda, and they loved having space to offer hospitality through traditional South African barbecues. Hannelie's family was happy here, and she didn't want to leave.

She tried to picture their family in a small apartment. The tiny kitchen and building were unsuitable for entertaining. The children wouldn't have freedom to move around, and the Afghan workers would be present constantly. The prospect of moving looked unappealing, but Hannelie knew they would be able to save on rent, utilities, and the salaries of their two gate guards.

Friends and coworkers warned Werner and Hannelie about the danger of combining their office and home in one building. It would leave them exposed as a family in the event of an attack, but the Groenewalds knew they had no other option. Hannelie remembered their days preparing to leave South Africa for Afghanistan, when they canceled their life insurance policies and were struck by the harsh reality of their new chosen home. Through the years, the South African government had made it clear they were not prepared to help any citizen who ended up in trouble abroad. Hannelie and Werner knew they were on their own as a family if anything were to happen to them.

Life in Afghanistan had always been a risk, though, and God was with them. Hannelie knew their transition to this new apartment would be no different.

⟋⟍

SHANGHAI, CHINA
OCTOBER 2014

Over the summer, Werner was invited to speak in China at a special summit for humanitarian workers. The Groenewalds' coworkers frequently visited other countries to attend inspiring conferences, but they never had. As the date approached, Hannelie could tell Werner wanted to attend, but he didn't want to go without his family, so they made plans to travel together to China. It would be a good opportunity to spend time together away from the stress of life in Kabul, especially since they'd had to miss a planned vacation in June. It also was a needed break from the rigors of the children's exam preparation back home.

Now, Hannelie sat with her son and daughter in the audience and waited for her husband to take the stage. During the previous ten days, the family had traveled throughout China, visiting the Great Wall and Tiananmen Square and consuming local street food—unfamiliar dishes they explored with enthusiasm.

Hannelie watched as her husband walked to the podium, looked out at the gathered audience, and then began to preach. She felt inspired as she listened to his sermon, "Counting the Cost for Christ." The message reminded her not to lose sight of the very reason they were called to endure hardships and pain in ministry. They had served in Kabul for more than a decade, and their work was rarely easy.

Soon, Werner's sermon drew to a close, and Hannelie nodded as her husband spoke the final words of his message: "We die only once. It might as well be for Christ."

Werner had encouraged his listeners to count the cost of following Jesus, and exactly one month later, Hannelie would realize just how steep that cost would be.

ele

THE MORNING OF THE ATTACK

When Hannelie woke at 7:00 a.m. Saturday, Werner had already been awake for several hours. He typically spent quiet time with the Lord early in the morning, usually around 5:30 a.m., while the rest of the household slept. Sometimes he went outside and stood on the rooftop to watch the sun rise over the beautiful mountains skirting the city.

But on this particular Saturday, Werner was up even earlier, around 4:30 a.m. He'd been sleeping less the past week, communicating less, and working harder. Ever since he'd returned from the conference in China, he seemed withdrawn and focused on the work he had to complete before the family's holiday departure for South Africa on December 12.

Hannelie dressed and walked quietly downstairs, careful not to wake the children. She prepared to spend her Saturday in the clinic, and she wondered if the predicted attack would come to pass.

For weeks, nearby bomb attacks had rattled the Groenewalds' neighborhood. Security in Kabul was deteriorating as the Taliban gained more ground, especially after the inauguration of the new president of the Islamic Republic of Afghanistan.

On two other occasions, as Hannelie's driver drove her to the medical clinic, the car had narrowly missed being struck by devastating explosions. Hannelie knew God had protected her.

Just before 8:00 a.m., Werner said goodbye to his wife and then disappeared into his office. The Afghan staff began to arrive. Hannelie left for work, unaware that this was the last time she would see her husband alive.

ـ ele ـ

HOURS LATER

Hannelie looked up again at her apartment as the sun began to set. No one had turned on the evening lights. She was consumed by an overwhelming desire to burst through the police barricade and enter the compound gate by force. Worried for her husband and children, she sat down outside the building, and she prayed ceaselessly for the safety of her family and everyone in the building.

At 5:45 p.m., just after sunset, an eruption of gunfire shattered the silence, followed by an explosion that shook the ground.

Realizing the noise came from inside the building, Hannelie burst into tears. Onlookers in the street scattered for cover, but Hannelie didn't move until police officers ushered her away from the scene and to a neighbor's home, two houses away from her own.

Gunfire and explosions continued for the next hour, rattling the windows on the far end of the neighbor's house. Finally, the Afghan police fired two rocket-propelled grenades into the top-floor apartment where she lived with her family. The explosion ignited the structure, and for half an hour, the building burned. Never in her life had Hannelie felt so petrified and helpless. She texted a few close friends, desperately pleading with them to pray.

In the darkness, she stared at the glow of her smartphone. Between texts and calls from concerned loved ones, she sought comfort from reading God's Word on her Bible app. Over and over, Hannelie pored over Psalm 91, reciting the words and believing that her family was, somehow, okay. "*Whoever dwells in the shelter of the Most High will rest in the shadow of the Almighty. I will say of the Lord, 'He is my refuge and my fortress, my God, in whom I trust.' Surely, He will save you from the fowler's snare and from the deadly pestilence. He will cover you with His feathers, and under His wings you will find refuge; His faithfulness will be your shield and rampart. You will not fear the terror of night . . .*" (NIV).

From Psalm 91, Hannelie reminded herself that "*If you say, 'The Lord is my refuge,' and you make the Most High your dwelling, no harm will overtake you, no disaster will come near your tent. For He will command His angels concerning you to guard you in all your ways*" (NIV).

Soon, she felt calm. She trusted with her whole heart that her family was alive and well, that they were just hiding, and that she would see them within an hour or two. This was just an ugly nightmare that would soon end.

But a deep-seated fear lurked in the back of her mind. *What if they aren't okay?*

At 7:30 p.m., a friend following the news informed Hannelie that the attack was over, and six hostages had been released unharmed. One was a boy. Relief washed over Hannelie. *This can only be Jean-Pierre!* He was the only boy in the house.

Minutes later, in the midst of her intense relief that her son was safe, a high-ranking police officer and his colleague approached to ask her a seemingly endless list of questions: What were the Groenewalds doing in Afghanistan? Who did they work for? How many employees did they have? What kind of projects were they running?

Hannelie responded to each question, certain that her cooperation would lead to information on the status of her family, but the officers refused to tell her anything. Nevertheless, she expected that Jean-Pierre was now safe, and she hoped Werner and Rodé would surely be right behind him.

When the two men left, Hannelie's phone rang once more. Two close friends and coworkers, James and Ron, asked if they could come retrieve her. When they arrived, though, she noticed they both looked grim.

The men guided Hannelie toward a group of chairs, and all three sat down. James cleared his throat and clasped his hands, struggling to convey the terrible news they had received. Finally, he spoke, hesitantly. "Hannelie," he said, "this is going to be the longest night of your life."

Hannelie looked back in confusion. "Why?" she asked. "Which one has been injured?"

James' eyes filled with tears. "Hannelie," he said, "all three of them have been killed." With the back of his hand, he wiped his eyes. "I am so very sorry."

Hannelie stared in disbelief. *It can't be true!* She felt as if someone had punched her hard in the stomach. Hadn't she just learned that Jean-Pierre was freed? Her chest felt like she was suffocating under the weight of a massive boulder. Finally, she nodded, but inside her mind swirled.

Lord, what about Your promise of protection in Psalm 91? I believed nothing would happen to them! I believed You were with them to protect them! Lord, where were You?

Where are You now?

⟳

Immediately, the Taliban took full credit for the attack on the Groenewalds' home. A Taliban spokesman explained that they targeted the specific building because it was "a hub for missionary activity." Knowing her family abroad would soon hear the devastating news, Hannelie made the most difficult phone calls of her life, depleting any energy she had left.

That night, Hannelie stayed in the home of James and his wife, Lauren. She spent most of the night wrestling with God. She was overwhelmed by waves of intense nausea throughout the night, and as she hung her head over the toilet to vomit bitter bile, she could identify with Jesus' agony on the cross: "*My God, my God, why have You forsaken me?*"

Hannelie wished she could just release her emotions. If she could cry, maybe the heaviness would lift. But she couldn't. She tried to think of her family members, to remember Werner, Jean-Pierre, and Rodé as they'd been the previous day, and anxiety welled up inside her when she struggled to recall their faces.

Hannelie became convinced that God had left her alone, and that she must have done something terribly wrong to make Him this angry. At one point, she even questioned whether God existed at all. *Maybe He was just an illusion.* But each time the thought crossed her mind, she rejected it. Even in this unspeakably tragic situation, Hannelie knew Satan was trying to plant seeds of destruction in her vulnerable heart.

Another thought plagued her mind. *Lord, I was supposed to be there too!* she cried. *I was supposed to die with them! Why wasn't I there? I've always been at home on Saturdays. Why didn't You allow me to die with my family today?* Exhaustion hung like a heavy blanket around her, but sleep refused to come.

The next morning, Hannelie's colleagues gathered to discuss how to handle the situation. She needed to leave the country quickly and safely, but her passport and visa had been destroyed in the fire, and the closest South African embassy was in Pakistan. She was at the mercy of the Afghan government.

After countless phone calls by Hannelie, her family, the South African Ministry of Foreign Affairs, and the South African embassy in Pakistan, Hannelie received a miracle. For years, the South African government had made it clear they were unprepared to help any South African citizen who ended up in trouble abroad— but now, the embassy agreed to cooperate and issue her new travel documents. The embassy spokesperson was a kind African lady who was deeply touched by Hannelie's situation. She would later admit that it prompted her to want to know more about Jesus.

In the days to come, messages of condolence poured in from all over the world. People were sad, angered, and outraged. Chain messages of prayers circulated among smartphones, and Christians created social media pages dedicated to praying for Hannelie.

Not all of the outcry was supportive. The South African public criticized the Groenewalds' obedience to God's call because, to them, the couple's decision to live in Kabul seemed unwise. People ridiculed the family, especially Werner, and the media published heartless statements: "You never take your family to a war zone," they said. "It is irresponsible. They deserved it. They got what they were looking for, and I don't feel any sympathy for them."

The words hurt Hannelie deeply, but they did not sway the certainty of her family's calling. *Do these people really comprehend that every person has been created to fulfill a special life purpose for God's glory?* Hannelie realized how many people were still stumbling in the dark, unaware of their own true spiritual health, and she became convinced that the criticism was part of the persecution of Jesus' followers. It was part of counting the cost of obedience.

The day arrived for Hannelie to go back to what remained of her family's home and office. Utter chaos greeted her in the yard. Shattered glass and destroyed furniture and appliances were scattered everywhere.

Inside, she climbed over huge piles of building rubble. A strange chemical smell mixed with smoke hung in the air, burning Hannelie's nostrils. She looked at shoes strewn across the entrance hall floor and spotted one of Rodé's blue sneakers, which she'd purchased a few weeks earlier in China. In the entryway, tables and chairs lay upside down, and bullet holes were visible across the shrapnel-pierced walls. Hannelie had learned two suicide bombers detonated themselves within the home during the attack. She looked around and realized this must have been where it happened. In her son's room, Hannelie found more bullet holes and dark blood stains.

Hannelie searched for things to save—anything of value—but all she could find was a copy of Werner's passport, a few medical supplies, and a Mother's Day card from Jean-Pierre. With her heart racing, she shoved the meager items into a bag. *Is this all that I can save? After almost twelve years in Afghanistan?* An overwhelming reality struck Hannelie: her time in Kabul had come to an end.

In her final days in Afghanistan, Hannelie was told the attackers were most likely terrorists who had come to Werner for training. For four weeks, several men from Jalalabad—a fundamentalist city in the eastern part of Afghanistan—had come to Werner for weekend training sessions. They disguised themselves as friends and brothers in Christ.

These men had been in Hannelie's home, eaten at her table, and watched her family's every movement. Her family's killers memorized the floor plan of the house and office and secretly put their plan of action together. They knew exactly what the family's daily routine looked like, and they had been given explicit instruction to eradicate the family—a nuisance, stirring up too much trouble in Muslim circles and contributing to an unwanted spiritual revolution.

ele

As Hannelie made final preparations to leave the country, she was called to identify the bodies of Werner, Jean-Pierre, and Rodé at the International Security Assistance Force military base near Kabul International Airport. The base was the only place in Kabul with refrigeration facilities capable of preserving the bodies.

Hannelie's heart pounded in her throat and against her temples. James and Ron, the friends who had delivered the terrible news that night, stood silently behind her in support. She wasn't prepared for what would follow in the next half hour. *Can anyone be?* Her friends' presence—just being there—encouraged her, lifting her up before God's throne of love, grace, and strength.

An employee opened a refrigerated compartment, transferred a body onto a stainless-steel trolley, and pushed it toward Hannelie. Her eyes fixed anxiously on the zipper. When the employee unzipped the bag to reveal Werner's face, Hannelie was overcome with emotion and fought hard against the tears, battling to keep it all inside. She hated hysteria and promised herself to stay in control, no matter what.

Quietly, Hannelie gazed at Werner's face, swallowing the choking tears. He looked as if he were sleeping peacefully, no sign of anxiety on his face. Suddenly, her medical training took over, and the power of the Holy Spirit filled her, and she asked for a pair of gloves. She searched Werner's body to feel with her own fingers where he'd been shot. It became evident to Hannelie that the attackers hadn't aimed for the life-sustaining organs in the chest, but had instead fired at her husband's lower body and legs. It was as if they wanted him to suffer as he heard his children being slaughtered.

Next came Jean-Pierre's body, and then Rodé's. Hannelie studied her children, trying to decipher from their bodies how they had spent the moments leading up to death. Her son's face was stained with thick, black blood, and his whole body, including his chest, was full of bullet holes. What she saw didn't look like her son. Shock wrenched the air from her lungs, and her heart missed several beats as it appeared to her that he struggled to die. She examined his chest and discovered her son had drowned in his own blood.

As she viewed Rodé's small, fragile body, Hannelie was struck by the dried leaves in her beautiful, long, wavy hair. *Was she outside? Where was she found?* Hannelie wondered. She appeared to have died like her brother—suffocating and drowning in her own blood. Signs of her intense battle as she struggled to die were visible on her face.

Hannelie still couldn't cry. She buried her pain deeply, where no one could see it.

Days later, she and her friend Kate traveled to the Department of Medical Forensics, and in one final act of love, Hannelie helped prepare her family's ravaged bodies for transport back to South

Africa. As she did, she overheard a conversation in Dari among the Afghan men assigned to assist. They were astounded she was able to be present to help work on her own family members.

Hannelie looked up. "They were indeed my family," she told them. "I have forgiven the Taliban who did this to them."

Forgiveness? The men were surprised. In Islam, the idea of forgiveness meant nothing compared to the idea of "an eye for an eye and a tooth for a tooth"; forgiveness is not extended to the one who did harm to a person.

Hannelie didn't say anything further to the men and turned to Kate. "Kate, do you see that foreigners' lives here are worth nothing? They don't want us in this country, even when we are here to help. Are you ready if your time has come to die tonight? Do you know where you will spend eternity? Are you right with God?"

Kate shook her head and looked away. "I am not," she admitted. "I will not spend eternity in heaven. I have done so much wrong in my life—there is no redemption for what I have done."

"Kate," Hannelie said, "that is not true. The day when Jesus was crucified, He told the criminal on the cross next to him that on that day, because he believed in Jesus to redeem him, he would be with Him in paradise. Faith is all that you need for eternal life. Jesus did everything on the cross for us to be saved. All you need to do is believe in Him and accept the gift of eternal redemption."

In her cloud of emotions, Hannelie was amazed by this wonderful opportunity to share Christ's sacrifice for humanity. No sin was too big for Christ to forgive. And in that moment as Hannelie talked about forgiveness, the process of healing unknowingly began to take place in her own heart.

℮

Six days after her family was killed, Hannelie found an online blog Jean-Pierre had begun just two months before his death.

In his third and final post, he wrote these words that soothed Hannelie's heart:

All in all, I love this country. I love the life I'm living. I wouldn't change any of it, even if I could. I've grown in myself, and in God. The tough times are only temporary, but God is there permanently and He is constantly blessing us.

Shortly after that, a British woman shared with Hannelie a vision she'd had a few days after the attack. In it, Werner, Jean-Pierre, and Rodé were standing with Jesus and watching Hannelie deal with the terrible situation she now found herself in. They weren't sad, however, because they knew what was ahead. They were excitedly cheering her on.

"Come on, Mom! Come on, Hannelie! We're waiting for you! There's more for you to do there, but your turn will soon come! Keep going! Keep running! You'll soon be with us, and it's fantastic here!"

The vision comforted Hannelie, and it became more vivid and real to her as time passed. It motivated her to tirelessly focus on the finish line, running with the torch of "life through Christ" held high in her hand. Hannelie was running toward Jesus and toward her family. Even in the midst of her grief, her goal was not to give up. She would be a living witness of God's love, care, protection, and faithfulness. She would find purpose in why her life had been spared, and she would live that purpose to God's glory.

For several months after her family's murder, Hannelie felt unsure about what God really expected of her. *Am I supposed to continue with life as an international aid worker, or am I supposed to stay in South Africa and create a new life?* There were so many opportunities, so many voices offering guidance, but she felt no clear direction.

Soon, one thing became clear to Hannelie: she had to share her story. Prior to the attack, she shied away from public speaking and gladly let Werner have those opportunities. But now, she shared with confidence and zeal.

"The biggest challenge for me," Hannelie said, "is not only to be willing to die for Jesus, but to continue to live for Him, to be His ambassador in the world in a way that will make Him proud.

"I definitely don't understand much about how things really work in life, how things work in the spiritual realm, why God decides to allow some things and not others. I don't know why He blesses some people while others suffer. I don't know why He protects some people and others are killed.

"All I can say is that God takes each of us on an individual journey with Him to accomplish His purposes in and through us. My journey forces me on my knees to become quiet at His feet while His voice resonates in my ears: 'Be still and know that I am God.'"

ele

Just six months after the deaths of her husband, son, and daughter, Hannelie reflected on the tremendous loss. "I was not prepared to lose my husband and children in one single attack," she said. "Can anyone be? I knew something could happen, but only after it had happened did I realize that God gave me His grace to overcome this." Comparing receiving God's grace to a boarding pass a traveler receives, she said that "we get the boarding pass just before boarding the plane. Not a week before. This is just the same."

Then Hannelie said something that demonstrated the profound way the Lord was shaping her perspective on her family's deaths. "I am so glad that Werner, Jean-Pierre, and Rodé were chosen to die as martyrs for Christ. What a wonderful honor. As a family, we lived for Christ. They died for Christ.

"From a human perspective, it doesn't make sense. From an eternal perspective, it was gain, and God will be glorified in this. Satan tried to steal their lives and my joy; he murdered my family. His name is Murderer and Thief.

"But he forgot that God always has the last move. The blood shed by my family and the two Afghan brothers who died in the attack was not shed in vain. It will deliver a big harvest of Afghan people who will come into God's kingdom.

"That, I am absolutely sure of."

EPILOGUE
Hannelie returned to her native South Africa to bury her family and mourn, eventually writing a book about her experience. She remarried and continued to travel and speak in South Africa and abroad until coronavirus brought her travels to a halt. She now serves full time in a medical practice and still shares her story and her faith with troubled patients facing difficulties.

In Her Words:
Maria

Maria and her husband are front-line workers advancing God's kingdom in Cuba. They've been detained and interrogated multiple times during their years of ministry inside the Communist country.

When I was about 13 years old, my dad was a pastor in the Cuban city of Holguin. We had gotten copies of a book called *Tortured for Christ*. It was forbidden by the government to read this book. One of the church leaders got word that government officials were coming to check the house, so he and I started burning those books. Afterward, we cleaned up the ashes so when the government came, they couldn't find the books.

If they had found my dad with those books, he would have gone to prison. We didn't even understand why that book was so dangerous. We hadn't even read it yet. When I was older, I read the book. Pastor Wurmbrand suffered so much, much more than we had suffered. In that book, I discovered that I would freely die to take the gospel. It is worth the price.

When we were in difficulties, I felt the power of prayer. There was a season when I was afraid. During interrogations with Cuban officials, I would shake when they were asking me questions. I felt like I couldn't breathe. But then one day, I started praying. *God, listen, You have chosen me for this job. You have to take this fear away.* God worked in me and I am no longer afraid. I don't even know how this happened. I used to be afraid of flying in airplanes, and I have lost my fear of flying.

Now when I travel to Cuba, my family doesn't want me to go back there. "Aren't you afraid?" they ask. "No, what can they do to me?" I respond. "If they send me to prison, well, good, because I will be famous for being in prison for Christ, just like the apostles. I have seen how they died." So, I continue to go back, and though I know the Cuban government is following me, they never say anything to me. And the fear has left.

You can listen to the interview with Maria and her husband Pedro by visiting vomradio.net/maria.

Helen Berhane

"Why Don't We Sing?"

MAI SERWA PRISON
NEAR ASMARA, ERITREA
2003

Helen Berhane's emaciated wrists ached from being bound behind her back for most of the previous day.

"Why is this so hard for you to do, Helen?" the interrogator asked, shaking his head in disappointment. She could hear the exasperation in his voice.

"All I want is for you to stop singing," he said.

He then took a single sheet of paper and slid it across the desk to Helen. He tapped his pen on the document, drawing her eyes downward.

"Read this, Helen," he said.

She scanned the paper. It stated that she would stop believing in her new faith, that she would stop singing, preaching, and spreading the gospel. When she reached the bottom of the page, her eyes rested on the blank space awaiting her signature.

"I will not sign it," the twenty-nine-year-old said defiantly, looking her interrogator in the eye. Helen knew the risks involved in refusing to sign the statement. She'd likely spend years in prison, possibly even die there. But even so, she would never renounce her relationship with Jesus Christ.

The interrogator tried once more. "All you have to do is give up being a Christian, and we will let you go. Just say the word," he urged, "and we will believe you."

Helen said nothing. The man sighed. "Return this woman to her cell to collect her belongings," he told the waiting guard.

Helen was not about to be released.

∽ℓℓ

Helen grew up in Asmara, the capital city of the East African country of Eritrea. As a child, she loved to sing. Her parents worked as nurses in the large local hospital, and the family attended the Orthodox church near their home. By the time Helen turned eight, she knew the Scriptures and knew she was a Christian.

When Helen's younger sister was born, their father built a larger home across town for his growing family. There, the members of her new church nurtured Helen's singing gifts, and the young girl began writing praise songs and performing them before the congregation. When she turned fourteen, Helen was baptized and decided to devote her life to doing the work of God.

Music continued to play an important role in Helen's life, and she used her singing talents as an integral part of her gospel ministry. She also spent significant time caring for sick neighbors in their homes, especially those who turned to witch doctors for healing. When she saw the telltale signs of a witch doctor's involvement—a prayer or curse folded into a scrap of leather and tied around the patient's neck—Helen shared the gospel and prayed for the patient. Often, these men and women abandoned the witch doctor's remedies after Helen prayed. She knew God was using her in powerful ways to accomplish His work.

Just after her sixteenth birthday, Helen returned home from school eager to finish composing a song for that week's church service. But before she made it to her bedroom, the family's maid, Ruth, intercepted her with a message. "Helen, your mother wants to see you."

Helen found her mother preparing dinner in the kitchen. "We've arranged a holiday for you," her mother told her. "You are going to Ethiopia, to Addis Ababa." Helen would be staying with family friends.

Addis Ababa! Helen thought excitedly. She'd never traveled far beyond her home, and now she would have the chance to meet new people in a new city. Helen hurried to her room to begin packing. But just before she left the kitchen, she saw a look of apprehension flash across her mother's face.

When the day of Helen's journey arrived, her parents walked her to the door. "I hope you will enjoy your time away," her mother said, smoothing her daughter's hair and smiling uneasily. Helen caught the brief glance exchanged between her parents. "You are going to meet someone who is very important to our family," her mother continued, "and who will also be very important to you." She then explained to Helen the real purpose of her trip: to marry a man twenty years older.

As Helen traveled to Addis Ababa, she thought about the arranged marriage. She knew it wasn't unusual for parents to make such arrangements, as they still occurred in Eritrea. In her culture, the bonds between families were significant. The man she was to marry was an important friend of Helen's family, and the marriage would further strengthen the bonds between the two families. Plus, she wanted to respect her parents' wishes.

Not long after her arrival in the new country, and just as she'd started to adjust to the idea of the arranged marriage, Helen's parents unexpectedly arrived. While she was happy to see them, she wondered what had prompted their visit since she assumed she would be returning home soon. But that was not the case. They were there for her wedding. It would happen sooner than Helen realized, and she would not be returning to Asmara.

Helen swallowed her fear and prepared for marriage. *I wish I'd had the chance to say goodbye to my school friends,* she thought.

ℕ

Helen, at age sixteen, wed the thirty-six-year-old man she barely knew and began her newlywed life in Ethiopia. Her new husband was not a Christian, and the marriage was unhappy. The couple had little in common. After a year, they moved back to Helen's hometown of Asmara in Eritrea.

Several years later, Helen gave birth to her daughter, Eva. When Eva was six months old, Helen's husband left for Sweden, where he'd spent some of his bachelor years. Initially, Helen wasn't concerned. But when he continued to make frequent trips and his time at home grew shorter, Helen knew there was a problem. On his final trip home, he presented Helen's father with an envelope containing divorce papers. With this act, her husband initiated the process of family arbitration that would, eventually, dissolve her marriage.

Helen was crushed. She viewed marriage as sacred in the eyes of God, and now hers had ended. But she had no choice in the matter. Even though she knew her husband had felt obligated to get married, just as she had, and they were both unhappy, she could never regret a relationship that produced her beloved daughter.

When the divorce was finalized, Helen's husband provided some money to help support her and Eva. Almost immediately,

Helen knew just what she wanted to do with the settlement money. She bought a beauty salon in the affluent part of the city of Asmara where she could help others and share her faith.

But life as a divorced woman wasn't easy; divorce is generally frowned upon in her culture. Helen hadn't made the decision to get married, and she hadn't made the decision to get divorced; yet, she was still blamed. "Oh, look," ladies in her church whispered to each other. "Here comes The Divorcee. What does she think she's doing here?"

Helen tried to explain her situation to the members of her church, but they still ostracized her, leaving her to sit alone in the back of the room. She was not allowed to sing or preach or be involved in any church business. Eventually, several church members approached her to let her know she should no longer take part in the services. "A divorcee can have no place in the church," they insisted.

Helen left and was so hurt she didn't return to church again. Instead, she prayed alone at home, often throughout the night. She missed the fellowship of other Christians and felt terribly lonely, but soon God gave her a gift: the words of a new song. No matter how alone she felt, Jesus was on this journey with her. Although other people rejected her, God never abandoned her.

With a newfound fervor in her faith, Helen pored over the story of Paul in the Bible. *As a Christian*, she thought, *I must be prepared to face far greater suffering than this.* She came across Richard Wurmbrand's book, *Tortured for Christ*, and soon felt God was preparing her to suffer in His name. While enduring rejection by her Christian friends, when she had only God to turn to for comfort and companionship, Helen became convinced of one certain truth: *I need to be ready to serve Christ, even if it costs me my life.*

⁓ℓℓ

Helen flourished at her new beauty salon. She was able to talk about her faith as she braided hair and applied makeup. Her heart warmed each time she saw young brides smiling at their reflections in Helen's mirror.

But the peaceful future she'd hoped and prayed for did not become reality. Conflict brewed between Ethiopia and Eritrea, and to Helen, the atmosphere felt uneasy.

In 1998, when Eva turned four, war with Ethiopia broke out again. A small dispute erupted over a border village and escalated into full-scale fighting. The violent conflict lasted two years, and many of Helen's friends who were called up to serve in the military were killed. The bloodshed felt like a terrible waste of people's lives. *Surely God intends something better for us*, Helen thought.

At the same time, Helen began studying theology at a nearby Christian training center. She traveled to the surrounding towns and villages to sing in small churches and share her faith. Gradually, her reputation as a singer spread, and more and more churches invited her to come perform. Helen was overjoyed as she continued to have opportunities to serve God.

However, before long, Helen would find herself an enemy of the government.

⁓ℓℓ

EARLY SUMMER, 2000

Helen was walking through the busy streets of Asmara one Sunday around 8:30 p.m. She had just left a Bible study and was enjoying the summer evening, watching people bustle about.

Sensing an unmistakable prompting from the Lord, Helen knew she must obey. "Hold this for me," she said, handing her purse to a friend. "I'm going to preach."

Helen climbed the stairs to the top of a taxi stand, clapped her hands loudly, and began to speak. "We live in a great country," she said. "We may be small, but we are determined, and we have much to be proud of.

"But this war is tearing us apart. We have all lost someone. Even some of you here may not have long to live. So I believe that what our country needs now is reconciliation. God does not want to see more of His people die. Didn't Jesus tell us that we should love our neighbors? We must all pray that Eritrea and Ethiopia can find peace, and that this war will end very soon."

Looking out among those gathered, Helen saw that some of the people were crying. After a few minutes, she finished speaking and walked back down the steps. Halfway down, she noticed two men staring at her. As she stepped onto the road, the two men lunged forward and grabbed her by the shoulders, one on each side.

Secret police.

Soon, Helen found herself in front of the chief of police. One of the men who had apprehended her filed a false report that Helen had been speaking against the imprisonment of Eritreans and that the president and government should step down.

The chief waved away the two officers and then sat at his desk, folding his arms across his uniformed chest.

"Is this true?" he asked. "Were you preaching against the government?"

Helen shook her head. "I only spoke about how Jesus says we should love our neighbors, and how sad I was that so many are dying in the war. I am loyal to my country and only want to see it prosper, and I believe that for that to happen, people must have faith in God."

Late in the evening, after talking to witnesses who were present while Helen preached, the chief took Helen's name and address and told her to return the next morning.

But before she returned, Helen called her parents to let them know what was happening in case the police detained her. She wanted to ensure they and Eva knew where she was and that someone would manage the salon.

Later, as Helen sat before the police chief, he gave her an official warning: "You must never preach again."

Helen knew the man wanted her to meekly agree, but she couldn't deny God. She held her head high and said, "I will never stop preaching. The gospel cannot be stopped."

Helen left the police station with no intention of obeying the order. Soon, the strength of her conviction would be tested again.

ele

Just a week later, Helen was at a Christian gathering where she was scheduled to sing. The meeting was in a residential part of the city, and almost immediately after the group began worshiping, there was a loud banging on the door. A man stood there complaining about the noise.

"Don't you know people are trying to sleep?" he demanded. "Why should we be disturbed by your loud singing?"

The man was simply passing through the neighborhood, and though no residents had complained, the host promised the group would make sure to sing quietly.

Just as Helen began singing, she heard loud banging on the door once again. When the host opened the door this time, a group of police muscled their way into the room. Helen kept singing, refusing to let them stop her from worshiping.

The police herded the twenty Christians to the police station for interrogation.

"Why were you meeting there?" they wanted to know. Suddenly, one of the officers pointed at Helen.

"That one—she's the leader. Ask her what she was doing there."

"We only gathered there to preach and hear the gospel," Helen said. "We were not causing any disturbance, and it is not a crime to worship God. You should release us, as we have not done anything wrong."

But the police held the Christians until late that evening. Many of those detained with Helen became increasingly worried. The next day was Monday. They would lose their jobs if they were kept in prison overnight and missed work the next morning.

The group tried to encourage each other as they sat and prayed. At last, the police released them with a stern warning to stop meeting together.

But Helen would not be deterred. A month later, as she visited the local hospital to minister to the sick, she encountered a wealthy man. She saw him at the hospital frequently, waiting for patients to die so he could purchase coffins for them, claiming to do so out of charity.

Why doesn't he spend his money on medicine instead of coffins? Helen wondered, noting his odd act of generosity. She wasn't sure whether he was mentally ill or involved in one of the Eritrean "death cults" that venerate death. But his presence upset the hospital staff and the patients and their families who knew he was waiting for someone to die. Helen decided to share the gospel with him. As she began talking to him, he erupted in an angry tirade.

"You have no right to speak to me about that! How dare you humiliate me in front of these people?" He pressed his face close to Helen's and glared at her in anger as spit flew from his mouth. "Take her to the police station!" he shouted.

He was so angry that the hospital security guards decided it would be best if they did call the police. Helen soon found herself handcuffed and thrown into solitary confinement. The cell was tiny—just wide enough for her to lie down on the floor—and it was dark, hot, and airless. As the door closed behind her, Helen suppressed a cry of panic.

Leaning against the wall, Helen slid down to the floor, unable to find a comfortable position. The metal handcuffs held her arms behind her back and tightened if she so much as twitched her hands. Her fingers tingled as the circulation was cut off, and she grew dizzy.

Helen was imprisoned twenty-four hours before a guard finally came to take her to the bathroom. This pattern went on for several days. Though Helen's family brought her home-cooked food in a metal pan, the guards dumped it into a plastic bag and pushed it into her cell.

After eleven days, the guards took Helen to the courthouse to face the man from the hospital who had lodged a case against her. In front of the judge, he demanded that Helen apologize to the court, hospital staff, and her church congregation. He wanted her to admit she was wrong for telling him about the gospel and humiliating him.

When she refused, the guards returned Helen to the police station. This time, she was taken to a large cell with a group of women. Happy to be somewhere light and airy, and with other women, she passed the time singing to keep their spirits up.

Later that day, Helen was taken back to court where she asked to speak privately to the judge. He was a calm, elderly man, and he listened carefully as she told him about herself and her faith and what had actually happened at the hospital.

"As you seem so keen to help others," the judge said, "perhaps you could give me some advice?" The judge described a problem he was having with his wife. It worried him. Helen listened and tried to help as best she could.

When she returned to the courtroom, the judge ruled in Helen's favor. *Surely God is watching over me and intervened to have me released!*

الكه

Though the war with Ethiopia was officially over and life in her country was more peaceful, tensions still remained between the two countries. Her government, led by President Isaias Afwerki,[1] was becoming stricter and less tolerant. He failed to ratify the constitution, canceled presidential elections, outlawed other political parties, and effectively closed the national press. In keeping with his Marxist governmental policies, he also embraced atheism.

By May 2002, the Eritrean government issued a decree that only four religious groups would be recognized—the Ethiopian Orthodox Church, the Catholic Church, Islam, and the Lutheran-affiliated Evangelical Church. Helen and the other members of the church she attended were discouraged, as the government now considered their church illegal.

The government began broadcasting propaganda against the church, accusing Christians of accepting bribes from foreign organizations like the CIA. Soon, private homes and small meetings, as well as social gatherings among known Christians, were raided. Many Christians were arrested for conducting family devotions in their own homes, and others were arrested for simply

---

1. President Isaias Afwerki studied in China during the Cultural Revolution (1966–1976), absorbing Chairman Mao Zedong's strong-arm approach to governance. Upon his return to Eritrea, Afwerki founded his own Marxist revolutionary movement—the Eritrean People's Liberation Front, later renamed The People's Front for Democracy and Justice. Afwerki and his followers joined in a 30-year battle for independence from Ethiopia that resulted in defeat for Ethiopia, independence for Eritrea, and a presidency for Afwerki in 1993.

owning a Bible. Asmara became oppressive, and an atmosphere of distrust developed among the people. Anyone could be a member of the secret police.

How can our government imprison law-abiding, hardworking people simply because of their personal beliefs?

Amid the rising oppression, Helen devoted herself to writing worship music, and in 2003, she completed her first CD. The church she attended had gone underground, but they still supported her by distributing the album. She was delighted that her songs would reach a wider audience and help spread the gospel. For Helen, fear and the gospel did not go together, and she was determined that whatever happened, she would continue to do God's work.

The release of Helen's album brought new opportunities to lead worship and teach the Bible. Three times a week, late at night in the cellar of a home, she secretly taught a group of young people. Helen's family would sit with little Eva while she slept back at home. Though Helen's ministry was dangerous, she was determined to carry out the mission God had given her.

One night, as she locked her bicycle and prepared to go inside to conduct Bible study, she overheard two young men talking nearby.

"She's the one," one of them said.

Helen hurried into the home, and as she saw the eager faces of the group, her concern dissipated. *This is where the Lord wants me.*

Helen and the fifteen young people crowded into the small stone room, and just as she began to speak, the cellar door burst open. A group of secret police, too many to count, filled the cellar. The men, who reeked of alcohol, herded the group into the center of the room and began beating them mercilessly with batons and thin plastic whips.

Helen felt one of the men's fingers close around her arm, hard enough to bruise, and he dragged her up the stairs. Her shins jarred painfully against the stone steps. Later, Helen would learn that when the men first burst into the house, they had shouted, "Where is the singer? We're going to execute her!"

Once outside, the officer shoved Helen and her bicycle into a waiting truck and drove to the police station. There, they pushed her into a large cell. The female guard yanked the white shawl from Helen's shoulders. "See how you like being cold," she sneered.

By now, it was after 2:00 a.m., and the cell was full. One of the women, a red-lipped prostitute named Zula, introduced herself. When she learned Helen was a singer, she clapped her hands in delight. "Will you sing for us?"

For the next week, in between periods of questioning by the secret police, Helen sang for the other prisoners. Her singing was an unwelcome presence for the guards in the prison.

Late at night, the guards took Helen and the other prisoners outside and made them kneel in the wet, muddy grass. The female guard walked over to Helen and leaned forward, squeezing Helen's nose painfully between her fingers and pulling her around the grass.

"Stop singing!" the woman hissed, as Helen's eyes watered with pain.

The next morning, Helen was sent to her official interrogation. She answered questions about where her beauty salon was located and her future plans. But when the man asked about her religious beliefs, Helen answered: "I am willing to die for my faith."

Following the interrogation, Helen was surprised when she wasn't returned to her cell. Instead, the guards took her outside and forced her into a military truck. As she settled in among the other captives, Helen was horrified when she overheard the guards mention the name Adi Abeito—a notorious prison reserved for soldiers and military personnel.

Why would they send me, a civilian, there?

The truck jolted along the outskirts of Asmara until it finally stopped outside the prison gates. Helen prayed silently, determined not to show any fear.

One by one, Helen and the others were taken to be interrogated. Eventually, the guards came to take her to her cell.

Along the way, the guard took her outside into the daylight of the main prison compound. Before her were huge, corrugated iron halls, like army barracks. As they passed through one of the halls, Helen could see hundreds of starving prisoners, suffering etched on their faces.

Helen found it impossible to sleep at night. She could hear prisoners coughing and vomiting, and she felt compelled to help them clean themselves. The cells were infested with rats and fleas, and without any toilets, prisoners were forced to use the bathroom in an open space behind the prison.

Many of those confined were sick and could hardly walk. One inmate, a man with an intravenous drip who slept in the corridor because of his diarrhea, needed to be helped outside to the bathroom. So, each night, Helen stayed awake to assist him; for weeks, she hardly slept.

One night Helen was suffering from diarrhea, and a guard took her outside. It was after midnight, and clouds covered the moon. As they walked to a place for Helen to relieve herself, she spotted three shapes on the ground. *Are those sacks of potatoes or tied-up sheep?* As she got closer, though, she realized they were people. Helen could make out their contorted bodies, with their handcuffed wrists stretched tightly behind their bodies and tied to their ankles. She thought the three people were dead until she heard one of them groan.

Helen was shocked. "What have they done?" she blurted out. "Will they have to stay there all night?"

The guard pointed silently at the waste ground and refused to answer.

Back in the cell, Helen asked the other prisoners about what she'd seen. It was a common form of torture, she learned, one called the "helicopter position." Her heart mourned for the men and women who were treated so inhumanely, just a few feet from her own cell.

Three weeks after arriving at the military prison, Helen was told to gather her belongings. She was assembled with a small group of Christians and again loaded onto a military truck.

"Where are we going?" Helen asked the woman next to her.

"I heard a guard say 'Mai Serwa,'" the woman answered, her voice unsteady.

Mai Serwa. The prison and military camp reserved for dangerous, long-term prisoners and serious criminals.

Helen exhaled slowly as the truck began its bumpy journey.

 freshening

Located in a deserted area outside the city, Mai Serwa contained a few primitive mud-brick huts that appeared to be army barracks. Upon Helen's arrival, prison guards carried out a full body search — checking for weapons, money, and Bibles — but she was determined the guards would not see her flinch.

Helen and the other prisoners were then walked through the camp and down into the valley. There they came across row after row of metal shipping containers, the kind used to transport goods overseas.

As Helen and the others stood in line, waiting to be taken to their cells, Helen caught a flash of movement in the container nearest her. A small hole had been cut in the side, just near eye level, and she could see people looking out.

A shocking realization hit Helen. *The containers* are *the cells.*

Forcing herself to breathe deeply, Helen soaked up the warmth of the sun and the feeling of wide-open space around her. She didn't know if or when she would experience these things again.

One guard ordered the women to march forward as another struggled to wrench open the rusty double doors of a container. Helen and her new cellmates walked inside. She turned back just in time to see the guard grin as he pushed the doors closed. The heavy metal doors slammed together with a clang, leaving a thin strip of light. Then, as a guard worked the bolts into place with a terrible screeching noise, the doors shut with a final *pop* as the rubber seal trapped the women inside. Helen's heart pounded as she thought about what was to come.

The container was no more than twenty feet long. The eighteen women inside were packed closely together. Within moments, Helen felt an itch on her leg and reached down to scratch it. As she did, she noticed other women doing the same. The container was infested with hungry fleas and lice. Helen panicked as she ferociously brushed the insects from her body, but it was no use.

As the day wore on, the container began to heat up until it was almost too hot to bear. The women grew despondent, and many of them were now angry. Helen struggled to remain calm in such a small space that was so overcrowded with other frightened people.

"What should we do, Helen?" one of them cried.

While Helen knew they were expecting her to say they should shout or bang on the container to let their captors know they weren't going to tolerate this treatment, she had a different message for the women. She remembered a passage in Richard Wurmbrand's book, *Tortured for Christ,* about how Christians, like nightingales, could not be prevented from singing—even in captivity.

"Why don't we sing?" Helen asked. "We should praise God in spite of the fleas, in spite of the lice, in spite of the heat. We should thank God despite our circumstances."

Slowly, the women began to sing and pray. Then, Helen shared verses of Scripture that she had memorized.

At night, the temperature inside the shipping container dropped quickly, and the women shivered. They pushed their toilet bucket to the corner, but the smell was so horrible they slept in shifts to ensure no one spent the whole night beside the bucket. At 5:00 a.m., the guards opened the container doors and marched their prisoners to an open area half a mile away. There, they could use the bathroom and empty their bucket.

As she lined up with the other women to go back into the container, Helen saw more prisoners, all male, spilling out of the container next to her. She looked around at the containers surrounding her and counted more than twenty. She calculated that if each held eighteen people, there were easily several hundred prisoners in the camp. Most seemed to be between the ages of twenty and thirty. Helen felt anger rise up. *How could locking away so many young people in containers possibly help our country grow and flourish?*

When the container doors slammed shut once more, many of the women burst into tears. Helen felt the same emotions, but she was determined to minister to her cellmates. She encouraged the women to sit on the floor in a circle. "Remember that the walls of Jericho came down because of praises. If we keep complaining, we cannot win. Instead, we must continue to pray, praise, and sing. Satan wants to use discouraging words as a weapon against us, so we must continue to praise God in all circumstances." Helen was relieved to see the women nodding. She knew they weren't all Christians, but each seemed grateful for Helen's encouragement.

At night, though, in the quiet of the container cell, Helen had only the Lord for comfort. She thought of little Eva. Helen's sister was caring for her daughter, but Helen couldn't stand the thought of her little girl crying for her mother. *Does she understand where I've gone? Is she scared at night as she drifts off to sleep?* All Helen could do was pray.

ele

For days, the women sat in their container and sang. One morning, they heard the bolts on the metal doors grinding as they were loosened. The doors were flung open, revealing three angry guards standing outside.

"Who was singing?" one demanded.

Helen's heart pounded as several women, including herself, admitted they had been singing. The guards pulled them from the container, made them remove their shoes, and instructed them to run around on the sandy ground. Small, sharp pebbles cut their feet.

The guards then made the prisoners squat on their haunches and leap forward like frogs. "Jump!" the guard shouted as Helen struggled to keep her balance. When she kept falling over, the guard beat her with his stick.

"Since you cannot stand on your feet, you will lie down," he ordered Helen, who lay down on the gravel.

After the torture, the guards asked the women one by one to agree never to sing again. Helen knew the guards viewed this refusal to give up their faith as disloyalty to their country. She took a deep breath and spoke.

Helen Berhane: "Why Don't We Sing?"

"I am a singer," she said, "so I cannot give it up. I will sing quietly so as not to disturb the other containers, but I will not stop." Half of the other women refused as well.

The guards led the women back into their container for an hour at midday, then called them out once more. They grabbed one of the women and beat her with a police baton. Helen winced as the woman writhed in pain. Gradually, most of the women became afraid, worn down by the torture, and they agreed to stop singing. They were returned to the container. Soon, only Helen and two others remained outside.

The guards ordered the three women to hold heavy stones above their heads as they knelt on the gravel. Helen thought about Eva as she struggled to keep the rocks aloft. She thought about her brothers and sisters in Christ who were also suffering for their faith in places just as horrible or even worse. She prayed for strength. It was late in the evening when the guards finally ended the women's agony and put them back in their cell.

But the guards' torture proved unsuccessful, and Helen and the women began to sing again as soon as the guards shut the doors. At 10:00 the next morning, the guards called out the singers, tied their hands behind their backs, and made them lie flat on the ground.

Helen's circulation stopped, and her hands turned blue. She felt dizzy and expected to faint. Periodically, the guards untied the women and asked them if they would stop singing; when they refused, the men tied them up again. Throughout the day, the torturous pattern continued. Through bouts of dizziness, Helen continued to pray for strength.

When night fell, the guards left the women scattered about the yard so they could not take comfort from each other. At 2:00 a.m., the guards finally led them back to their container cell. Helen couldn't believe how terribly the guards treated the women. Back inside, the Christian prisoners prayed together, thankful they could forget their troubles for a little while and draw strength from their faith.

Later in the day, a guard took Helen to the interrogator. He placed a form before her that promised she would not preach, praise, sing, or spread the gospel. When she refused to sign it, he decided he would need to make her life even more difficult if there were any chance of persuading her to renounce her faith.

The interrogator had her moved to another container. This one held just two other prisoners—a woman who had been caught sneaking over the border into Sudan and a woman who suffered from mental illness. Helen's heart rate quickened. Before, she had support from other Christians in her cell; but now, she felt alone.

Helen would spend the next ten months in the container with this madwoman.

ele

Helen felt compassion for her troubled cellmate, but living with the woman was nearly unbearable. She talked and cried all day and night without ceasing. She would swear at and insult the guards through the small window in their cell. Often, she flung herself against the walls to rock the container. She stuffed her blanket into the small window, cutting off their air supply.

Eventually, the guards brought more women to Helen's new container. Many of them were the other Christians who had refused to abandon their faith. Unfortunately, Helen's unstable cellmate became increasingly agitated. One night, Helen jerked awake when she felt the woman squeezing her neck in an uncontrolled fury. After the strangling incident, the woman continued attacking other cellmates each night. The rest of the prisoners began taking turns staying awake at night to keep an eye on the volatile woman.

Helen was unable to sleep, and her body couldn't cope with the stress. She lost weight, and the guards teased her for how thin she'd become. The guards often salted the prisoners' food so heavily that it was inedible.

When Helen's sister, who worked for the Ministry of Defense, was finally given permission to visit Helen, she brought young Eva to see her mother. Helen was delighted to see them both. But she quickly realized how horrific she must look when her two visitors burst into tears.

"Will you die?" Eva sobbed. Helen felt her heart breaking, and she was unable to answer. She left the visit feeling more despondent than she'd ever felt in her life.

And her circumstances as a prisoner continued to deteriorate. Once, when a guard caught Helen peeping through the small window in her container cell, he dragged her outside and beat her mercilessly. Helen held the man's gaze as he punched her, his fists pummeling every part of her frail body. The beating was so severe that Helen's menstrual cycle stopped for the next four months.

Gradually, the guards transferred Helen's Christian friends out of the container, and soon she was the only Christian remaining. Whenever they brought new prisoners, the guards made an example of Helen by torturing her in front of them.

After another especially intense interrogation, the guards moved Helen to a new container, one already holding eighteen other Christian women who, like Helen, had refused to renounce their faith. There, Helen tried to keep her cellmates busy and maintain a routine of preparing breakfast—a meager meal of rolls, weak lentil soup, and a cup of tea—and then singing and studying the Bible, which she had managed to sneak past the guards in five small sections.

She also managed to smuggle in some writing supplies and began exchanging letters with other Christian prisoners. But when the guards discovered her clandestine communications, they beat her and left her handcuffed on the icy floor of an empty container all night long. That night, Helen thought she might freeze to death in her thin dress, and her whole body ached from the cold and the beating.

So, Helen began to sing. She composed a song and repeated it all night.

I love You, that's why I draw myself closer to You.
I know that it's worth following You.
I am not only ready for prison, but I trust You until death.
Even in a closed space or in a pit, I will not surrender to
evil spirits.
Not even if I am bound or I am chained and I am suffering
from cold.
I will sing and I am not going to tire of singing, nor give up.
My heart is burning with Your love,
And my heart declares I will never stop respecting You or
lifting You up.
I will sing again and again.
I will sing a melody for You.
My soul is pleased to sing for You.

The next morning, the guard returned and ordered Helen to stop writing letters to other prisoners, but she refused.

"I was arrested because I preached and spread the gospel," she said, "and even now, I will not stop. I will continue to write and speak about my faith."

For her obstinance, Helen was sent to solitary confinement.

Through each hardship, Helen found that God always sent someone to help her, and her experiences continued to draw the attention of the guards and other inmates. By now, she had been in prison for a year and a half—and in her solitary cell for months.

Helen occasionally had brief encounters with other prisoners. When she went to empty her toilet bucket, she passed other inmates in the yard and found some of them to be especially kind. One group of inmates, former army officers now serving long-term prison sentences, were allowed access to newspapers. When they finished each edition, they passed them along to Helen.

Helen, in turn, was delighted to have news of the world outside the prison. When she read a special series on people who had changed the world, she began fastening the articles around the walls of her container with chewing gum.

A guard came to her container and, looking in, asked Helen about the articles. When she explained they were inspiring stories, the man made a surprising comment: "Don't you realize that you are one of these people?"

Four long months after Helen first entered solitary confinement, an interrogator came to her container and ordered her to gather her belongings. She would be moved to a new container, one with seven other inmates, on the strict understanding that she would not teach, preach, or sing.

"I can't comply with that," Helen said, but he had already begun to collect her things.

ele

In her new "home," Helen continued to sing, and it wasn't long before there was a rattling at the door. "Who is singing?" a guard shouted.

Helen was about to speak when Liya, a new Christian prisoner, took responsibility. The guard led Liya outside, chaining her for the whole evening. The next morning, the man came to the container once more. "She wasn't singing alone," he said, gesturing toward Helen and another Christian woman named Esther. He dragged both women from the container and chained them outside with Liya, leaving them there until 2:00 a.m. The next day, he did the same thing.

After two days, the guard returned to the container and threatened the women. "If I hear you sing once more, I will take you to sleep with the male prisoners." Helen swallowed nervously. It was the worst threat he'd made so far.

The guard released Helen and Esther but not Liya. Back inside the container, Helen felt deep compassion for Liya. She was new to the prison and had been punished for protecting Helen. When the guard walked away, Helen slipped back outside to sit with her.

When the guard saw Helen, he walked back over. "What do you think you are, Helen? A priest comforting your people? I told you to get back in the container."

"Please," Helen said, "let me stay with her, or chain me on her behalf."

The guard was astonished. He'd never had a prisoner quite like Helen, and he called for three other higher-ranking guards to help talk sense into her.

"I would like to either be punished in her place or to be allowed to stay and comfort her," Helen explained.

The senior guards didn't know what to make of Helen, either.

"If you're this serious about your faith," the first guard said, "you must be prepared for the harshest punishment. You would be wiser to give up your beliefs before it is too late."

In the months to come, unspeakable torture continued, with the harshest punishments reserved for Helen and the other Christians.

After a while, guards escorted Helen and the other Christians to the office. One of the prison chiefs presented them with a piece of paper, and Helen scanned the document.

"*I will keep on preaching and believing,*" it said. Helen furrowed her brows. It was a positive confession, the opposite of the last paper they'd been asked to sign. As she tried to understand the significance of this new confession, the chief spoke.

"This is your last chance," he said. "If you sign this paper, you will have to stay in prison, and we will send you to one of the secret prisons—you will never be released. If you do not sign it, then we will let you go." He stared at each of the women. "If you choose to sign, I wash my hands of you; you will have decided your own fate. What happens to you will not be my fault."

Helen sat up straight in her chair. "I cannot abandon my faith," she said. "If you puncture a sack of grain, the only thing that pours out is the type of grain that was in the sack. It is the same with me. I can only say what is inside me; everything that is in my heart must come out of my mouth." Helen looked the man square in the eyes. "So, give me the paper, and I will sign it. Then you can send me wherever you want.

"The more you punish me, the stronger I will be. If you keep hammering on a nail's head, it just becomes harder to pull out of the wall. Give me the paper."

Helen signed the sheet and went back to her container, confident that God was using her terrible situation for His glory.

⁓ℓℓ⁓

Helen continued teaching the other inmates about Christ, and she also began teaching some of the guards. When she was discovered, the guards punished her ruthlessly, binding her with excruciating handcuffs that cut deep into her wrists.

"Look at Helen!" the guards jeered. "She looks like a sheep prepared for the holiday slaughter!"

Afterward, the guards took her to interrogation. She was so stiff she could barely walk.

"Why have you been teaching members of staff?" the chief asked.

"I am always looking for opportunities to talk about my faith and to spread the news about Jesus," Helen replied. "I am not ashamed of the gospel, and I will talk to anyone and to everyone. Jesus does not just want me to tell the prisoners about Him; He wants me to tell the guards too. Even if the president were to visit the prison, I would tell him about the gospel."

The chief was furious. Though Helen's whole body ached, she continued. "I am not afraid of you. You can do what you want to me, but ultimately, all you can do is kill my body. You cannot touch my soul. You cannot even kill me unless it is God's will that I die."

The guards returned Helen to her container, but that was not the end of the matter. Soon, the guards recruited a desperate prisoner to spy on Helen, and his first task was to trap her breaking the rules.

The man, a prisoner who lived in a nearby container, asked Helen to write some Christian teachings on a piece of paper for him, and she agreed. When she'd prepared the paper, she folded it and hid it inside a matchbox, waiting for a safe time to throw it to the man.

When the man gave her the signal, Helen tossed the matchbox, but the handoff had not occurred in secret after all. When she saw a guard rushing toward her, she knew she'd been set up.

"Now we have evidence against you," said the guard as he pulled Helen from her container. "What are we going to do with you?"

Instinctively, Helen raised her hands to protect her face, but the blows were swift. She felt as though something exploded against the side of her head as the man kicked her repeatedly. When she finally limped back to her container, Helen knew her thin body would be covered in bruises.

But the punishment was far from over.

The prison chief summoned Helen to his office where another guard waited, this one a terrifying Muslim man named Suleiman who had a reputation for his ruthless beatings. He raised his baton and struck Helen relentlessly. When she remained silent, he redoubled his efforts, certain he wasn't beating her hard enough.

Finally, he paused. "We shall have a break so that you can think about your actions," he said. Helen lay on the floor. Her muscles twitched involuntarily. "Helen, you must stop believing."

How can he still think that I will stop, after all that has happened to me? Does he really think that a beating will make me abandon my faith? Helen wasn't afraid of dying, but she shuddered at the thought of leaving Eva.

"Suleiman," she said, "you can do whatever you like to me, but I will believe and be faithful to my God, even if you kill me."

When Suleiman finished, Helen's body was battered beyond anything she had ever experienced. The cruel man then chained her outside of her container in the broiling sun. She couldn't even manage to sit upright.

"I'm dying," she moaned to the other prisoners.

"What can I do for you?" one woman asked, beginning to cry.

"Tell them to take my chains off," she whispered, "so I can at least have a comfortable death."

Moments later, Helen's world faded into darkness.

ℓℓ

When she regained consciousness, Helen was carried to the prison medic. By now, her whole body was black with bruises. When she told the man what had happened, he stepped outside and wept.

It was late at night when the guards carried Helen back to her container. For days, she lay still, mostly sleepless with the pain. She thought a lot about what had happened and about how cruel humans could be to each other.

Yet, she could not hate Suleiman. He had beaten her in anger, and she wondered if now he was ashamed. She did not want him to be punished for what he had done to her, but she prayed that one day he would find faith in the Lord and come to repent of what he had done.

While Helen was still suffering, Suleiman sent another Muslim guard to beat her again. When he struck her wounds, the pain was unbearable.

Helen's condition worsened until she could no longer urinate. She was unable to stand, let alone walk. The guards brought a stretcher and carried her from the container back to the medic. "Her body is shutting down," he told the chief interrogator. "If we leave her here, she will die."

Helen's condition continued to worsen until, finally, Suleiman allowed the medic to take her to the hospital.

It was 2006, and Helen had been in prison for nearly three years.

～ℓℓ～

The truck rolled out of the prison, but Helen was in too much pain to feel truly relieved. As they entered the city, she began to look around. It helped distract her from the jolts of pain as the truck rumbled down the street.

Helen hadn't seen the city in more than two years, and she had missed it. After all this time, it looked older to her, more haggard and careworn. Like Helen, the city had deteriorated.

At the hospital, Helen explained to her doctor that her injuries were the result of torture, and the man's expression darkened.

"I will make sure that you are admitted as a patient," he said. "They cannot send you back to prison in this state."

Helen's mother was a nurse at the hospital and learned that her daughter was now a patient. When Helen saw her mother, she burst into tears. She was so relieved to see her but couldn't believe how much older she looked.

One of the prison guards watched the reunion and spoke. "Helen, you are human after all. We have never seen you cry before."

The doctors began treating Helen's injuries, and the hospital sent word that her health was too poor to return to prison. Helen knew what this meant. If she died in prison, the guards would be held responsible, so they released the severely ill prisoners in order to avoid that responsibility. Helen's parents took her home.

Though she had officially been released from prison, she was still under surveillance. The house was surrounded by secret police.

"How is Helen's leg?" the men asked her parents as they walked to and from the house. "Is she improving?"

Helen and her family knew if the police felt she had improved sufficiently, there was a good chance they would take her back to prison—where she would surely die. So she made the difficult decision to leave Eritrea. Helen went to the Sudanese Embassy and begged for a visa. She was shocked when the embassy granted her request. If the authorities had known she was planning to leave, they would have stopped her. And although they followed her everywhere, they seemed blind to what she was actually doing. *God's hand is protecting me.*

Since it would be too dangerous for Helen to take her daughter with her, plans were made for Eva to stay with her grandparents. *How much longer will I be separated from my daughter?* Helen knew her only hope of being reunited with Eva was by successfully escaping Eritrea, but it would be nearly impossible.

Helen's anxiety grew as the day of her departure approached. Most people escaped the country by crossing the border with the help of smugglers, but with her crippled leg, she knew she'd never make it. Instead, she would have to travel by plane, and there was almost no chance she would be able to leave without being caught.

When the day arrived, she hugged her family and said goodbye, promising her daughter that she would see her again soon.

All along, Helen felt God had directed her path. He had allowed her to survive her long imprisonment, to be released from prison and from the hospital, and He had allowed her to secure a visa at the embassy. Now, she prayed He would continue to protect her in this last stretch toward freedom.

At the airport, as Helen leaned on her crutches and waited to board her flight, she noticed a security guard staring at her. Helen's heart beat furiously, and beads of sweat formed on her brow. *Does he somehow know who I am and what I'm doing?* The man walked toward her, and Helen's legs began to shake. Instead of apprehending her, though, the man reached out a hand to steady her.

"Let me help you," he said. Helen was nearly in a panic, but she murmured her thanks, and the man smiled. "We must help those who fought so bravely for our country."

He thinks I have been handicapped in the war with Ethiopia! Once again, Helen knew God was with her. When she handed her passport to the gate attendant, the man barely glanced at it. *God is blinding the people who might have stopped me!*

On the plane, Helen sat in a seat reserved for the disabled. As the plane took off, she looked out the window and saw Asmara spread out below her. She scrunched her eyes against the sun. In the distance, she glimpsed the prison where she had spent more than two years suffering for God.

Helen could barely believe that now she was leaving her beloved country. She felt as though at any moment, she would wake up on the cold, hard floor of her prison container to find her freedom was just a dream.

But it was real, and by God's grace, Helen was free.

ele

Helen's older sister, who lived and worked in Sudan, met her at the airport and took her to her home. Even though she was free, Helen still was not safe. Most days when Helen answered the phone, the voice on the line warned, "We are watching you."

Helen's leg had healed a bit, but she was still unable to walk. She was also worried about Eva, who was still back in Eritrea with Helen's parents. Helen was afraid that if Eva stayed much longer, the government might try to hurt her, and she would never see her daughter again. Helen also knew that in five years, when Eva turned seventeen, she would have to join the Eritrean military. Helen wanted a better future for her daughter, so she decided it was time to smuggle twelve-year-old Eva out of Eritrea.

The secret police were still watching Helen's family, making it impossible for Eva to escape Eritrea the same way Helen had. Instead, Helen made other plans: a smuggler would drive Eva from Asmara across the desert into Sudan. The journey terrified Helen. She knew the horror stories of traffickers who led their group into the desert only to rob them and leave them to die. Even if this man was honorable, he and her daughter could still be caught.

Helen sat in Khartoum and prayed as her daughter and several other refugees were driven through the night in a vehicle with no lights—the smuggler's son lying on the roof hissing directions to his father below. Eva's journey was long and hard. Helen had made arrangements for food to be delivered to her daughter en route, but the meals she paid for never turned up. At one point, the group had to walk for a time, and Eva was so weak that one of the other refugees carried her on his back.

Once Eva crossed the border, she spent several days in a detention center where, tragically, a refugee girl in her group was raped by a Sudanese security officer. From the detention center, Eva moved to a refugee camp. The whole time, her mother waited to be reunited with her daughter once again.

Finally, Helen's sister found Eva and brought her home. Helen hobbled on her crutches to greet her daughter at the door. Through tears, she thanked God for keeping her daughter safe and for the good men who had smuggled her out.

✧

Helen had already made plans for the two of them to leave Sudan. In the five months that she'd lived there, she'd been forced to move four times as the threatening phone calls persisted.

Although Helen was not singing at churches in Sudan, an Eritrean pastor asked her to sing at a gospel concert at his church in Khartoum. Without telling her, he printed large posters with Helen's face and distributed them throughout the city. When the Eritrean government heard about it, she had to move once more.

An organization that helps Eritrean Christians was working hard to find Helen and Eva asylum in America or Europe. "We'll take the first successful application," Helen said. It turned out to be Denmark, which welcomed Helen and Eva in part because of Helen's disability.

The two soon landed in Copenhagen. Denmark felt like a different world to Helen. Their new home was nestled in a small community in the countryside, not far from the sea, and the village people cared for Helen as if she were one of their own.

Helen was nearly immobile when she arrived, but once she was well enough to walk with two sticks, she began her spiritual ministry again. She sang, attended Bible studies, and ministered in churches nearby. Miraculously, Helen slept well and didn't suffer any lasting psychological trauma, as so many survivors of torture do.

With good healthcare and miraculous intervention from the Lord, Helen's body also healed. Her teeth had suffered in prison without sufficient nutrients for so long, but in Denmark, she received proper dental care. Soon, her legs healed as well, and she no longer needed crutches to walk.

As she recovered, Helen realized that she had experienced what she read in the Bible in Paul's second letter to the Corinthians: "Though our outer self is wasting away, our inner self is being renewed day by day" (4:16).

Helen was finally able to live without fear. She could leave her home and return safely. In prison, every aspect of her life was controlled; but now, she was free to take a bath whenever she wanted. As she grew accustomed to freedom once more, she prayed fervently for all those still suffering in prison, that one day they, too, would have the freedom she now enjoyed.

Helen also prayed for the men who had tormented her in prison. "I want to tell you that I love you, and that I hope one day you will believe in the Jesus that I serve."

Years after her release from prison, Helen penned a message for Christians living in the free world. "You must not take your freedom for granted," she said. "Use every opportunity to praise the Lord every day. If I could sing in prison, imagine what you can do for God's glory with your freedom." She was reminded of the lyrics to a song she'd written in prison: "Christianity costs you your life, but in the end, its outcome is victory."

Helen still dreams that one day she will be able to return to her beloved country and sing a song of praise in the stadium in Asmara. Today, she remains one of the most vocal advocates for religious freedom in Eritrea.

"With God, all things are possible," she said, "and so I pray that one day, it may be so."

Acknowledgments

In addition to The Voice of the Martyrs' interviews with the women whose stories and testimonies are featured in this book, the following titles were used as sources.

Bianca: Jesus, Her Constant Companion
Some content taken from *Serving God in Hostile Territory* by Bianca Adler, edited by Kaye Hollings. Copyright © 2003. Used by permission. All rights reserved.

Gracia: We Must Run
Some content taken from *In the Presence of My Enemies* by Gracia Burnham with Dean Merrill. Copyright © 2003, 2004, 2010. Used by permission of Tyndale House Publishers. All rights reserved.

Marziyeh and Maryam: Two Ordinary Girls
Some content taken from *Captive in Iran* by Maryam Rostampour and Marziyeh Amirizadeh. Copyright © 2013. Used by permission of Tyndale House Publishers. All rights reserved.

Hannelie: The One Who Was Spared
Primary source of content from *Tragedy in Kabul* by Hannelie Groenewald. Copyright © 2019. Used by permission of Hannelie Groenewald. All rights reserved.

Helen: "Why don't we sing?"
Some content taken from *Song of the Nightingale*. Copyright © 2009 Helen Berhane. Published by Authentic Media Ltd, Milton Keynes, UK.

About The Voice of the Martyrs

The Voice of the Martyrs (VOM) is a missionary organization dedicated to serving persecuted Christians in the world's most difficult and dangerous places to follow Christ while inspiring all members of the global body of Christ to enter into fellowship with one another. VOM was founded in 1967 by Pastor Richard Wurmbrand (1909 – 2001) and his wife, Sabina (1913 – 2000). Richard was imprisoned 14 years in Communist Romania for his faith in Christ, and Sabina was imprisoned for three years. Soon after their imprisonment, they founded VOM and established a family of missions dedicated to assisting persecuted Christians worldwide.

To be inspired by the bold faith of our persecuted brothers and sisters in Christ who are working to advance the gospel in hostile areas and restricted nations, request a free subscription to VOM's award-winning monthly magazine. Visit us at vom.org, or call 800-747-0085.

To learn more about VOM's work, please contact us:

United States	vom.org
Australia	vom.com.au
Belgium	hvk-aem.be
Brazil	maisnomundo.org

Canada	vomcanada.com
Czech Republic	hlas-mucedniku.cz
Finland	marttyyrienaani.fi
Germany	verfolgte-christen.org
The Netherlands	sdok.nl
New Zealand	vom.org.nz
Poland	gpch.pl
Portugal	vozdosmartires.com
Singapore	gosheninternational.org
South Africa	persecutionsa.org
South Korea	vomkorea.kr
United Kingdom	releaseinternational.org